Wrong Again, Doglips

ROGER AUSTIN

Library of Congress Control Number: 2025918268
ISBN: 978-1-969422-00-3 (Paperback)
　　　978-1-969422-05-8 (Hardback)
　　　978-1-969422-01-0 (Ebook)

Olympus Story House

Contents

For my unbelieving relatives and friends

August 2 This Is Your Brain on God
Acts 8:1-3, 9:19-31

You know, I think one of the most effective anti-drug abuse commercials that the Partnership for a Drug-Free America put out was one of their earliest ones. You remember it: it opens with a man, standing behind a stove with a frying pan sitting on it. The man proceeds to hold up an egg, points to it, and matter-of-factly says, "This is your brain," and if you'd never seen the ad before, you'd probably be thinking at that point, "Who *is* this guy, calling me an egghead?" He then cracks the egg open and drops the yolk and the white of the egg into the frying pan, and it immediately starts to fry up, sizzling, cracking, and popping, like a raw egg is supposed to, in a hot frying pan.

After the camera then focuses up close on the egg, frying away, it goes back to showing the man, who then says, while pointing to the egg, "This is your brain *on drugs*." It's then that you're thinking, "That's *gross*. That hurts my head just *thinking* about it." He then finishes making his point by asking the viewer, "Any questions?" Now, I don't know about you, but my response to him after seeing such a demonstration would most likely be, "Nope, that pretty much sums it all up right there, thank you very much!"

The point, of course, of that commercial is that abusing drugs alters your mind in such a way that it makes it impossible for you to think straight. Substances such as that, when they enter a human body, have the ability to make that person's mind a lot less able to function as it is meant to function, and so it powerfully affects that person's brain—much for the worse.

But when a person's brain is "on G," when a person's mind is controlled by G and his direction for them, it's a much *different* story, and for the better. That truth is demonstrated, then, by the passages contrasting the apostle Paul—before and after his conversion experience.

1

The pre-Jesus Paul, the man before his mind and life-altering experience with Christ, is seen in the first three verses of Acts 8. It's there the Jerusalem Bible plainly states, "Saul entirely approved of Stephen's killing. That day, a bitter persecution started against the church in Jerusalem, and everyone except the apostles fled into the country districts of Judea and Samaria. There were some devout people, though, who buried Stephen and made great mourning for him. Saul worked for the total destruction of the church; he went from house to house, arresting both men and women and sending them to prison."

Yes, before his conversion to the faith, Paul, then known as Saul, was pretty much of a rascal, at least toward Christians, wouldn't you say? But during the first portion of the very next chapter, we see him on his way to Damascus, with the intent of arresting followers of J and hauling them off to jail, breathing out murderous threats against the disciples. But it's as he is on his way to Damascus that J sees to it that he's knocked to the ground and blinded, and then J speaks to him, revealing who he is and what he has planned for Saul from that time forward. It's at this point that Saul becomes a believer in and a follower of J's.

Now, remember, we just got through examining a portion of scripture that described him as if his brain had been on the "drug of the world," being hateful, cruel, and judgmental, among other nasty characteristics, having it out for anyone who had anything to do with the church. But now listen to what happens when the Bible describes him shortly after having come to faith in J, according to Acts 9:19–30: "After he had spent only a few days with the disciples in Damascus, he began preaching in the synagogues, 'Jesus is the Son of G.' All those who heard him were amazed. 'Surely,' they said, 'this is the man who organized the attack in Jerusalem against the people who invoke this name, and who came here for the sole purpose of arresting them to have them tried by the chief priests?' Saul's power increased steadily, and he was able to throw the Jewish colony at Damascus into complete confusion by the way he demonstrated that J was the Christ.

"Some time passed, and the Jews worked out a plot to kill him, but news of it reached Saul. To make sure of killing him, they kept watch on the gates day and night, but when it was dark, the disciples took him and let him down from the top of the wall, lowering him in a basket.

"When he got to Jerusalem, he tried to join the disciples, but they were all afraid of him; they couldn't believe that he was *really* a disciple. Barnabas, however, took charge of him, introduced him to the apostles, and explained how the Lord had appeared to Saul and spoken to him on his journey and how he had preached boldly at Damascus in the name of J. Saul now started to go around with them in Jerusalem, preaching fearlessly in the name of the Lord."

You see, once he met J personally, Saul was no longer lost in a sea of selfishness and self-centeredness; he was a new creature in Christ. Instead of his mindset being focused on his own self-righteousness, then his brain was on G.

You see, the person whose brain is on G has a mindset and a worldview like that described in Galatians 5:22 when the scripture says at that point, "But the fruit of the Spirit is love, joy, peace, patience, kindness, goodness, faithfulness gentleness and self-control." That's—in a large part—what it means for a person to have their brain on God.

Chuck Swindoll says that for a number of years, he served on the board of Dallas Seminary with Tom Landry, formerly of the Dallas Cowboys. While the board was talking about the importance of character among the young men and women going into the ministry, Landry leaned over and said to me, "You know, Chuck, for the Cowboys, when we draft men for our team, we look for five things, and the first is character."

Swindoll then replied, "Well, let me ask you something. What if you find a terriffc athlete who *lacks* character?"

Landry answered, "Chuck, that's easy. We don't draft him." Landry also said something at lunch that Swindoll will never forget. He said, "I've noticed that there's never been an exception. When any one of our men gets involved in drugs, their character leaves. They're finished. It's just a matter of time."

Swindoll then pondered to himself later, how come guys with all that talent, money, and time would get involved with drugs? And those people who are trying to get you into abusing drugs are saying, "Look, this is like no high you've ever had. This'll turn your life around." And then they make promises they can't keep. They *ruin* your character.

In his book, *Root of the Righteous*, A. W. Tozer wrote that Dr. Harold C. Mason once said, "Man was made to dwell in a garden, but through sin, he has been forced to dwell in a field, a field which he has wrestled from his enemies by sweat and tears, and which he preserves only at the price of constant watchfulness and endless toil. Let him but relax his efforts for a few years and the wilderness will claim his field again. The jungle and forest will swallow his labor and all his loving care will have been in vain.

"Every farmer knows the hunger of the wilderness, that hunger that no modern farm machinery and no improved agricultural methods can ever quite destroy. No matter how well prepared the soil, how well kept the fences, or how carefully painted the buildings, when the owner neglects for a while his prized and valued acres, and they will revert again to the wild and be swallowed up by the jungle or the wasteland. The bias of nature is toward the wilderness, never toward the fruitful field. That, we repeat, every farmer knows."

So for our purposes this morning, we might sum up what Tozer said there nice and neatly by saying that, unfortunately, the easiest course through life, the natural tendency that people will have is to live with their mind on sin, rather than G.

Don't believe me? Would you rather believe that it's more natural for people to do good rather than evil? I'd like to think so, too. But former secretary of education Bill Bennet once published *The Index of Leading Cultural Indicators*, revealing how shockingly we have drifted as a nation. His book states, "In the past thirty years, violent crime has increased 560%; illegitimate births, 400%.There has been a tripling of the percentage of kids living in single-parent homes. Teen suicide increase more than 200%." Interesting also, in the past thirty years, there has been a drop in SAT scores by almost 80%.

Maybe for all those reasons and more, whenever we're tempted to think that we're *hot stuff* and that we've really got our act together in so many ways, we ought to take the advice found in Romans 12:3, when the Good News Bible warns, "And because of G's gracious gift to me, I say to all of you: Don't think of yourselves more highly than you should. Instead, be modest in your thinking, and each one of you judge himself according to the amount of faith that G has given him."

But another problem in the area we've been talking about today is that it's simply *not enough* to have our brain partially on G and partially not. Our minds need to be *fully* focused on him and his will for us. At a particular children's hospital, a boy gains a reputation for wreaking havoc with the nurses and staff. One day, a visitor who knew about his terrorizing nature made the boy a deal: "If you are good for a week, I'll give you a *dime* when I come in again." A week later, she stood before his bed. "I'll tell you what," she began, "I won't ask the nurses if you behaved. You have to tell me yourself. Do you deserve the dime?"

After a couple seconds of pause, the boy looked at her in the eye and said, "Gimme a *penny*."

When I was a kid, I used to like to watch auto racing on TV, and I remember seeing A. J. Foyt drive during those days. Well, when you put some race car driver like A. J. Foyt in a race car on the Indianapolis 500, get out of the way. But most of Foyt's life is not spent at the I-500. He has to drive a car on city streets and highways just like the rest of us, paying attention to speed limits just like the rest of us.

Now let's say Foyt pulls up to a stop sign one day, and some young kid with a grin on his face pulls up next to him, not knowing who Foyt is. The kid thinks his car is fast and cool. Foyt is just sitting in his passenger car, but the kid says, "Hey, wanna race?" The kid has no idea he's talking to A. J. Foyt. Of course, Foyt could blow the kid away in the drag race. But when the traffc light turns green, Foyt has to apply a whole lot of restraint. There are speed limits on the street, so he has to sit on his pride as this other kid peels off in the distance. Exhibiting that sense of restraint, then, is big way of showing that our brain is on G and not under the influence of the ways of the world.

Yes, the Bible does indeed encourage us to have our brains on God in one of the most widely recognized passages in the New Testament letter of Romans 12:1–2. It's in the Good News Bible's version of those verses that the Bible says, "So then, my brothers, because of G's great mercy to us, I make this appeal to you: Offer yourselves as a living sacrifice to G, dedicated to his service and pleasing to him. This is the true worship that you should offer. Do not conform outwardly to the standards of this world, but LET G TRANSFORM YOU INWARDLY BY A COMPLETE CHANGE OF YOUR MIND. Then you will be able to know the will of G—what is good, and is pleasing to him, and is perfect."

And remember, everybody, once we do acquire the mind of Christ, once we have our brains on G, as 2 Corinthians 5:17 explains: "If anyone is in Christ, he is a new creature: old things are passed away; behold, all things are become new."

So for the person who's trying to overcome giving into temptations and thus showing forth the mindset of having a brain on sin, let me give you some suggestions on how we can maybe overcome that mindset and begin to have a brain on G instead.

1. Stop rationalizing: Refuse to make comments like "Oh, well, that's just the way I am, always have been, always will be." Such excuses encourage us to completely ignore the Spirit's work of conviction in our life.
2. Apply a strategy: Approach your target with a rifle, not a shotgun. Take on each habit one at a time, not all at once.
3. Be realistic: It won't happen fast. It won't be easy. And the change won't become permanent overnight. Periodic failures, however, are still better than habitual slavery.
4. Be encouraged: Realize you're on the road to ultimate triumph, for the first time in years! Enthusiasm strengthens self-discipline and prompts an attitude of stick-to-it-iveness.
5. Finally, start today. This is the best moment thus far in your life. To put it off is an admission of defeat and will only intensify and prolong the self-confidence battle.

You know, if I had the appropriate visual material and necessary equipment to show it to all of you with. I'd finish this message this morning by showing you about a dozen pictures or so of people in the midst of less-than-godly activity—people stealing, fighting and arguing, committing crimes, acting self-righteously toward others, committing acts of vandalism, etc.—and then I'd say to you, "This is your brain, in its naturally sinful, fallen state."

Then I'd show you a bunch of pictures of people in the midst of doing good, godly, Christlike things—scenarios like Billy Graham preaching the gospel to hundreds or thousands of people at a time, Mother Theresa ministering to the poor, groups of people banding together to build Habitat for Humanity houses. And then I'd say, "*This* is your brain on God."

Any questions?

The One Thing You Can't Put into a Box
Genesis 18:6-15; Luke 1:37; 1 Kings 22:16

Look what I've got, everybody—I've got a box (hold up a cardboard box). Boxes are great, aren't they? Why are boxes so great? Because you can stick all kinds of stuff in them. For example, you can put food in a box (proceed to put some food items in the box). Look—beans and oranges, right in there. Take it with you, and you've got your own portable grocery store. Or you can put tools in a box—screwdrivers, flashlights. Take it with you now and you have your own take-it-with-you hardware store. You can even put clothes in a box. If you put socks in a box, you can sound like Dr. Seuss when you do that. But you know, there's one thing that you can't possibly put into a box, no matter how hard you try, and that's God.

Now, what in the world do I mean by that? Of course you can't put God in a box. Who'd be ridiculous enough to try something like that? Oh, you'd be surprised. You see, "to put something in a box" can mean something other than simply physically packing something up for storage or travel. "To put something in a box" can sometimes mean that we've figuratively wrapped something up and taken care of it, that we've brought something to a conclusion. Whatever had posed a problem for us before no longer does because we've "taken care of it, gotten it under control." We now call the shots, not this thing that once posed more of a challenge for us than we wanted to have for ourselves. But we can't put God in a box, now can we? God will always be who he wants to be and do whatever he wants to do. Amen?

Now, one way in which is attempt to put G in a box is to lessen his power and might in our minds—in other words, doubt that G can do the unlimited amount of things that we know deep down inside that he can indeed do. You know the kind of thing I'm talking about. We Christians, though we should know better, do this all the time whenever we think to ourselves or say out loud things like "Not even God can heal the illness I have," "It would take more than the power of God to repair the damage that's been done to my relationship with my particular loved one," or even "I'm so far in debt, there's no way that even G himself is able to get me back onto solid financial footing." Excuse me, but do know what a person who says that kind of thing is doing? They're basically trying to put G in a box, claiming that the great G we serve, contrary to what scripture tells us over and over again, is powerless against whatever type of difficulty we're facing at that point.

But when we are faced with such a scenario, what we need to do, then, is to call to mind what the Bible tells us in passages such as Luke 1:37, which deals with the fact that both the virgin Mary and her aged cousin Elizabeth would both conceive and give birth, when the angel spoke to Mary then saying, "With G, nothing is impossible." And J Himself makes the exact same statement, according to Matthew 19:26 and Mark 10:27, when questioned about the rich man who would not give up everything to follow J, and the people there asked then, "Who can be saved?"

J responded to them saying, "With man, this is impossible, but with G, all things are possible."

But one of the earliest demonstrations of this truth in the Bible comes from the story of G revealing to Abraham and Sarah that elderly Sarah would also give birth to a son. It's in Genesis 18:6–14, then, we read, "So Abe ran back to the tent and said to Sara, 'Quick! Get three measures of your best flour, and bake some bread.'

"Then Abe ran out to the herd and chose a fat calf and told a servant to hurry and butcher it. When the food was ready, he took some cheese curds and milk and roasted meat, and he served it to the men. As they ate, Abe waited on them there beneath the trees.

"'Where is Sara?' they asked.

"'In the tent,' Abe replied.

"Then one of them said, 'About this time next year, I will return and your wife Sarah will have a son.'

"Now Sarah was listening to all this from a tent nearby, and since both Abe and Sarah were elderly, Sarah was long past the age to have children. She laughed silently to herself. 'How could a worn-out woman like me have a baby when my husband is also so old?'

"Then the Lord said to Abe, 'Why did Sarah laugh? Why did she say, "Can an old woman like me have a baby?" IS ANYTHING TOO HARD FOR THE LORD?'"

But even after the Bible tells us again and again, in various ways, that nothing is impossible with G, many times, we just can't seem to trust G to be powerful enough to help us out. For example, there's the story of a tourist who wandered too close to the edge of the Grand Canyon, lost his footing, and plunged over the side, clawing and scratching to save himself. Well, just before he fell into to the bottom, he encountered a shrubby bush which he desperately grabbed with both hands. Filled with terror, he called out toward heaven, "Is there anyone up there?"

Well, a calm and powerful voice came from out of the sky, "Yes, there is."

The tourist pleaded, "Can you help me?"

The calm voice replied, "Yes, I can. Do you have faith?"

"Yes, yes, I have *strong* faith."

The calm voice said, "Well, in that case, simply let go of the bush and everything will turn out fine."

There was a tense pause, and then the tourist yelled, "Is there anyone else up there?"

Yeah, it's sad to say, but we often put G in a box by not being able to trust him with our lives. However, we also put him in a kind of box whenever we trust him *too* much, by expecting him to do *everything* for us, by instantly and completely answering *all* our requests. Then when we don't get what we want, when and how we want it, we blame G. It's kind of like a fellow named Mike, who faithfully went to church every Sunday and prayed, "G, please let me win the lottery." Months passed, and although Mike *fervently* repeated his prayer weekly, it went unanswered—until one Sunday, when Mike hears a deep voice from above utter his name. "Is that you, G?" Mike asked.

"Yes, Mike," the voice responded, "it's me."

"God," Mike then implores, "why won't you let me win the lottery?"

"You have to meet me halfway, Mike," G answered. "At least buy a ticket!"

So that point that we are very well able to do something about the needs we have and are completely capable of fulfilling some of the requests we throw at G was seen in an exchange that G. K. Chesterson and some of his literary friends had when they were asked once what book they would prefer to have with them if stranded on a desert isle. One writer said without hesitation, "The complete works of Shakespeare." Another said, "I'd choose the Bible." (That sounds right, doesn't it?) But then Chesterson spoke up and answered, "In a case like that, I'd choose Thomas's *Guide to Practical Ship Building.*"

But for all those times where we just "can't be of real help to ourselves," G is there to do the miraculous, it if is indeed within his will to do so. Job acknowledged about as much, as he spoke to G after G confronted him about his self-righteous opinions. Convicted by what G told him, Job confessed, "I know that you can do anything, and no one can stop you."

Not only Job, however, was able to see the extent of G's power, in the Bible. Jeremiah is recorded in the Bible book named after him, in the seventeenth to the twentieth verses of the thirty-second chapter as having prayed aloud, "O Sovereign Lord! You have made the heavens and earth by your great power. Nothing is too hard for you! You are loving and kind to thousands, though children suffer for their parents' sins. You are the great and powerful G, the Lord Almighty. You have all wisdom and do great and mighty miracles. You are very aware of the conduct of all the people, and you reward them according to their deeds. You performed miraculous signs and wonders in the land of Egypt—things still remembered to this day! And you have continued to do great miracles in Israel and all around the world. You have made your name very great, as it is today." Now, I ask you, according to that passage of scripture, does it sound like G isn't able to help us deal with whatever we're going through, presently?

In addition, Romans 4:20–21 reassures us, "Abraham never wavered in believing G's promise. In fact, his faith grew stronger, and in this, he brought glory to G. He was absolutely convinced that G was able to do anything he promised." And G himself declared in both Isaiah 50:2 and Jeremiah 32:27 together, "Was I too weak to save you? Is that why the house is silent and empty when I come home? Is it because I have no power to rescue? No, that is not the reason! For I can speak to the sea and make it dry! I can turn rivers into deserts covered with dying fish…I am the Lord, the God of all the peoples of the world. is anything too hard for me?"

And of course, we're all familiar with miracles in the Bible where G overrode the laws of nature, to accomplish his purposes, like when he explained he would, in 1 Kings 3:15–18: "While the harp was being played, the power of the Lord came upon Elisha and he said, 'This is what the Lord says: This dry valley will be filled with pools of water! You will see neither wind nor rain, says the Lord, but his valley will be filled with water. You will have plenty for yourselves and for your cattle and your other animals. But this is only a simple thing for the Lord, for he will make you victorious over the army of Moab!"

Now, the *other* major way, as I see it, that people try to put G in a box is when they try to have him all figured out, when they've come to the conclusion that because they have a personal relationship with G, they *think* they've come to have all the answers to all of life's tough problem questions. The spiritual people who really concern me are those who act as if they can answer *any* difficult theological question you ask them. *Never* do they admit that they don't know, nor will they say in response to a debatable question about something in the Bible, "Well, your question can't be answered with absolute certainty." Instead, people in religious cults and today's false prophets have an answer for *everything*.

You see, what they are trying to do is to put G in some kind of nice, neat little theological box, so that they can have a false sense of peace of mind and security, believing that with G, we can have *all* our questions answered. The problem, though, is that that's not possible. Even though we might have a solid relationship with Christ, we're still sinful, fallen human beings, unable to answer all the tough questions of the universe.

In 1 Kings 22:15 and 16, the prophet Micaiah came to pay king Ahab a visit to prophesy some tough words to him. Scripture tells us here that when Micaiah arrived, Ahab asked him, 'Should we go to war against Ramoth-Gilead or not? And then Micaiah answered, "Go right ahead. The Lord will give the king a glorious victory." Now, here, the part I appreciate. Verse 16 says that Ahab replied sharply, "Whenever you speak to me in the name of the Lord, tell me the truth. How many times do I have to tell you that?" You don't know how many times I have said as much to JWs and Mormons who've spoken with me about their beliefs.

Yes, we can know certain things about G: that he is loving, powerful, the Creator of everything, and that he has ultimate control of everything that happens, whether he initiates a certain event that takes place or not. The Bible tells us these kinds of things over and over in many different passages. But we really need to be careful not to try to put G in any kind of box, since there are things about him that we just don't know.

To illustrate what I mean, look at what G himself said to Job, in Job 38–42, after having listened to Job go on and on about all he *thought* he knew about who G is and how he operates. From selected verses out of those two chapters, here are some of the things G told Job: "How great is G—beyond our understanding! The number of his years is past finding out…He does great things beyond our understanding…Then, the Lord answered Job out of the storm. He said…Where were *you* when I laid the foundations of the earth? Have the gates of death been shown to you? Have you seen the gates of the shadow of death? Have you comprehended the vast expanses of the earth? Tell me, if you know all this…Surely you know, for you were already born! You have lived so many years! Then the Lord spoke to Job out of the storm: 'Brace yourself like a man; I will question you, and you shall answer me.' Then Job said to G, 'I know that you can do all things. Surely I spoke of things I did not understand, things too wonderful for me.'"

You see, it's a fact of human nature that the things of the Unknown scare us. Those many people are adventurous and like to explore new and unknown things. But face it, by and large we like things that are familiar to us, things that we can get a handle on and control, for the most part. But we can't do that with G. Think about, for a second, what G told Job in that exchange we just went over. In contemporary terms, I can just hear G now tell Job, "Where were you, Job, when I hung the stars in the sky? Oh yeah, that's right. You weren't there, because I, your Creator, hadn't made you yet. But if I *had* brought you into being before I had created the world and you had been there when I hung the stars in the sky, I can imagine you—with the attitude you have right now—telling me that I had hung some of the stars in the sky too close together and that I needed to *move* some of them away from others in the sky. But you know what, Job? If you had been there and said something like that to me, I would have had to say that I was the one in charge, that I created everything there is, *including you*, and that the way I've hung the stars in the sky is just fine, thank you very much."

As we read in Romans 9:20–21, "But who are *you*, O man, to talk back to G? Shall what is formed say to him who formed it, 'Why did you make me like this?' Does not the potter have the right to make out of the same lump of clay some pottery for noble purposes and some for common use?"

Everyone, as tempting as it might be sometimes, we really need to refrain from either doubting G's available power for our lives, thinking that he isn't able to help us handle the difficulties before us, or the temptation to try to get a handle on him and reduce him to something simple and easy to figure out even in difficult to understand circumstances. You see, G's going to be who he is and do what he wants to do. There's no need for us to try to fool with that.

I don't know about *your* G, but *my* G isn't powerless or helpless or unable to come to my rescue when I need him. And my G also isn't so easy to explain away or get under control. No, my G can't be put in any kind of box— cardboard, iron, steel, or any other kind. So, folks, whenever we think of G, it's time to think *outside the box*. Amen? Amen.

January 11 The Coyote and the Sheepdog
Exodus 34:6-7; John 8:42-47

When I was a kid, I used to love to watch cartoons on TV—actually I *still* do. I was a fan of almost all different types of cartoons, but there were some that made a special impression on me, to the point where I remember some of the very episodes I'd watch. One of these began by show a coyote and a sheepdog, both making their way, in the early morning, toward the front of a large meadow, filled with grazing sheep. Oddly enough, there was a *timeclock*, posted on the ground, at the front of the meadow, and as the sheepdog and coyote gave each other a "good morning" greeting, they took turns "punching in" for the day.

After wishing each other to have a good day, then, they both went to work—the sheepdog taking his position in order to guard the sheep, and the coyote got busy setting up various means in which to catch and kill some sheep in order for him to have something to eat for that day. However, throughout the course of the cartoon, the sheepdog foils the coyote's efforts to catch any sheep, and the coyote thus finds himself in numerous instances of trouble—being weighted down enough to sink to the bottom of the river, being fried by massive volts of electricity, being burned to a crisp by assorted sources of fire, etc.

Now the reason why they each did what they did is because coyotes are *natural predators*—they hunt in order to catch/kill for food. That's just what they are made to do. Likewise, the sheepdog just naturally *guards* who/whatever it's supposed to protect. In fact, the sheepdog will face danger on its own part, in order to protect whatever has been put under its guard.

Well, you know, G and Satan reflect that "natural instinct" of both the sheepdog and the coyote, respectively, as we see both described characteristically in the Bible. First, G is described, according to a vital passage found in Exodus 34:6–7: "G passed in front of Moses, saying, 'The Lord, the Lord, the compassionate and gracious G, slow to anger, abounding in love and faithfulness, maintaining love to thousands and forgiving wickedness, rebellion and sin. Yet, he does not leave the guilty go unpunished." And that's not the only passage in the Bible that describes G in that way. We'll look at several more throughout the sermon today, and one of those that's just a tad bit shorter than Exodus 34:6–7 is found in Numbers 14:18, which states, "The Lord is slow to anger, abounding in love and forgiving sin and rebellion." So G, according to those verses, is found to be like a "spiritual sheepdog" of sorts, being depicted as loving, faithful, forgiving, and yet, hard on sin.

The devil, Satan, on the other hand, reminds me of a sly, cunning, cold, and calculating type of coyote or wolf—a predator of souls. J himself laid out for us just what kind of an enemy we face in Satan, when he was recorded in John 8:42–47 as saying, according to the Living Bible, "J said to the them, 'If G were your father, you would love me, for I have come to you from G. I am not here on my own, but he sent me. Why can't you understand what I am saying?It is because you are prevented from doing so! For you are the children of your father, the devil, and you love to do the evil things he does. He was a murderer from the beginning and a hater of the truth—there is not an iota of truth in him. When he lies, it's perfectly normal; for he is the father of liars. And so when I tell the truth, you just naturally don't believe it! Which of you can truthfully accuse me of one single sin? Since I'm telling you the truth, why don't you believe me? Anyone whose Father is G listens gladly to the words of G. Since you don't, it proves you aren't his children.'

"'You Samaritan! Foreigner! Devil!' the Jewish leaders snarled. 'Didn't we say all along you were possessed by a demon?'"

Yes, as those words of J indicate, Satan is a liar and *therefore can't be trusted* in anything that he communicates to us. In connection with that truth, then, there's the story of a family that was driving one warm spring day on a road so thick with tress that they couldn't see the sun. The four-year-old boy in the family spoke up and commented, "There are so many trees here that I think I'm in Eden."

"Why do you say that?" the boy's mother asked. "Don't you know about Eden, Mom?"

"Why don't you tell me about it?" she answered.

So he did. "Well, there were lots of trees in the Garden of Eden, and in the middle of the garden was a fruit tree. G told A and E not to pick the fruit from that tree. But then a snake came along, and the *snake* said, 'It's okay, you can eat fruit from that tree.' And they did."

Then, the boy made an insightful comment: "I would *never* listen to a snake. I would listen to GOD. Mommy, why would anyone listen to a snake?" In later relating this story to a friend, the mother stated that she never told her son this, but there had been numerous times in her life when she herself had ignored G and instead listened to a snake.

And it's exactly because many people choose to ignore G that they do indeed wind up listening to a snake, or Satan, throughout their lives. They, then, are the children of the devil whom J was talking to and referring about in John 8. It's like the time when a pastor asked a lawyer, "What do you do if you make a mistake on a case?"

The lawyer responded, "I try to *fix* it if it's *big* and ignore it if it's *insignificant*. What do you do when you make a mistake, Pastor?"

The minister answered, "I do more or less the same thing. Let me give you an example: The other day, I meant to say, 'The devil is the father of *liars*,' but instead, I said, 'The devil is the father of *lawyers*,' so I just let it go."

Now, in order for us to continue to *properly* describe God, we need to understand that there are two sides to him: there's a righteous, just, and serious side, and then, there's the loving and compassionate side of G. So in speaking about G's judgmental side, C. S. Lewis wrote in his book *The Problem of Pain*, "We want, in fact, *not* so much a Father in heaven as a grandfather in heaven—a senile benevolence who, as they say, 'likes to see people enjoying themselves,' and whose plan from the universe was simply that it might be truly said at the end of each day, 'a good time was had by all.'"

You see, that's, unfortunately, how a lot of people view G—or at least *want* to view him, as an overly permissive being who lets us do whatever we want, rather than acknowledge that G will make sure that people will pay dearly for their unrepented sin. G is righteous and just after all, and he's not about to put up with any spiritual foolishness on our part. Remember, the Bible tells us in Romans 6:23 that the penalty of sin is *death*—spiritual as well as physical.

On the other hand, I believe it's just as wrong to view G as being all about judgment, harshness, and punishment. They forget about—or maybe neglect to realize to begin with—that G is *love*. These are the kind of people that Chuck Swindoll was describing when he once said, "Have you ever served in the military? I remember how wonderful it was to go into the office of the company commander, ha-ha. I remember doing that one time. He didn't say, 'Oh, Chuck, how *nice* of you to drop by! Come on in, son. Have a seat. Now, what's on your heart?' No, in fact, the first words I heard that I can repeat to you were 'What do *you* want?' Now, there's a wonderful greeting for a guy who's standing there with his knees knocking against each other. You know what? I couldn't even *remember* what I wanted, which made the whole thing that much worse."

Swindoll then continued, "When I was a little kid, I had that feeling about G. I'd got it from a Lil Abner cartoon. This little guy is walking around with a club, and it had a *nail* in it, or more like a *spike*, actually. He was always walking around, looking for people to smack with it. And when I was a little kid, I used to think, 'That's G! He's just looking for people and saying, "There he is!" Then *whomp*!'"

So we mortal humans need to realize that there are truly two sides to G—a *powerful* side and a *loving* side, as a group of third and fourth graders at Wheaton, Illinois, Christian Grammar School expressed when they were given the assignment to complete the phrase "By faith, I know that G is." Here are some of their answers:

Forgiving, because he forgave in the Bible, and he forgave me when I went in the road on my bike without one of my parents. *Providing-ful* (interesting word, eh?), because he dropped manna for Moses and the people, and he gave my dad a job. *Caring*, because he made the blind man see, and he made me catch a very fast line drive that could have hurt me. He probably sent an angel down. *Merciful*, because my brother has been nice to me for a whole year. *Faithful*, because the school bill came, and my mom didn't know how we were going to pay it. Two minutes later, my dad called, and he just got a bonus check. My mom was in tears. *Sweet*, because he gave me a dog. God tells me not to do things that are bad. I need someone like that.

Well, let's take another look at what the Bible itself has to say about Satan. There are a couple of extremely important passages in the Old

Testament that help us to see just exactly how in G's originally all-good creation there ever came to be such a being—Isaiah 14:12–15 and Ezekiel 28:11–17: "How you have fallen from heaven, O morning star, son of the dawn! You have been cast down to the earth, you who once laid low the nations! You said in your heart, 'I will ascend to the heaven; I will raise my throne above the stars of G; I will sit enthroned on the mount of the assembly, on the utmost heights of the sacred mountain. I will ascend above the tops of the clouds; I will make myself like the Most High.' But you are brought down to the grave to the depths of the pit...You were the model of perfection, full of wisdom and perfect in beauty. You were in Eden, the garden of G; every precious stone adorned you. You were anointed as a guardian cherub—I ordained you as such. You were on the holy mount of G; you walked among the fiery stones. You were blameless in your ways from the day you were created until wickedness was found in you. Through your widespread trade, you were filled with violence, and you sinned. So I drove you in disgrace from the mount of G and I expelled you, O guardian cherub, from among the fiery stones. Your heart became proud on account of your beauty, and you corrupted your wisdom because of your splendor. So I threw you to the earth; I made a spectacle of you before kings."

Ironic, isn't it? After all, everything that G creates is good, including Lucifer in his original state. But part of G's love for us is the freedom he gives *all* his human and angelic creations to decide to love him back or not. We don't know how long it was after Lucifer's creation before he decided to rebel against G, but we do know that ever since that time, he's done everything he could to oppose G in every way possible. So the closer we get to following S's will for our lives, the more spiritual peril we get ourselves in. As Augustine once put it, "The devil is like a chained-up mad dog. He is powerless to harm us when we are outside his reach, but once we enter his circle, we expose ourselves again to injury and harm."

And don't forget, it's not like we can just *ignore* S and he'll go away. He's persistent in trying to harass J's followers. As Ewald Plass wrote in his book, *Volume 1 of What Luther Says*, "The devil doesn't take a holiday; he never rests. If beaten, he rises again. If he can't enter in front, he steals in the back door. If he can't enter at the back, he breaks through the roof or enters by tunneling under the threshold. He labors until he's in. He uses great cunning and many a plan. When one miscarries, he has another at hand and continues his attempts until he thinks he's won."

J. Dwight Pentecost used to say, "Mercy is G's ministry to the miserable. It's both intensely personal and immensely practical. For when I am treated unfairly, G's mercy relieves my bitterness. When I grieve over loss, it relieves my pain and anger and denial. When I struggle with disability, it relieves my self-pity. When I endure physical pain, it relieves my hopelessness. When I deal with being sinful, it relieves my guilt."

So you see, no matter how powerfully evil S is, G's mercy *still triumphs*. I guess that we could say that the only reason we're important to S is that we're the focus of all the pain, suffering and misery he can throw at G's creation. But as you know, we're much more important to G, and in a good, positive way. Frank Capra, who directed the classic movie, *It's a Wonderful Life*, was asked once about the central message of the film. He responded, "I believe the real message of *It's a Wonderful Life* is this: that under the sun, nothing is insignificant to G." Now, the next time you see the film, you know that everything that happens has intended and unintended consequences. Everything, because it happened, causes something else to happen. Everybody in that story is important, because he or she relates to everyone else. Nothing is insignificant to under the sun to G. Maybe we need to be reminded, every once in a while, that not only are *we* important to G, but everyone *else* around us is important to him, too.

Now, we've spent a lot of time, today, defining both G and S, but once more, let me quote some additional Bible passages helping us to make even clearer just exactly who G is and what he's all about. Jonah 4:2, and Psalms 86:15 and 103:8 are shorter versions of our original passage for today, the one from Exodus 34:6–7. So together, those verses from Jonah and Psalms say, "Jonah said, 'I *knew* G, that you are a loving and merciful G, always patient, always kind, and always ready to change your mind and not punish...' But you, O Lord, are a merciful and loving G, always patient, always kind and faithful...The Lord is merciful and loving, slow to become angry and full of constant love." And as the New Testament puts it in 1 John 4:7–8 and 16, "Dear friends, let's love one another, because love comes from G. Whoever loves is a child of G and knows G.

Whoever does not love does not know G, for G is love… And we ourselves know and believe the love which G has for us. G is love, and whoever lives in love lives in union with G and G lives in union with him."

A man named Phil Watson once put it like this: "The fundamental biblical opposition isn't between flesh and the Spirit, creature and Creator, but between the *Creator* of the flesh and its *Destroyer*, between G and the devil, Christ and Satan, the HS and the unholy." And I might add between the sheepdog and the coyote.

A kindergarten teacher told the kids to draw a picture of what was important to them. In the back of the room, little Johnny began to labor over his drawing. The teacher eventually made the rounds, looking over shoulders and at what the kids had produced.

She eventually asked, "What are you drawing, Johnny?"

"God," he replied.

"But, Johnny," she began to say gently, "no one knows what G looks like."

"They will when I get through," he answered.

None of us may know what G *looks* like, but we know what he *acts* like, through the depiction of him in scripture. Do you know G for yourself?

Dealing with Christmas Mourning
Matthew 2:13-18; Jeremiah 31:13-17

You know it's going to be a bad day when you see a new *60 Minutes* crew walk into your office. You call the suicide prevention hotline, and they put you on hold. You turn on the news, and they're in the process of show escape routes out of the city. Your twin sister forgot your b-day. Your car horn goes off accidentally—and remains *stuck*—as you follow a group of Hells Angels on the freeway. Your boss tells you not to bother to take your coat off, as you get to the office.

Now, we *laugh* at those scenarios, even at this special time of the year. But you know, Christmas is *anything* but merry and jolly for many people, and that fact is due largely to those who've experienced the death of a family member of other loved one during the previous year—whether the death took place earlier in the month of December or much earlier in the year. Ironically and sadly, this was the situation during the time of Christ's incarnation on earth.

Matthew 2:13–18 reports, "When they had gone, an angel of the Lord appeared to Joseph in a dream. 'Get up,' he said, 'Take the child and his mother and escape to Egypt. Stay there until I tell you, for Herod is going to search for the child to kill him.'

"So he got up, took the child and his mother during the night and left for Egypt, where he stayed until the death of Herod. And so was fulfilled what the Lord had said through the Prophet Isaiah: 'Out of Egypt I called my son.' When Herod realized that he had been outwitted by the Magi, he was furious, and he gave orders to kill all the boys in Bethlehem and its vicinity that were two years old or under, in accordance with the time he had learned from the magi. Then what was said through the prophet Jeremiah was fulfilled: 'A voice is heard in Ramah, weeping and great mourning, Rachel weeping for her children and refusing to be comforted, because they are no more.'"

Interestingly enough, the same description of someone who lost a child in death, whom also refused to be comforted, is found in Genesis 37:35, in the case of Jacob's sons deceiving him, leading him to believe that his son Joseph had killed by a wild animal. It's there the Bible states, "All his sons and daughters came to comfort him, but he refused to be comforted."

James Dobson once said that in a hospital where he was ministering, a five-year-old boy was dying of cancer. His mother was a devoted Christian, and though it was painful for her to do so, she stayed right by his bed every day. One night after she had left to go back home, the hospital staff could hear the boy from in his room calling out, "I hear the bells, I hear the bells. They're ringing." He repeated that phrase through the night, though the staff didn't pay much attention.

When the boy's mother came to visit the next day, asking at the nurse's station how her son was doing, she was told, "He seems to be hallucination. He keeps talking about hearing bells. It must be the medication talking."

The mother stopped and said sternly to the nurse, "He's *not* hallucinating. He's not out of his head. I *told* him weeks ago that when the pain got so bad that he couldn't breathe, he was soon going to heaven to be with J. Then I said that when it got really bad, he was to look up in the corner of his room toward heaven and listen for the bells, because they'd be ringing for him."

She then swept down the hall, turned into his room, saw her little boy, and immediately picked him up in her arms to rock him. Then, he talked about hearing the bells until they were just an echo.

Horatio Spafford, a Chicago businessman, sent his wife and three daughters to Europe by ship, while he remained back in the US, intending to join them later. En route, there was a terrible storm, and the ship wrecked, drowning all three daughters. Mrs. Spafford, however, made it to safety and wired back to her husband, saying, "All of our daughters have been lost. Only I have been saved."

Spafford then took the very next ship, and as they neared the place where the accident had occurred, the skipper of the boat Spafford was on pointed that fact out to him. It was there on the deck of that ship that Spafford penned these very familiar words: "When peace like a river attendeth my way, when sorrows like sea billows roll; whatever my lot, thou hast taught me to say, 'It is well, it is well with my soul.'"

You see, one thing we can get out of suffering due to the death of a loved one (at Christmas or any other time of the year) is that we can come to realize the truth that joy and happiness very rarely have anything to teach us, but pain and suffering have a way of helping us to grow, personally, by teaching us numerous lessons of life. For example, in his book *A 20th Century Testimony*, Malcolm Muggeridge wrote, "Contrary to what might be expected, I look back on experiences that at the time, seemed especially desolating and painful with particular satisfaction. Indeed, I can say with complete truthfulness, that everything I have learned in my seventy-five years in this world, everything that has truly enhanced and enlightened my existence has been through affliction and not through happiness." In other words, if it ever were to be possible to eliminate affliction from our earthly existence by means of some drug or other medical mumbo jumbo, as Huxley envisioned in *Brave New World*, the result would not be to make life delectable, but to make it too plain and trivial to be endurable. This, of course, is what the cross signifies. "And it's the cross," Muggeridge concluded, "more than anything else, that has called me to Christ."

Along these same lines, a man by the name of Ross W. Marrs once pointed stated, "Take away my ability to fail, and I would not know the meaning of success. Let me be immune to rejection and heartbreak, and I couldn't know the glory of living." And Ralph Waldo Emerson once observed that "Bad times have a scientific value. Those are occasions a good learner would not miss." John Calvin even recognized that when we suffer, it makes us a more effective witness for J when he said, "No one is fit to preach the gospel, seeing that the world is against the message, until that man is prepared to suffer."

All right, so we've talked about pain and suffering at Christmastime, for the first half of today's message. Let's get to what the Bible says, then, about the fact that the Christmas message is Good News to those who do suffer at any point during the calendar year. Well, as you know doubt know, the Bible is *full* of encouragement for times such as when we feel in the midst of a typically joyous season more than just a little depressed. For instance, Psalm 30:5 reminds us that "weeping may remain for a night, but rejoicing comes in the morning." Isaiah 40:1 states, "Comfort, comfort, my people, says your God." David penned in Psalm 30:11–12, "You turned my wailing into dancing; you removed my sackcloth and clothed me with joy, that my heart may sing to you and not be silent." And Isaiah 51:11 proclaims, "The ransomed of the Lord will return. They will enter Zion with singing; everlasting joy will crown their heads. Gladness and joy will overtake them, and sorrow and sighing will flee away."

Dr. R. A. Torrey, founder of the Bible Institute of LA, lost his twelve-year-old daughter in an accident. The funeral was on a rainy day. They stood there, beside that hole in the ground, surrounded by loved ones. It was dark and dismal. Mrs. Torrey said to her husband, "I'm so glad Elizabeth is *not* in that box." Their grief went home with them as they tried to sleep that night.

Well, Dr. Torrey got up the next morning and went for a walk. A wave of grief broke over him, the loneliness of her absence, the terrible feeling knowing they would never hear her laughter again, never see her face, witnessing her growth. He couldn't take it. He leaned against a street light and looked up and began to pray. This is what he experienced: "And just then, the fountain, the Holy Spirit, whom I had in my heart, broke forth with such power as I think I had never experienced before. And it was the most joyful moment I had ever known in my life! It is an unspeakably glorious thing to have within you a fountain ever springing up, springing up, springing up, *ever* springing up 365 days in every year, springing up under *all* circumstances."

Well, possibly, it's *not* us who are suffering at the present time. Maybe everything's okay, as far as we're concerned. But maybe we know of someone else who is suffering, someone who we feel like we should try to help out this Christmas season, to try to help make the holiday a little more bearable. In his book *The Last Thing We Talked About*, Joseph Bayly recalled, "I was sitting, torn by grief. Someone came and talked to me a G's dealings, of *why* it happened, of hope beyond the grave. He talked constantly, he said things I knew were true. I was unmoved, except to wish he'd go away. He finally did. Another friend came and sat beside me. He *didn't* talk. He *didn't* ask any leading questions. He just sat beside me for an hour or more, listened when I said something, answered briefly, prayed simply, then left. It was then that I was moved. I was comforted. I hated to see him go."

And remember this truth: when we take the care and time to help be an encouragement to someone who needs it, *everyone involved* in the situation becomes blessed by the situation, one way or another. The story is told of a lady missionary, who was sitting one day at her window, going through her mail. As she opened one envelope, a $10 bill fell out. But as she reached down to pick it up, her eye caught the sight of shabbily dressed stranger on the street below. Thinking that he might be in more financial stress than she was, she put the bill on a plain envelope, writing on the front of it the phrase, "Don't despair." She then threw it out the window. The stranger below sure enough picked it up, read it, looked up, and smiled as he tipped his hat to her and went on his way.

The next day, she was about to leave the house when a knock came at the door. She found the same shabbily dressed man smiling as he handed her a *roll of money*. When she asked what that was for, he replied: "That's the $60 you won, lady. 'Don't despair' paid five-to-one odds at the track."

But just remember, G can help us recover from difficult times much more effectively than any human being ever could. After all, it's been suggested that you should bother telling other people your troubles. Half of them don't care, and the *other* half figure that you probably had it coming, anyway.

One thing to consider, though, is when tough times hit, we can choose to attempt to either make something good out of them *or* something rotten. It's all up to us. James Lowell put it like this: Troubles are like knives—they either serve us or cut us, depending on whether we grab them by the blade or the handle. Along those lines, there's the story of a second-grade boy named David, who was bumped as he was getting on the bus one day, and as a result suffered a cut on his cheek. At recess, he collided with another boy and lost a tooth in the process. At noon, he was sliding on ice, fell, and sprained his wrist. Later at the hospital, his dad noticed him clutching a quarter in his good hand. David then said, "I found it on the ground when I fell. It's the first quarter I've ever found... this sure is my lucky day!" Now, I realize that it would take a *lot* of good to happen in the same time frame in which a loved one of ours has passed away in order for us to feel as though we're having a good day. But I think you know what I'm getting at. Even in the darkest of times, G can give us the strength to nevertheless rejoice.

Most, if not all, of us are familiar with J's words from Matthew 11:28–30. In Today's English Version, the Bible records there, "Come to me, all of you who are tired from carrying your heavy loads, and I will give you rest. Take my yoke and put it on you, and learn from me, because I am gentle and humble in spirit; and you will find rest. The yoke I will give you is easy, and the load I will put on you is light." But maybe a lesser known passage is found in Psalm 68:19, which proclaims, "Praise be to the Lord, to God our Savior, who daily bears our burdens." In addition, Psalm 116:7 states, "Be at rest once more, O my soul, for the Lord has been good to you."

Oscar Wilde once said that once, while he was on vacation, he finished reading a book called *Adrift*. It was the story of a man who built a vessel that was to sail him through the whole of the Atlantic, sort of a large loop. He hit bad weather and his vessel went down. He existed on a raft for almost eighty days. The thing that kept him alive was *hope*. His lowest days were the days when he could see no hope and he could not see the possibility of being rescued or making it to the islands or coming into the shipping lanes and being found by one of those vast vessels on its way on the trade routes. His hope kept him alive. Someone once said, "We can live forty days without food, eight days without water, four minutes without air, but only a few seconds without hope."

Isn't it great, then, to read Bible passages like Isaiah 30:19, where it's written, "O people of Zion, who live in Jerusalem, you will weep no more. How gracious G will be when you cry for help! As soon as he hears, he will answer you." Also, from Isaiah 25:8 says, "The Sovereign Lord will wipe away the tears from all faces."

Think of peace, then, as that calm of mind that is not ruffled by adversity, overclouded by remorseful conscience, or disturbed by fear.

October 28, 2007 Deliver Us from Evil
Ephesians 6:10-18

You know something? I did my best to try to find a funny and humorous illustration to open up with for today's message. I figured that with Halloween just three days away, I'd do a creepy sermon on demons, demonic possession and evil in general. But it's an interesting thing: there aren't too many funny and humorous illustrations, stories, or jokes about demons and evil. Gee, I can't imagine why. Well, it probably has something to do with the fact that Satan, demons and evil are *anything* but funny.

Maybe that's why Ephesians 6:10–18 says what it does. Taken from an assortment of Bible versions, that passage says, "Finally, be strong in the Lord and in the strength of his might. Put on the whole armor of G, that you may be able to stand against the wiles of the devil. For we are not fighting against human beings, but against persons without bodies—the evil beings and great evil princes of darkness who rule this world, and against huge numbers of wicked spirits in the spirit world.

"So take up G's armor now! Then, when the evil day comes, you will be able to resist the enemy's attacks, and after fighting to the end, you will still hold your ground. Stand firm, then, with the belt of truth buckled around your waist, with the breastplate of righteousness in place, wearing for shoes on your feet, the eagerness to spread the gospel of peace, and always carrying the shield of faith, so that you can use it to put out the burning arrows of the evil one. And the you must accept salvation from G to be your helmet and receive the word of G from the Spirit to use as a sword. Pray all the time and ask G for anything in line with the HS's wishes. Plead with him, reminding him of your needs, and keep praying earnestly for all Christians everywhere."

Since this is the last Sunday before Halloween, I'd like to talk to you about a pretty *creepy* subject that really doesn't get spoken of much from the pulpit in church, and that's the topic of demonic possession. Even though the gospels record J's exorcism of numerous people who were possessed by demons, we tend not to talk about demon possession much in the church today, especially in *contemporary* applications. It's just too weird for many of us to deal with. But I actually got the idea for this sermon from a book I read about a year and half ago, *Hostage to the Devil: The Possession and Exorcism of Five Contemporary Americans*, by Malachi Martin.

Now, we might tend to think that people who are possessed by demons have absolutely *no* connection with the church whatsoever, but the first main point that Martin made in the book that really struck me was that a demonically possessed person can be found in a family in which religion occupies a prominent place in their lives. In one of the five cases presented in his book, Martin points out that morning and evening prayers were part of this particular family's routine. This family's love and loyalty were based on Christian beliefs and the pastor of their church had, for them, ultimate authority. Now, I don't make that point to scare anybody in the room, today. I'm not trying to suggest that everybody in the room better be on edge, because one of your family members might need an exorcism, but you know this—just because someone grows up in a Christian home, that's no guarantee that they are protected from that particular spiritual danger. A person isn't saved through the family they belong to, but only through their expressing faith in the one, true G of the universe—G the F, S, and HS.

Make no mistake about it. As our Scripture passage from Ephesians points out today, we're dealing with powerful evil beings in the spiritual realm. As J said to the chief priests and the officers of the temple guard at the time of his arrest, according to the Living Bible's version of Luke 22:53, "This is your moment, when Satan's power reigns supreme." We recognize the power of the statement made in 1 John 5:19, where the Bible points out, "We know that we are children of G and that all the rest of the world is under Satan's power and control." We are warned in 1 John 3:12 "not to be like Cain, who belonged to the evil one and murdered his brother." And 2 Corinthians 2:11 encourages us "to keep Satan from gaining the advantage over us; for we are not ignorant of his schemes."

So just what exactly *are* some of Satan's schemes that he employs in order to try to prevent the kingdom of G from growing? Well, J pointed out in his parable of "The Sower and the Seeds," according to Matthew 13:19, that "the hard path where some of the seed fell represents the heart of the person who hears the Good News about the Kingdom and doesn't understand it; then Satan comes and snatches away the seeds from his heart." So the devil keeps people out of the kingdom of G by causing them not to understand the preaching and teaching of Christ when they have the chance to receive it. Likewise, to further come to see that one of S's strategies is to keep people from simply understanding and comprehending the gospel, 2 Corinthians 4:3–4 points out, "If the Good News we preach is hidden to anyone, it is hidden from the one who is on the road to eternal death. Satan, who is the god of this evil world, has made him blind, unable to see the glorious light of the gospel that is shining on him, or to understand the amazing message we preach about the glory of, who is the image of G."

Now, one of the most striking comments Malachi Martin made in his book *Hostage to the Devil*, was when he was relating the story of an actual exorcism. On page 178, he quotes someone who was directly involved in the exorcism, and this is what the man had to say: "While true cases of Exorcism take their toll on the people involved in them, they are not simple horror tales for frightening readers and moviegoers. For all that evening, we were delving deeper and deeper *not* into horror, but into the frame of love that makes it possible to expel horror." In other words, when attempting to help release someone from the awful grip of demonic possession, as terrifying as attempting to do something like that might be, *love* is the key, the answer, to successfully completing an exorcism. As the Bible so plainly states in 1 John 4:18, "There is *no* fear in love, but perfect love drives out fear."

So besides the attitude and the mindset of love, another powerful weapon against Satan and demons, whether we're facing the need to get involved in an actual exorcism or not, is to make *prayer* an important part of your spiritual warfare battle plan. Seriously, deliberately pray for your—and your loved ones'—safety, against any attacks the devil might throw your way. For instance, Paul wrote in his second letter to the church in Thessalonica 3:2–3, "Pray too that we will be saved out of the clutches of evil men, for not everyone loves the Lord. But the Lord is faithful; he will make you strong and guard you from satanic attacks of every kind."

In addition to that passage, don't forget that J—while leading in the Lord's Prayer, according to Matthew 6:13, prayed, "Don't bring us into temptation, but deliver us from the evil one." And finally, it's exemplified for us that we ought to pray for each other and our loved ones in this same fashioned, according again to a prayer of J's, found in John 17:15—"I'm not asking you take the ones you have given Me, Father, out of the world, but to keep them safe from Satan's power."

Now, two of the most important—and fascinating—points that are brought out in Martin's book, are the emphasis on the importance and power of the symbol of the cross and of J's name. We're all familiar, I'm sure, with the story of Dracula and how in Bram Stoker's novel the vampire was absolutely repelled by a crucifix or the sign of the cross. Well, considering the fact that Stoker meant for his main character to symbolize "the devil on earth," at least that part of his famed piece of fiction seems totally accurate. There was a man with the first name of George, whose sister was demonically possessed. Her increasingly corresponding behavior not only puzzled George, but it frightened him as well. George didn't normally frighten easily, and he *never* had felt fear toward any of his immediate family.

Geo's sister, Marianne, at one point was laying on her bed, and she got up in order to use the bathroom. Now, Geo and M's mother had requested of Geo, at some point, to hide a crucifix somewhere in Marianne's room, so he decided to do just that. When Marianne went to the bathroom, Geo hid a small crucifix under her mattress. No sooner had she returned and sat on the edge of the bed, then she turned white as chalk and fell rigidly to the floor, where she lay jerking her pelvis back and forth as though in great pain. In seconds, the expression on her face had changed from dreamy to almost animal-like; she foamed at the mouth and bared her teeth in a grimace of pain/anger. Obviously, we can see by that example, demons cannot tolerate being near the cross, the most sacred and important symbol in all of Christianity.

Another similar instance is related in Martin's book, in which the power—as well as the antagonizing character—the symbol of the cross has against the demonic realm is clearly demonstrated. A priest by the last name of Hearty holds a crucifix up for a dying (and demonically possessed) man to see. The effect of the sight of the cross on the man was both instantaneous and catastrophic. It was at this point where Hearty and a friend (an army captain) of the dying, possessed man heard strange, guttural sounds coming from the man's throat.

"Padre, he's cursing the cross!" the friend of the dying man said to the priest.

"Go away," the dying man continued, "take yourself and all you signify away from us. You serve what we hate!"

Obviously, a plurality of demons had invaded the man's body and mind. "Ask him a question for me, Captain," Hearty said to the officer. "Ask him why he hates the cross." The officer had no sooner asked the question than the possessed man started to get up. His right hand flashed up to the bandages covering his chest wounds, tearing them off in a convulsive movement.

"Himiko! Himiko!" was as much as Hearty could catch of his shout before the man fell back.

The intelligence officer could not understand the curious word but thought it must be a name of some sort. In a matter of seconds, the dying man's eyes opened with the sightless stare of the dead.

It wasn't until later that Hearty found out what *Himiko* meant. But then knowing that the dead man had spent significant time in a certain part of the jungle, Hearty had a dawning realization that the man who had just died had been dedicated to some sort of evil spiritual power or force, from which his hate of the cross had come.

So you see, as this story illustrates, we ought to be encouraged, if we should ever come up against a full-blown case of demonic possession in someone we know, because the power of the cross will triumph. No, to actually face up to something like this can be a formidable thing, to say the least. But remember, the Bible reminds us that G is there, even is situations like that backing us up, in passages like the Living Bible's version of 1 Peter 5:8–9 and the Phillips Modern English Translation's version of James 4:7: "Be careful—watch out for attack from Satan, your great enemy. He prowls around like a hungry, roaring lion, looking for some victim to tear apart. Stand firm when he attacks. Trust the Lord and remember that other Christians all around the world are going through these sufferings, too...Be humble, then, before G. But resist the devil, and you'll find that he'll run away from you."

But it's not just the cross that demons shrink back from. The name of Jesus also has incredible power when it comes to doing spiritual battle with the demonic realm. Once more, Martin's book brings to life some perfect examples from actual instances of exorcism on just how effective J's name is in spiritual warfare. In relating the story of a man who had performed numerous exorcisms who was instructing a younger exorcist-in-training, the point was made that a person attempting to perform an exorcism is *never* to try to take the place of Jesus. It was only by the name of Jesus that a demon can be exorcised.

A second instance of the power of J's name in the matter of facing up to demonic attacks in the book deals with a boy who was being harassed by a demonically possessed man. At one point, the man came to the boy and began to verbally harass him, confusing and mentally tormenting the youngster. The torment of the man's voice was starting to be more than the boy could handle, but then he remembered a strategy that his minister had passed on to him, and the thing for the boy to do in this situation was to spell out the name of Jesus, over and over, which the boy immediately began to do: J-E-S-U-S. As he began to do this, the boy then discovered that those letters and their piecemeal pronunciation meant more to him than just simply a gimmick. The pain of the old man's chanting diminished. The boy then began to cry but doing so *sweetly*, more as a *relief* than a sign of suffering.

In one last example from the book, another boy who was constantly being spiritually attacked by demons was advised that whenever he felt this strange grip come upon his mind, memory and imagination, he was to spell the name of Jesus out letter by letter, over and over. When the boy asked his counselor if *any other name* would do, the boy was told that he would find that only J's name would be effective in giving him relief.

So what does all this tell us, this morning? It tells us that G is more powerful than Satan, and that one day, G will triumph completely over him. I know you're familiar with John 1:5: "The light shines in the darkness, and the darkness has never overpowered it."

Lastly, as Hebrews 2:14 relates to us, "Since the children have flesh and blood, he too shared in their humanity, so that by his death, he might destroy him who holds the power of death—that is, the devil."

May 2, 2010 Different Responses to the Gospel
John 6:48-52; 7:11-12, 28-31, 40-43

(Before preaching this message, Roger plays "Amazing Grace," on guitar, classical style.)

So what'd you think of my guitar rendition of "Amazing Grace"? What was your reaction? What were you thinking/feeling as I was playing? Did the soft, soothing music make you want to *fall asleep?* Maybe you got *angry*, because maybe you not only hate guitar music, but maybe you even hate just to look at guitars. Maybe my "performance" was so bad and I made such a mess of such a beloved hymn that you felt like *crying*. Or maybe the whole thing was just so *goofy* to you that you felt like *laughing*. I'm willing to bet that there were a variety of reactions among you, as to my playing the guitar just now.

Well, you know, the gospel gets different reactions from different people all the time. A particular group of people can all hear the *exact same* message from the Scripture, and yet the different people within that group can have very different reactions to it. Case in point is seen in various passages, starting with John 7:11–12, 28–31, and 40–43; 9:13–16; and 10:1–21. It's in those places the Bible states, "The Jews kept looking for him at the festival and asking, 'Where is that man?' And there was an undercurrent of discussion about him among the crowds. Some would say, 'He is a good man.' Others maintained that he was not but that he was 'misleading the people.' Then, as J taught in the Temple, he cried out: 'Yes, you know Me and you know where I came from. Yet I have not come of myself: no, there is one who sent Me and I really come from Him, and you do not know him, but I know Him, because I have come from Him and it was He who sent Me.' They would have arrested him then, but because his time had not yet come, no one laid a hand on him. There were many people in the crowds, however, who believed in Him; they were saying, 'When the Christ comes, will he give more signs than this man?'

"When the crowds heard him say this, some of them declared, 'This man surely is the prophet who will come just before the Messiah.' Others said, 'He is the Messiah.' Still, others said, 'But he can't be! Will the Messiah come from Galilee? For the Scriptures clearly state that the Messiah will be born of the royal line of David, in Bethlehem, the village where David was born.' So the crowd was divided about him.

"Then, they took the man to the Pharisees. Now as it happened, this all occurred on a Sabbath. Then the Pharisees asked him all about it. So he told them how J had smoothed the mud over his eyes, and when it was washed away, he could see! Some of them said, 'Then this fellow J is *not* from G, because he is working on the Sabbath.' Others said, 'But how could an ordinary sinner do such miracles?' So there was a deep division of opinion among them."

"'I tell you the truth: the man who does not enter the sheepfold by the door, but climbs in some other way, is a thief and a robber. The man who goes in by the door is the shepherd of the sheep. The gatekeeper opens the gate for him; the sheep hear his voice as he calls his owns sheep by name, and he leads them out. When he has brought them out, he goes ahead of them, and the sheep follow him, because they know his voice. They will not follow someone else; instead, they will run away from him, because they do not know his voice.' J told them this parable, but they did not understand what he was telling them.

"So J said again, 'I tell you the truth: I am the door for the sheep. All others who came before Me are the thieves and robbers, but the sheep did not listen to them. I am the door. Whoever comes in by me will be saved; he will come in and go out, and find pasture. The thief comes only to order to steal, kill and destroy. I have come in order that they might have life, life in all its fullness.

"'I am the good shepherd. The good shepherd is willing to die for the sheep. The hired man, who is not a shepherd and does not own the sheep, leaves them and runs away when he sees a wolf coming; so the wolf snatches the sheep and scatters them. The hired man runs away because he is only a hired man and doesn't care for the sheep. I am the good shepherd. As the Father knows me and I know the Father, in the same way, I know my sheep and they know me. And I am willing to die for them. There are other sheep, that belong to me that are not in this sheepfold. I must bring them, too; they will listen to my voice, and they will become one flock with one shepherd.

"'The Father loves me because I am willing to give up my life, in order that I may receive it back again. No one takes my life away from me. I give it up of my own free will. I have the right to give it, and I have the right to take it back. This is what my Father has commanded me to do.'

"Again, there was a division among the Jews become of these words. Many of them were saying, 'He has a demon! He's crazy! Why do you listen to him?' but others were saying, 'A man with a demon could not talk like this! How could a demon open the eyes of a blind man?'"

You see, to simply sum up the meaning of the previous passages, whenever J spoke, he *always* got a reaction out of people, and it wasn't always the same reaction from every person. In fact, many times, the reactions varied widely.

Now, I've had numerous types of reactions to my guitar playing, believe it or not, and one of those reactions has been to literally *put people to sleep*, who've heard it. Case in point is my cousin Jonathan. Jon and I worked a lot together, during our college years, during the summer at our family's hotel/resort in Capon Springs, West Virginia. Numerous times when I'd be practicing my guitar in my room at my family's house on the hotel property, Jonathan would come listen to me practice. The only chair in my room was the one I used to sit on as I practiced, so Jon would start out by sitting on my bed, listening to me practice. But the soft, gentle sound of classical guitar eventually would make him so relaxed, he eventually would end up laying down on the bed and actually falling asleep—without fail.

Of course, one of the oldest things joked about in church is the way that some church members routinely fall asleep during church services. One such biblical example comes from Acts 20:7–12. It's there the Good News Bible says, "On Saturday evening, we gathered together for the fellowship meal. Paul spoke to the people and kept on speaking until midnight, since he was going to leave the next day. There were many lamps in the upstairs room where we were meeting. A young man named Eutychus was sitting in the window; and as Paul kept on talking, Eutychus got sleepier and sleepier, until he finally went sound asleep and fell from the third story to the ground. They picked him up, and he was dead. But Paul went down and threw himself on him and hugged him. 'Don't worry,' he said, 'he is still alive!' Then he went back upstairs, broke bread and ate. After talking with them for a long time until sunrise, Paul left. They took the young man home alive, and were greatly comforted."

Two things that story shows: (1) It can be downright *dangerous* to fall asleep in church, and (2) that is exactly what some people do with what should be considered the most exciting and enthralling of all messages on earth, the Gospel—they fall fast asleep when presented with it.

Now, another way people react oftentimes to the gospel message is with *anger*. I honestly don't recall any time where I actually made anybody mad with my guitar playing, but I guess anything's possible. Well, a biblical example of such a reaction to the gospel is seen in the Good News Bible's version of Acts 24:24–27. It's there the scripture reads, "After some days, Felix came with his wife, Drusilla, who was Jewish. He sent for Paul and listened to him as he talked about faith in Christ Jesus. But as Paul went to discussing about goodness, self-control and the coming Day of Judgment, Felix was afraid and said, 'You may leave now. I will call you again when I get the chance.' At the same time, he was hoping that Paul would give him some money, and for this reason, he would call for him often and talk with him."

Now that particular version of that passage states that Felix was *afraid*, not angry, at Paul's preaching. But I think you'll agree that there was probably a lot of tension in his voice when he told him to leave, and then basically tell Paul on his way out, "Don't call me, I'll call you." And ever since *before* Felix spoke those words to Paul, there have been people who've reacted with anger toward the Gospel message. Why have they done so? Because *it convicts them*. As a lost sinner, they don't like having pointed out to them that they're lost in sin and headed for hell, so it makes them upset and they react with anger in their voice and attitude. But it's not only the *lost* who often respond to the gospel message this way. Christians sometimes, when hearing a portion of the message that has a disciplining tone to it, react much the same way. I've heard many Christians say, from time to time, that they actually *want* their minister to preach sermons that step on their toes and convict them of sin and wrongdoing, but then when the minister does just that, they get offended and act out angrily.

Well, another way, but in a more positive light, that people react to the gospel is when they respond to the message with sadness and sorrow, then coming to understand their need to draw closer to J. I remember once when I was practicing my guitar in the auditorium on the property of my extended family's hotel, in West Virginia. All of a sudden, when of the guests who was staying there that week happened to walk into the room. Noticing that I was in there practicing, she quietly took a seat in the back of the room and simply watched me and listened to me practice. That was fine; it didn't bother me a bit—that is, until she got out a handkerchief and started dabbing her eyes and wiping tears away from them. I'm thinking at that point, "Great, I've put people to sleep before, with my guitar playing, but I've never made anybody cry before!" I wondered if I was playing so badly that it was just simply bringing tears to her eyes. Well, she explained to me later that my playing classical guitar reminded her of another person in her life she used to know and love who also played guitar in a similar fashion, who eventually died under tragic circumstances.

But honestly, the gospel message, at times, has the power to bring people to the point of tears, when they come to recognize the depth of sin in their lives and their need for a savior. It is said in 2 Corinthians 7:8–11, "For even if that letter of mine made you sad, I am not sorry I wrote it. I could have been sorry when I saw that it made you sad for a while. But now, I am happy—not because I made you sad, but because your sadness made you change your ways. That sadness was used by G, and so we caused you no harm. For the sadness that is used by G brings a change of heart that leads to salvation—and there is no regret in that! But sadness that is merely human causes death. See what G did with this sadness of yours: how earnest it has made you, how eager to prove your innocence! Such indignation, such alarm, such feelings, such devotion, such readiness to punish wrongdoing! You have shown yourselves to be without fault in the whole matter."

Maybe one of the best contemporary examples of such a situation involved the well-known evangelist, Jimmy Swaggart. Many of you remember back a number of years ago when he was caught in a compromising position in the company of an unsavory character. One of the most enduring images of that whole episode was his televised, tearful confession, "I have sinned." Now, many people then blasted Swaggart, saying that he was sorry only because he got caught. But I'd like to give him the benefit of the doubt that he truly learned a sharp lesson and realized that he had a lot to repent of, in order to grow closer to J, so he did just that.

Well, a final way that people often react to the gospel message is to be thankful with *joy*. J himself encouraged the seventy disciples of his that he was about to send out into the surrounding area to witness, preach, and teach, in Luke 10:18–20 when he said there, "I saw Satan fall like lightning from Heaven. I have given you authority to trample on snakes and scorpions and to overcome all the power of the enemy; nothing will harm you. However, do not rejoice that the spirit submit to you, but rejoice that your names are written in heaven." Rejoice that your names are written in heaven. *Rejoice.* Do you realize how many times the word "rejoice" is mentioned in the Bible? Well, the word "rejoice," in its various forms and tenses, is used 266 times in the scripture— 266 times—and many of those instances are where the people are *instructed* to rejoice, due to the reality of G's demonstrating his love for them in some fashion.

Now, I've never made anybody actually rejoice/laugh at my guitar playing (that I know of), but I *did* have an instance back in college when I was still a music major when I did manage to bring some levity to a couple of people due to my piano playing. You see, my major instrument was guitar, but piano was my minor instrument. On the day of my final exam for piano class for the semester, I ended up having to take the time slot for the end of the second day out of three days for the final. What this means is that I went into the assigned room to play my assigned pieces for the two teachers who had been stuck in that room for two long days, listening to student after student struggle through the same pieces of music over and over again.

Well, after greeting the two professors, I sat down at the piano, as nervous as all get out. I then began to struggle to play through the exercises and songs I was supposed to do. As I was about half through one of the songs, I heard this noise. I stopped playing and looked up. The one teacher looked at the other, smiled, and they both cracked up laughing. They actually allowed me to go ahead and leave the room *before* I was technically finished playing through every song I should have played through.

So when we share the gospel with an unbeliever—or share a portion of the Bible message with a believer—we hope that they won't fall asleep on us, or that they will end up getting angry or upset with us. But if they should shed some tears (recognizing their need to repent) or heartily rejoice because of the good news that's come to them, then we can recognize that the Spirit has made its way successfully into the heart of that person. Those are the kinds of responses we need to hope, work, and pray for.

January 10, 2010 Wrong Again, Doglips!
Luke 12:13-21; 1 Samuel 17:4-11; Matthew 26:57-67

I sang in the choir at the church where I served as a youth/children's minister in Rocky Mount. One night at choir practice, the fellow sitting next to me, Cary Frommel, and I were talking. I can't remember what we were talking about, but I do remember that he eventually made a statement that was absolutely erroneous and false. Well, Cary and I liked to kid around with each other, so once he made this false statement, I looked at him and said, "Wrong again, doglips!" He then started laughing at my comment and said, "Doglips? I'm not doglips. *You're* doglips!"

Well, forget about the doglips part of this story. Here's a book by a lady named Jane O'Boyle (hold up the book) entitled *Wrong Again! More of the Biggest Mistakes and Miscalculations Ever Made by People Who Should Have Known Better*. It's great, and we'll hear from it later on. But I want to say to start off this morning that many times, people make definitive statements as if they know 100% what they're talking about, when, in fact, they couldn't have been further from the truth.

Now, many times, this kind of thing happens with people who have absolutely *no* connection with J whatsoever. So an example of that kind of person comes from the Jerusalem Bible's version of J's parable of the rich fool, found in Luke 12:13–21. It's there that the Bible records: "A man in the crowd said to him, 'Master, tell my brother to give me a share of our inheritance.

"'My friend,' he replied, 'who appointed me your judge, or the arbitrator of your claims?' Then he said to them, 'Watch and be on your guard against greed of any kind, for a man's life is *not* made secure by what he owns, even when he has more than he needs.'

"Then he told them a parable: 'There was once a rich man who, having had a good harvest from his land, thought to himself, 'What am I to do? I don't have enough room to store my crops.' Then he said, 'This is what I will do: I will pull down my barns and build bigger ones, and store all my grain and my goods in them, and I will say to my soul: My soul, you have plenty of good things laid up for many years to come; take things easy, eat drink, and have a good time.'

"But G said to him, 'Fool! This very night, the demand will be made for your soul and this hoard of yours, whose will it be then?' So it is when a man stores up treasure for himself in place of making himself rich in the sight of G."

In other words, after this guy went on and on about how safe and secure he was, due to his vast earthly wealth, G looked at him and said, "Wrong, again!"

You see, how we live expresses our Christian faith. Personal lifestyle is made up of attitudes and values, activities, conduct patterns, goals and specific uses of material possessions. The world insists that the good life consists of accumulating possessions and indulging in luxuries. J showed that life is fulfilling only when we seek to extend his kingdom by loving, serving, and giving to others. J's teachings and his lifestyle denounced getting wealth as the main goal in life. He reminded his followers that owning material riches is temporary and that spiritual riches are eternal.

Now, obviously, the man in this parable was living with the false religion of materialism. One of the unfortunate characteristics of false religion is that it can lead people to believe that they are in a situation that will cause them to overcome death on their own. But only the true God of the universe controls death and has the power to give victory over it. I know this can be hard, but somehow, we need to get that message across to those who have no belief in G whatsoever. We all know people like this—*because* they don't believe in G at all, they rely on themselves for sufficiency. Big mistake. Whenever somebody lives with that kind of mindset, I believe G just looks at them, shakes his head, and says, "Wrong again."

Now, another type of person who might talk and act like they have the world by the tail and have all the answers to life they need is the one who *does* believe in a god, but just not the God of the Bible, the Christian God, the *only* true God there is. Now, this might not always be the case, but sometimes, these believers in false gods have a position of power or influence in their surroundings. But it doesn't matter how powerful a person might be in society. When you're wrong, you're wrong, no matter who you are.

For instance, a handful of CBS executives once flatly stated, "Any TV with a frog as the host won't work." They were turning down the pilot for Jim Henson's *The Muppet Show* in the early 1970s. No one thought these Sesame Street-style characters would appeal to adults. Rejected by all the networks, Henson resorted to production to England, and the show was then syndicated in the US. *The Muppet Show* was soon viewed in a hundred countries, by 235 million people, and became the inspiration for several feature films.

But a *biblical* example of someone who had a measure of power about them, and yet who was seriously wrong in the outlook on G, can be seen in the example of the formidable Goliath. It's in 1 Samuel 17:1-4, 20-24 and 32-51, then, that we read, "A champion named Goliath came out of the Philistine camp. He was over nine feet tall. He had a bronze helmet on his head and had worn a coat of scale armor of bronze weighing 125 pounds. On his legs, he wore bronze fittings and a bronze javelin was slung on his back. His spear shaft was like a weaver's rod, and its iron point weighed six hundred shekels. His shield bearer went ahead of him. Goliath stood and shouted to the ranks of Israel, 'Why do you come out and line up for battle? Am I not a Philistine, and are you not the servants of Saul? Choose a man and have him come down to me. If he is able to fight and kill me, we will become your subjects; but if I overcome him and kill him, you will become our subjects and serve us.' Then, Goliath said, 'This day, I defy the ranks of Israel! Give me a man and let us fight each other.' On hearing those words, Saul and all the Israelites were dismayed and terrified.

"Early in the morning, David left the flock with a shepherd, loaded up and set out, as Jesse had directed. He reached the camp as the army was going to its battle positions, shouting the war cry. Israel and the Philistines were drawing up their lines facing each other. David left his things with the keeper of supplies, ran to the battle lines, and greeted his brothers. As he was talking with them, Goliath stepped out from his lines and shouted his usual defiance, and David heard it. When the Israelites saw him, they all ran from Goliath in fear.

"David said to Saul, 'Let no one lose heart on account of this Philistine; your servant will go and fight him.'

"Saul replied, 'You are not able to go out against this Philistine and fight him; you are only a boy, and he has been a fighting man from his youth.'

"But David said to Saul, 'Your servant has been keeping his father's sheep. When a lion or a bear came and carried off a sheep from the flock, I went after it, struck it and rescued the sheep from its mouth. When it turned on me, I seized it by the hair, struck it, and killed it. Your servant has killed both the lion and the bear; this uncircumcised Philistine will be like one of them, because he has defied the armies of the living God. The Lord who delivered me from the paw of the lion and the bear will deliver me from the hand of this Philistine.

"Saul then said to David, 'Go, and the Lord be with you.'

"Then Saul dressed David in his own tunic. He put a coat of armor on him and a bronze helmet on his head. David fastened his sword on over the tunic and tried walking around, because he was not used to them. 'I can't go in these,' he said to Saul, 'because I am not used to them.' So he took them off. Then, he took his staff in his hand, chose five smooth stones from the stream, put them in the pouch of his shepherd's bag and, with his sling in his hand, approached Goliath.

"Meanwhile, Goliath kept coming closer to David. He looked David over and saw that he was only a boy, and he despised him. He said to David, 'Am I a dog, that you come at me with sticks?' And Goliath cursed David by his gods. 'Come here,' he said, 'and I'll give your body to the birds of the air and the beasts of the field.'"

Now, let's stop there for just a second. Old Goliath seemed pretty sure of himself, there, didn't he? He certainly was making a lot of assumptions, as if he absolutely knew what he was talking about.

Well, picking up at verse 45 of 1 Samuel 17, then, David basically tells Goliath, "Wrong, again, buddy," when he responds to Goliath's arrogant statement by saying, "You come against me with sword, spear and javelin, but I come against you in the name of the Lord Almighty, the God of the armies of Israel, whom you have defied. This day, the Lord will hand you over to me, and I'll strike you down and cut off your head. Today, I will give the carcasses of the Philistine army to the birds of the air and the beasts of the earth, and the whole world will know that there is a God in Israel. All those gathered here will know that it is not by sword or spear that the Lord saves; for the battle is the Lord's, and he will give all of you into our hands."

Now let me stop there for a pause. I know it may have sounded like David was speaking with the same level of confidence that Goliath had spoken with just a few minutes earlier. But the difference was that David wasn't trusting in himself and his own ability and power to be able to claim victory, like Goliath was. David, instead, knew that he couldn't have claimed victory in this battle beforehand unless G was really going to win it for him.

We pick up, then, again with verses 48–51: "As Goliath moved closer to attack him, David ran quickly toward the battle line to meet him. Reaching into his bag and taking out a stone, he slung it and struck Goliath on the forehead. The stone sank into his forehead, and he fell facedown on the ground. So David triumphed over Goliath with a sling and stone; without a sword in his hand, he struck down Goliath and killed him. David ran and stood over him. He took hold of Goliath's sword and drew it from the sheath. After he killed him, he cut off his head with the sword. When the Philistines saw that their hero was dead, they turned and ran."

You see, G's presence, *not* human strength, determines the outcome for G's people. The same Lord who delivered David from the paw of the lion and the bear and from the hands of Goliath can deliver us from every foe. Think about it—a small boy, David, armed with just a simple slingshot, killed Goliath, a giant who was heavily armed. Throughout the unfolding story of the Bible, G moved in dramatic ways to make his sovereign power known both to Israel and to the nations involved with Israel.

Well, we've seen, this morning, two groups of people—people who believe in a *false* god, and people who don't believe in any god at all—come to have to eat their words. Well, a third and final group of people who, sadly, often make overly confident statements, only to later be proven absolutely wrong, are people who *profess* to be followers of G/J. Such was the case of the Pharisees. No, they didn't follow J, that's true. But they were supposedly following G when they put J through the kangaroo court they put him through and sentenced him to death. That might be the biggest irony of all—when you have people who ought to be *enforcing* truth, honesty, and justice but who instead end up breaking and smashing those characteristics to pieces. I think people like that demonstrate the rationale former president Richard Nixon did, when he offered, once in 1974, a legal interpretation later echoed by President Bill Clinton, when he said, "When the president does it, that means is not illegal."

You know the Pharisees. Matthew 26:57–67 describes the hypocrisy demonstrated through their speech, in the Phillips Modern English Version of the Bible: "The men who had seized J took him off to Caiaphas the High Priest in whose house the scribes and elders were assembled. Peter followed him at a distance right up to the High Priest's courtyard. Then, he went inside and sat down with the servants and waited to see the end.

"Meanwhile, the chief priests and the whole Council did all they could find false evidence against J to get him condemned to death. They failed completely, even after a number of perjurers came forward. In the end, two men stood up and said, 'This man said, "I can pull down the Temple of G and rebuild it in 3 days."'

"Then, the High Priest rose to his feet and addressed J. 'Have you no answer? What about the evidence of these men against you?' But J was silent. Then, the High Priest said to him 'I command you by the living G to tell us on your oath if you are the Christ, the Son of G.'

"J said to him, 'You have said so. Yes, and I tell you that in the future, you will see the Son of Man sitting at the right hand of power and coming on the clouds of Heaven.'

"At this, the High Priest tore his robes and cried, 'That was blasphemy! Where is the need for further witness? Look, you've heard the blasphemy— What's your verdict now?'

"And they replied, 'He deserves to die.'"

Now, we could sit here and debate all day whether the Pharisees honestly, truthfully, felt like they were doing the right thing, or if they *knew* all along that they were living and working Satan's will and purposes. But no matter which case it was, they were dead wrong to believe what they believed and do what they did. But whichever the situation was, the fact remains that as wrong as they were in their belief about J, they were *the church* people of their day. So you see, even those of us who claim to be in a right relationship to Christ can, on occasion, find ourselves to be very, very wrong in our thoughts and beliefs.

The thing to do, then, before we let certain words come spilling out of our mouths, or before we actually carry out certain plans and ideas we have, we need to ask ourselves if we're truly about to do the will of G or if what we're about to do or say is completely our own idea and, as such, completely removed from the will of G for our lives.

Every once in a while, our dog, Princess, will misbehave in some manner. So there are numerous times when I want to look at her and say, "Wrong again, doglips!" You know, in all seriousness, the last thing I want to hear J say to me on judgment day is, "You really messed up in how you lived your life—you couldn't have been further from the truth in how you lived it. Wrong again!" Maybe there's someone here today who needs to come to have a right relationship with J before it's too late.

Dumb Crook News
Joshua 6:15-19, 7:1-26

There's a comedy segment on the morning radio show that I listen to, and it's called, appropriately enough, "Dumb Crook News." I say it's called that, appropriately, because that's exactly what it is, dumb crook news. It's story after story of true incidents in which criminals exhibited extremely stupid behavior. Case in point comes from a man on trial for assault. The man became less and less satisfied with the progress of the trial, so he asked the judge for a new court-appointed attorney. When the judge denied the man's request, the man head-locked his attorney and repeatedly punched him in the head. The attorney resigned from representing the man, and the judge wouldn't appoint a new attorney, so the man represented himself. Well, based on the demonstration of the man's brainpower, which I just described to you, you can tell how the trial turned out. Then, there was the man who held up a bank with his gun's barrel pointed at himself, which *might* have worked if he'd been playing a role in the movie *Blazing Saddles*.

Now, it's easy for us to laugh at the stupidity of some goofy criminals, but sometimes, people who are *supposed* to be true followers of J don't act much better. An example of that was seen in the sin of Achan, as told about in Joshua 6:15–19 and 7:1–26: "On the 7th day, they got up at daybreak and marched around the city 7 times in the same manner, except that on that day, they circled the city 7 times. The 7th time around, when the priests sounded the trumpet blast, Joshua commanded the people, 'Shout! For the Lord has given you the city! The city and all that is in it are to be devoted to the Lord. Only Rahab the prostitute and all who are with her in her house shall be spared, because she hid the spies we sent. But keep away from the devoted things, so that you will not bring about your own destruction by taking any of them. Otherwise, you will make the camp of Israel liable to destruction and bring trouble on it. All the silver and gold and the articles of bronze and iron are sacred to the Lord and must go into his treasury.'…But the Israelites acted unfaithfully in regard to the devoted things; Achan took some of them. So the Lord's anger burned against Israel.

"Now Joshua sent men from Jericho to Ai and told them, 'Go up and spy out the region.' So the men went up and spied out Ai.

"When they returned to Joshua, they said, 'Not all the people will have to go up against Ai. Send 2 or 3 thousand men to take it and do not wear out all the people, because only a *few* men are there.' So about 3,000 men went up; but they were routed by the men of Ai, who killed about 36 of them. They chased the Israelites from the city gate as far as the stone quarries and struck them down on the slopes. At this, the hearts of the people melted and became like water.

"Then, Joshua tore his clothes and fell facedown to the ground before the ark of the Lord, remaining there till evening. The elders of Israel did the same, and sprinkled dust on their heads. And Josh said, 'Ah, Sovereign Lord, why did you ever bring this people across the Jordon to deliver us into the hands of the Amorites to destroy us? If only who had been content to stay on the other side of the Jordan! O Lord, what can I say, now that Israel has been routed by its enemies? The Canaanites and the other people of the country will hear about this, and they will surround us and wipe out our name form the earth. What, then, will you do for your own great name?'

"The Lord said, 'Israel has sinned and has violated my covenant. They have taken some of the devoted things; they have stolen, they have lied, and they have put them with their own possessions. That's why the Israelites can't stand against their enemies; they turn their backs and run because they have been made liable to destruction. I will not be with you anymore unless you destroy whatever among you is devoted to destruction. This is what the Lord says: I will not be with you anymore unless you destroy whatever among you is devoted to destruction. You won't be able to stand against your enemies until you remove it.

"Early the next morning, Joshua had Israel come forward by tribes, and Judah was taken. The clans of Judah came forward, and he took the Zerahites. He had their clan come forward, and he took Zimri's family. Joshua had Zimri's family come forward man by man, and Achan was taken. Then, Joshua said to Achan, 'My son, give glory the Lord, the G of

Israel and give him the praise. Tell me what you have done; do not hide it from me.'

"Achan replied, 'It is true! I've sinned. This is what I've done: When I saw in the plunder a beautiful robe from Babylonia, 200 shekels of silver and a wedge of gold weighing 50 shekels, I desired to have them and took them. They're hidden in the ground inside my tent, with the sliver underneath. Then, Joshua and all of Israel took Achan, the robe, the silver, the gold wedge, his sons and daughters, his cattle, donkeys and sheep, his tent and all he had, to the Valley of Achor.

"Joshua said, 'Why have you brought this trouble on us? The Lord will bring trouble on you, today.' Then, all Israel stoned him, and after they had stoned the rest, they burned them. Over Achan they heaped up a large pile of rocks, which remains to this day. Then the Lord turned from his fierce anger. Therefore, the place has been called the Valley of Achor (which means, 'trouble'), since."

You see, a large group may sometimes have to suffer from the sin of just one of its members. The covenant relationship with G binds members together in mutual responsibility, sharing victory and defeat, joy, and shame together. The community is responsible to discipline itself and its individual members so that no sin disrupts the community and separates itself from G. Achan had to pay the supreme price along with his family, who had been corrupted in his sin. The community momentarily suffered defeat until it took care of the situation according to G's direction. The thing, though, is that Achan *knew* what he had done was wrong. But just like some of the "dumb criminal behavior" that you see on the news today, he not only allowed himself to do what he *knew* was wrong to begin with, but I guess that he also honestly believed that he could get away with it and not get caught.

It really is amazing how people can talk themselves into believing that they will be able to successfully escape getting caught if they should give in to a particular temptation that's been plaguing them. Granted, some career criminal are experts at avoiding detection, but others just don't seem to have a clue. For instance, a man once walked up to a bank teller and attempted to rob the bank. However, he failed to realize that the person standing behind him in line was a policeman. Sounds more like coincidence that it does sheer stupidity, doesn't it? Well, maybe, except for the fact that the cop was *in complete uniform*. Then, there was the case of a guy who broke into someone else's car, in order to make a getaway after having just robbed the car owner's house. However, after getting inside the car, the burglar *fell fast asleep*, where he remained until the police showed up. The cops found him still asleep behind the wheel, still clutching the items that he had just stolen a short time earlier.

You see, just as the foolish criminals we've seen some examples of, this morning, Achan did something foolish in two aspects: he first did something that he *knew* he shouldn't have done to begin with (remember, the Israelites had been warned about not taking certain items they came across for themselves) and he was also foolish enough to think that he could actually get away with that kind of action/behavior. But as the Jerusalem Bible so painfully points out to us in James 1:13–15, "Never, when you have been tempted, say, 'G sent this temptation on me'; G cannot be tempted to do anything wrong, and he does not tempt anybody. Everyone who is tempted is attracted and seduced by his own wrong desire. Then, the desire conceives and gives birth to sin, and when sin is fully grown, it too has a child, and that child is death." And as the first half of Proverbs 19:3 so adequately points out, "A man's own folly ruins his life."

You know, just as Achan did the extremely foolish thing by taking some of the conquered people's possessions for his own, people today often tend to do similar foolish things—things against the laws of man, as well as the laws of G —and they then thus receive the appropriate consequences. For instance, a man once posted bail on a traffic charge, but then got a whole new bail amount set when he posted that original bail with counterfeit money. He had been arrested for driving with a suspended license, after he had been stopped for making an illegal left turn. Why do so many people continue to drive after losing their license? Shouldn't that be a clue to them that they haven't yet come to have a handle on this whole driving thing? Well, the man posted bail and the officer immediately realizes that the money is fake—apparently, police can spot Monopoly money a mile away. Needless to say, the man had to go back to jail, on a felony charge, and no, I don't think he got to use a "get out of jail free" card.

See, if we are "dumb enough" to think that we can plot and carry out sinful activities, all while thinking that either G won't know, or if he does know He won't care, then we deserve to get what's coming to us.

It's kind of like what G told in Jeremiah 34:17–20: "Therefore, this is what the Lord says: 'You have not obeyed me; you have not proclaimed freedom for your fellow countrymen. So I now proclaim "freedom" for you, declares the Lord—"freedom" to fall by the sword, plague and famine. I will make you abhorrent to all the kingdoms of the earth. The men who have violated my covenant and have not fulfilled the terms of the covenant they made before me, I will treat them like the calf they cut in 2 and then walked between its pieces. I will hand them over to their enemies who seek their lives. Their dead bodies will become food for the birds of the air and the beasts of the earth." But on the other hand, if we trust G and follow him with all our heart, mind and soul, faithfully, then rather than *punish* us, he'll *deliver* us from certain tragedies, as when Psalm 22:8 points out when there the Bible says, "This man trusts in the Lord; let the Lord rescue him. Let the Lord deliver him, since the man delights in Him."

Now, part of the problem of our spiritual condition is that we're not smart enough to commit the "perfect sin." In other words, we're not capable of rebelling against G in any way, and then figure out a way to escape and all consequences. We're kind of like the robber who demanded his victim's wallet and car keys, forced the victim into the car trunk, and then withdrew cash with the man's bank card. Well, Martino Williams wishes now that he had taken Ira Sully's cell phone, too. You see, Sully called police from inside the car trunk and described both his car and Mr. Williams, who was caught a short time later when an officer matched him and the car to Sully's description. Man, *that's bad.* The only way it could've been any worse was if Williams had tried to steal the car without taking the keys during the hold-up. So police charged Williams with aggravated robbery, kidnapping and, of course, operating a cell phone while driving a motor vehicle.

The thing is, sometimes, we get so proud of ourselves in how we think we're balancing our sinful living with our appearing to be righteous that we actually give ourselves away to others, eventually, as to what we're really like inside. So it's either that pride or the outright shame that might pile up in on consciences after we've been living like that that gets us to admit our being out of line with G. As the Bible points out in Isaiah 3:9, "The look on their faces testifies against them; they parade their sin like

Sodom; they don't hide it. Woe to them! They will be paid back for what their hands have done."

But sometimes, it's not so much that we give ourselves away in how we really are spiritually, as it is that G ensures that, on occasion, we wind up giving ourselves our own punishment for our misdeeds—like the attempted murder suspect who accidentally shot himself after he put his gun back in its holster. The shooting occurred over an argument about $10. (Something tells me that this argument didn't involve words over two syllables each). The suspect tried to shoot his intended victim, but someone else pushed the gun out of the line of fire and he missed. He then managed to shoot himself after he put the gun in his pocket.

Once again, everyone, as sinful, fallen human beings, we'll never be able (no matter how smart we are or think we are) to figure out a way to pull one over on G. As the Bible so eloquently puts it, together in the verses found in Numbers 32:23 and Galatians 6:7: "You may be sure that your sin will find you out." "Don't be misled; remember that you can't ignore G and get away with it; a man will always reap just the kind of crop he sows!"

No, in a spiritual sense, let's not be fools ourselves, fooling ourselves into thinking that, somehow, we can mislead G and get away with it, because it just won't happen—just like it didn't happen for a fellow who wanted to rob a restaurant manager, who was just getting to work. The would-be crook told the manager to unlock the restaurant, and the manager proceeded to do just that as the crook stands waiting by the manager's car. Well, as soon as the manager let himself in the restaurant, he called the police, who promptly came and arrested the man.

If we can admit that we definitely know the difference between right and wrong in G's eyes, then none of us has any excuse for getting ourselves in the type of trouble that we saw Achan and criminals of today get themselves into, this morning.

February 22 It's Called *Dumb* Luck for a Reason
1 Samuel 14:24; Genesis 50:15-21

I had a roommate in college, who once commented to me that he would never wish anybody good luck because, he said, the word "luck" actually comes from the word/name *Lucifer*, whom we Christians know to be the devil, depicted in the Bible. I've never been able to determine if my roommate was right on stating that, but it makes perfect sense to me. After all, when one puts their faith and trust in things like "good luck, fate, destiny or fortune" they're totally leaving God and his will for them out of the picture. And yet, there seem to be times when G uses instances of chance, luck and even gambling to make his will accomplished.

As a matter of fact, one of those very instances comes from the Bible in 1 Samuel 14:24–45. It's in that passage of Scripture that the Bible states, "Now, the men of Israel were in distress that day, because Saul had bound the people under an oath, saying, 'Cursed be any man who eats food before evening comes, before I have avenged myself on my enemies!' So none of the troops tasted food.

"The entire army entered the woods and there was honey on the ground. When they went into the woods, they saw the honey oozing out, yet no one put his hand to his mouth, because they fear the oath. But Jonathan had not heard that his father had bound the people with the oath, so he reached out the end of the staff that was in his hand and dipped it into the honeycomb. He raised his hand to his mouth, and his eyes brightened.

"Then one of the soldiers told him, 'Your father bound the army under a strict oath, saying, "Cursed be the man who eats food today!" That is why the men are faint.'

"Jonathan said, 'My father has made trouble for the country. See how my eyes brightened when I tasted a little of this honey. How much better it would have been if the men had eaten today some of the plunder they took from their enemies. Would not the slaughter of the Philistines have been even greater?' That day, after the Israelites had struck down the Philistines from Micmas to Aijalon, they were exhausted. They pounced on the plunder and, taking sheep, cattle and calves, they butchered them on the ground and ate them, together with the blood. Then someone said to Saul, 'Look, they men are sinning against the Lord by eating meat that has blood in it.'

"'You have broken faith,' he said. 'Roll a large stone over here at once.' Then he said, 'Go out among the men and tell them, 'Each of you bring me your cattle and sheep, and slaughter them here and eat them. Do not sin against the Lord by eating meat with blood still in it.' So everyone brought his ox that night and slaughtered it there. Then, Saul built an altar to the Lord, it was the first time he had done this.

"Saul said, 'Let us go down after the Philistines by night and plunder them till dawn and let us not leave one of them alive.'

"'Do whatever seems best to you,' they replied.

"But the priest said, 'Let us inquire of G, here.'

"So Saul asked G, 'Shall I go down after the Philistines? Will you give them into Israel's hand?' But G did not answer him that day. Saul therefore, said, 'Come here, all you who are leaders of the army, and let us find out what sin has been committed today. As surely as the Lord who rescues Israel lives, even if it lies with my son Jonathan, he must die.' But not one of the men said a word.

"Saul then said to al the Israelites, 'You stand over there; and Jonathan my son will stand over here.'

"'Do what seems best to you,' the men replied.

"Then, Saul prayed to the Lord, the G of Israel, 'Answer me by drawing of the sacred stones. If the guilt is Jonathan, or mine, answer by the lots that the priests will draw in order to know your will.' Lots were chosen and drawn and the answer indicated Saul and Jonathan. All the rest of the people stepped back. Then Saul said, 'Decide, Lord, between my son Jonathan and me,' and Jonathan was indicated once more by the drawing of lots. Then Saul asked Jonathan, 'What have you done?'

"Jonathan answered, 'I ate a little honey. Here I am—I am ready to die.' Saul said to him, "May G strike me dead if you are not put to death!" But the people said to Saul, 'Will Jonathan, who won this great victory for Israel be put to death? No! We promise by the living Lord that he will not lose even a hair on his head. What he did today was done with G's help.' So the people saved Jonathan form being put to death."

So we can see from this portion of Scripture that even though sometimes people use methods of chance and luck in order to determine "their destiny" or the destiny of others, G *still* have ultimate control of what happens in the end. Amen? Amen.

Now, I want to preface what I'm about to say with a little disclaimer. Not only do I not believe that the Bible promotes the practices of gambling (taking great chances in order to make a significant profit), but I also believe that it would be foolish to believe that we could do something like predict the future anyway, and especially by using means of luck, chance and circumstance. In helping us decide what the future may hold for us, G speaks to us in a number of ways—typically through the reading and study of the Bible, what other people actually say to us, and through the many experiences we have and the things that happen to us—and not, usually, through "popular psychic methods" of fortune-telling. So no, I would not advise anyone here this morning to read their daily horoscope or to consult a fortune teller. But G can and does, from time to time, use unconventional methods of helping people determine where it is he wants them to go and what he wants them to do.

So maybe that's why we can read verses in the Bible like Proverbs 16:33, which states, "The lot is cast into the lap, but its every decision is from the Lord." Now to be perfectly honest, I'm not really sure what "casting a lot into a lap" actually means, but there's a study note printed in my Bible for Proverbs 16:33, and this is how that verse is explained: "Here is an ancient expression of the belief that G causes and controls everything that happens." He controls the lots—probably specially marked stones (a forerunner of today's dice, maybe?) —used in determining G's will.

The same technique—drawing lots—was used in the case of Jonah, as recorded in Jonah 1:1–12: "The word of the Lord came to Jonah, so of Amittai: 'Go to the great city of Nineveh and preach against it, because its wickedness has come up before me.' But Jonah ran away from the Lord and headed for Tarshish. He went down to Joppa, where he found a ship bound for that port. After paying the fare, he went aboard and sailed for Tarshish to flee from the Lord. Then the Lord sent a great wind on the sea, and such a violent storm arose that the ship threatened to break up.

All the sailors were afraid and each cried out to his own god. And they threw the cargo into the sea to lighten the ship.

"But Jonah had gone below deck, where he lay down and fell into a deep sleep. The captain went to him and said, 'How can you sleep? Get up and call on your god! Maybe he will take notice of us, and we will not perish.'

"Then the sailors said to each other, 'Come, let us cast lots to find out who is responsible for this calamity.' They cast lots, and the lot fell on Jonah." No surprise there, huh? "So they asked him, 'Tell us, who is responsible for making all this trouble on us? What do you do? Where do you come from? What is your country? Form what people are you?'

"He answered, 'I am a Hebrew and I worship the Lord, the G of Heaven, who made the sea and the land.'

"This terrified them, and they asked, 'What have you done?' They knew he was running away from the Lord, because he had already told them so. The sea was getting rougher and rougher. So they asked him, 'What should we do to you to make the sea calm down for us?'

"'Pick me up and throw me into the sea,' he replied, 'and it will become calm. I know that it is my fault that this great storm has come upon you."

Exposition for Jonah 1:4–7, then Judges 1:1–2: You see, the sailors saw in the storm the anger of one of the gods. Revelation of divine anger through creation was a belief Israel shared with her neighbors. The sailors attempted to find out who was responsible *by casting lots*. So we see here an example of the truth that when people seek G's will, there are *many* ways to discern his response.

Yes, the mystery of G's revelation was, at times, clear to Israel. G was understood when a prophet was consulted and spoke, or when lots were cast, as probably took here. The Israelites possessed sacred stones, given to them during the Exodus, and specifically designed to give the user a means of making a decision. The high priest, wearing them over his heart, was in a proper attitude to consult them and receive an answer, which was understood as G's answer. The most important issue in the consultation of these stone, however, was the seeker's attitude, that is, coming to G and to G's representative searching for G's will on a matter.

Yet once more in the Old Testament, the Bible states that G can use such methods to inform people of his will, specifically helping, at times, to settle arguments about just exactly what decision should be made among those who disagree on the best course of action, in Proverbs 18:18, where there, the Bible states, "Casting the lot settle disputes, and keeps strong opponents apart."

Let's just be careful not to credit what most people would call "luck" for any success we have, since we must recognize that it's *God* who gives us all we have. Let's not be like the farmer, then, who when asked when being interviewed by a newspaper reporter wheat he attributed the source of his success to said, with a twinkle in his eye, "It's been about 50% weather, 50% good luck, and 50% brains." Yeah, whatever.

The truly important thing about all this to remember, then, is this: G is going to accomplish his will and purposes, however he chooses to and however he decides to let us in on those plans. As Ephesians 3:11–12, Ephesians 1:11, and Proverbs 16:4 tell us, "According to his eternal purpose, which he accomplished in CJ our Lord…In him, we were also chosen, having been predestined according to the plan of him who works everything out in conformity with the purpose of his will…The Lord works out everything out for his own ends—even the wicked for a day of disaster." He even makes certain that when he chooses someone to be an instrument for his plan that they fulfill that plan to the best of their ability, as Exodus 9:16 demonstrates when the Bible says there, "But I have raised you up for this very purpose, that I might show you my power and that my name might be proclaimed through all their earth."

Now, it *is* unfortunate that, at times, it seems that G's direction is a little less than clear. It's kind of like Jo Guerrero once explained, "When my daughter was five, she disobeyed me and had been sent to her room."

After a few minutes, I went in to have a talk about why she was being punished. Teary-eyed, she asked, "Why do we do bad things?"

"Well," Guerrero began to answer, "sometimes the devil tells us to do something wrong, and we listen to him. We need to listen to God instead."

It was then that her daughter responded, "But G doesn't talk loud enough."

Oh, G *does* talk loud enough. It just may be that he's *intentionally* kept his will for us for the immediate future to himself, rather than filling us in on every detail. Admit it, even with having G to guide, lead, and direct us, much of the future remains a complete mystery. As Ecclesiastes 9:11

puts it, "I have seen something else under the sun: The race is not won by the swift, nor the battle by the strong, nor does food come to the wise, or wealth to the brilliant, or favor to the learned; but time and chance happen to them all."

Let's just be extremely careful about looking at a situation where it seems that "dumb luck"—good *or* bad—has struck, and then assigning a divine truth to it, claiming that we know for absolute certain what G's will was in all that took place. For example, there's the story of a Kansas man whose house was once blown away in a tornado. The local minister, seeing this as an opportunity to witness for Christ, told the man, "*Punishment* for sin is inevitable."

"Oh, *really*," said the man, "and did you stop to think, preacher, that *your* house was blown away, too?"

"Well," the preacher began to respond, "the Lord's ways are beyond understanding."

Yeah, right!

You know, just because our lives might take a nasty turn at some point, it doesn't necessarily mean that things will always continue to only get worse. As Joseph reminded his bros who had sold him into slavery before he—through a series of divinely led events—came to a position of leading in Egypt, in Genesis 50:20, "You intended to harm me, but G intended it for good to accomplish what is now being done, the saving of many lives."

As a man named Eric Liddell once put it, "Circumstances may appear to wreck out lives and G's plans, but G is not helpless among the ruins. Our broken lives are not lost or useless. G comes in and takes the calamity and uses it victoriously, working out his wonderful plan of love."

On the topic of G's guidance and his will, then, Hannah Whitall Smith once stated, "I lay it down as a foundation principle—that G's voice will always be in harmony with itself, no matter in how many different ways he may speak. The voices may be many, the message can be but one. If G tells me in one voice to do or to leave undone anything, he can't possibly tell me the opposite in another voice. Therefore, my rule for distinguishing the voice of G would be to bring it to the test of this harmony."

Yes, maybe at this point in our lives, we're wondering how we got here? Has "fate" dealt us a rotten hand? Well, I might remind you that God's the one in charge and he knows what he's doing. After all, things could be worse. It's like when Snoopy was getting dog food for his Thanksgiving Day dinner, and he's aware that all else in the family has having turkey.

He thought about this for a second and said to himself, "How about that?

Everyone is eating turkey today, but just because I'm a dog, I get dog food." He trotted away and positions himself on top of his doghouse and concluded, "Of course, it could have been worse—I *could* have been born a turkey."

Maybe the "luck"/God's plan of Snoopy had being born a dog wasn't so bad after all.

Forever Young
Ecclesiastes 12:1-7; Psalm 103:1-5

(Begin the time by playing a recording of Rod's Stewart's song, "Forever Young." The words are as follows: "May the Good Lord be with you down every road you roam / And my sunshine and happiness surround you when you're far from home / And may you grow to be proud, dignified and true / and do unto other as you'd have done to you / Be courageous and be brave, and in my heart you'll always stay forever young...May good fortune be with you, may your guiding light be strong. Build a stairway to heaven with a prince or a vagabond. And may you never love in vain, and in my heart you will remain forever young... And when you finally fly away, I'll be hoping that I served you well / for all the wisdom of a lifetime, no one can ever tell / But whatever road you choose, I'm right behind you, win or lose, forever young.

It's been said that you know that you're getting older when your dreams get to be reruns; the stewardess offers coffee, tea, or milk of magnesia; you sit in a rocking chair and can't get it started; everything hurts, and what doesn't hurt doesn't work; a pretty young lady (or a handsome young man) prompts your pacemaker to open the garage door or you sink your teeth into a juicy steak— and they *stay* there.

Well, all kidding aside, aging—going from being young to getting old—is literally the experience of a lifetime, something that we *all* must go through. Now not only do we need to recognize *that* fact, but we also need to admit that no matter what stage in life we ourselves might be in at the moment, none of us has the right to discriminate against—or look down on—anyone in a very different age bracket from ourselves. Yes, the Bible admonishes, at times, and encourages people on both ends of the human lifetime spectrum. For example, in speaking to both "the younger and the older generations," Ecclesiastes 12:1–5 gently warns, "Don't let the excitement of being young cause you to forget your Creator. Honor him in your youth before you grow old and no longer enjoy living. It will be too late, then, to remember Him, when the light of the sun and the moon and the stars is dim to your old eyes, and there is no silver lining lift among the clouds. Your limbs will tremble with age, and you strong legs will grow weak. Your teeth will be too few to chew your food, and your eyes too dim to see clearly. Your ears will be deaf to the noise of the street. You will barely be able to hear the mill as it grinds or music as it plays, but even the song of a bird will wake you from sleep. You will be afraid to high places and walking will be dangerous. Your hair will turn white; you will hardly be able to drag yourself along, and all desire will be gone." Boy, that wasn't exactly encouraging, now, was it?

But there *is* hope for us, even as we grow older, for G is with us, there to help, as indicated in Psalm 103:1–5, when there the Bible states, "Praise the Lord, my soul. All my being, praise his holy name. Praise the Lord, my soul, and don't forget how kind he is. He forgives all my sins and heals all my diseases. He keeps me from the grave and blesses me with love and mercy. He fills my life with good things, so that I stay young and strong like an eagle."

Yes, like it or not, we all must admit that being both young and old have their drawbacks, things about them that we'd rather not have to deal with. After all, as Lloyd Cory wrote in his book entitled *Quote, Unquote*, "When you get too old for *pimples*, you go right into *wrinkles*." Likewise, along the very same lines, Christian psychologist James Dobson was once quoted as saying, "By the time your face clears up, your mind gets fuzzy."

Now, as you probably know, young people tend to get a "bad rap" sometimes. As George Bernard Shaw was quoted in Ray Stedman's book *Solomon's Secret*, "Youth is a wonderful thing. Too bad it's wasted on young people." And Bob Bowen likewise commented, "We're only young once— that's all that society can stand!" But to those of us in the congregation, this morning, who are honestly *chronologically* younger, the Bible actually gives an *encouraging* word, rather than an obnoxiously insulting one, when it advises in 1 Timothy 4:12, "Don't let anyone look down on your because you are young, but set an example for the believers in your speech, your conduct, your love, faith and purity." In addition, 2 Timothy 2:22 advises, "Run from anything that gives you the evil thoughts that young people often have, but stay close to anything that makes you want to do right. Have faith and love, and enjoy the companionship of those who love the Lord and have pure hearts."

Yes, unfortunately, sometimes, it's all too easy just to *look* at person, and going by how old or young they look to us, *pre-judge* them. They may not be the kind/type of person we assume just because they appear to be in a certain age range. A lady named Shermalee Ochoa once explained, "When my greatniece was five years old, she once asked her grandmother, 'Grandma, are you *rotten* on the inside?'

"'No, sweetheart, why do you ask that?' Grandma answered with some surprise.

"'Because when apples are all wrinkly on the outside, they're all rotten on the inside,' she said."

Now, I don't think I know a single person who actually likes the idea of aging and getting older, myself included. But no matter how much that aging process might bother us, it is—for each of us—inescapable and unavoidable. That's the truth that Lucy pointed out to Schroder in a *Peanuts* comic strip, once.

Lucy quizzes Schroder, "Will you love me when I'm old and crabby?"

Schroder then responds, "You don't *have* to be crabby."

"I know," Lucy says, "but it's hard to change."

"Maybe you can be nice in the morning and crabby in the afternoon," Schroder suggests.

"Yes, but I'll still be old all day," Lucy points out.

Yes, Lucy was able to admit the inevitability of her getting older, very much unlike what Ray Stedman penned in his sermon called *Life Beyond Death*, which he preached on December 1, 1968. Stedman wrote, "Everything is farther than it used to be. It's twice as far from my house to the station, now, and they've added a hill which I've just noticed. The trains leave sooner, too, but I've given up running for them because they go faster than they need to. Seems to me they're making staircases steeper than in the old days. And have you noticed the small print they're using lately? Newspapers are getting farther and farther away when I hold them. I have to squint to make out the news. Now it's ridiculous to suggest that a person my age needs glasses, but it's the only way I can find out what's going on without someone reading to me, and that isn't much help because everybody seems to speak in such a low voice, I can hardly hear them.

"Times are changing. The material in my clothes shrinks in certain places. Shoelaces are so short, they're next to impossible to reach. And even the weather's changing. It's getting colder in the winter, and the summers are much hotter than they used to be. People are changing, too. For one thing, they're younger than they used to be when I was their age. On the other hand, people my *own* age are so much older than I am."

I ran into my old roommate, the other night, and *he* had changed so much, *he* didn't recognize *me*.

"You've put on weight, Bob," I said.

"It's this modern food," he replied, "it seems to be more fattening."

I got to thinking about poor Bob this morning while I was shaving. Stopping for a moment, I looked at my own reflection in the mirror. You know, they don't use the same kind of glass in mirrors, anymore."

Now, you might laugh at that description of aging, but a Bible character named Barzillai, was doing anything but kidding when he told King David, according to 2 Samuel 19:34–39, "How many more years will I live, that I should go up to Jerusalem with you? I'm now 80 years old. Can I tell the diff between what is good and what isn't? Can I taste what I eat and drink? Can I still hear the voices of men and women singers? Why should I be an added burden to you? Let me return, that I may die in my own town near the tomb of my father and mother." So the king and all the people crossed over. The king kissed Barzillai and gave him his blessing, and Barzillai returned home."

Poor Barzillai. He really made it sound like getting older was *all* totally awful. But face it—there's good as well as bad in aging, as demonstrated in Robert Raines set of verses, entitled, "Lord, Could You Make It Better?" "Middle-agers are beautiful! Aren't we, Lord? I feel for us—too radical for our parents, and too reactionary for our kids. Supposedly, in the prime of life, like prime rib / Everyone eating off of me, devouring me / Nobody thanking me, appreciating me / But still hanging in there, communicating with my parents and in touch with my kids, and getting more in touch with myself / And that's all good / Thanks for making it good, Lord, and could you make it a little better?"

Yes, maybe that's the key—to ask G to help us to deal with getting older a little better, as Dale Evans Rogers did in her piece from her book *Time Out, Ladies*, where she wrote, "Lord, you know me better than I

63

know myself, that I am growing older and will someday be old. Keep me from getting talkative, and particularly from the fatal habit of think I must say something on every subject and on every occasion. Release me from the craving to try to straighten out everybody's affairs. Keep my mind free from the recital of endless details— give me wings to get to the point. I ask for grace enough to listen to the tales of others' pains. Help me to endure them with patience. But seal my lips on my own aches and pains. They are increasing, and my love of rehearsing them is becoming sweeter as the years go by.

"I don't ask for improved memory, but for a growing humility and a lessening of overconfidence when my memory seems to clash with the memories of others. Keep me reasonably sweet. I don't wish to be a saint— some of them can be so hard to live with—but a sour old woman (or man) is one of the crowning works of the devil. Make me thoughtful, but not moody; helpful, but not bossy. Give me the ability to see good things in unexpected places, and talents in unexpected people. And give me, Lord, the grace to tell them so."

So how are we supposed to "stay young in our mindset" toward our relationship to G? Well, I'm not sure who came up with this suggestion, but it's been said that five tips for staying young are: (1) keep developing your *mind*, (2) keep enjoying your sense of *humor*, (3) take care of yourself *physically*, (4) keep pursing opportunities to serve G, and (5) keep *seeking* G to begin with.

No matter what age we are, there are great things to be done in J's name. After all, Golda Meir was seventy-one when she became prime minister of Israel. William Pitt II was twenty-four when he became prime minister of Great Britain. G. B. Shaw was ninety-four when one of his plays was first produced. And Ben Franklin was a newspaper columnist at sixteen and a framer of the US Constitution at age eighty-one. You're never too young/old if you've got G-given ability.

So for those of us who *are* getting considerably older, J is there give us the mental and physical sharpness we need to live day to day, as Job 33:23–25 indicates when there the Bible says, "If there is an angel on your side, like a mediator who tells a man what's right for him, who is gracious to him and says, 'Spare him from going down to the pit; I have found a ransom for him,' then your flesh will be restored like a child's; it is restored like in the days of his youth." I think we'd do well to remember that passage.

A group of senior citizens was lounging on the patio of their retirement community. One man looked up as a large flock of birds flew overhead. He nudged a nearby friend who had dozed off. "Frank," the first man said, "you'd better move around a little bit. Those look like buzzards closing in on us." And if those two old coots had really wanted to, they could have got moving.

You see, the young and the old really need to have respect for each other, as difficult as that might be to do. It *is* hard, sometimes, to see the point of view of someone on the opposite spectrum of age. As Bertrand Russell once noted, "When I was a young man, no one had any respect for youth. Now that I'm an old man, no one has any respect for age." Well, whether we find ourselves young *or* older at this point in our lives, it would do us well to have at least a little bit of that other age range in our minds and lives. Along those lines, Cicero once admitted, "As I approve of the youth who has something of the old man in him, so I am no less pleased with an old man who has something of the youth." Yes, the young and the old need to learn to appreciate and learn from each other as Lyman Bryson wisely observed when he said, "The error of youth is to believe that intelligence is a substitute for experience, while the error of age is to believe that experience is a substitute for intelligence."

A lady named Teri Leinbaugh said, "Upon arriving in our new home, my seven-year-old son, Jason, decided to explore the neighborhood. Back within an hour, he stated he'd made some new friends. 'Good, are they boys or girls?' I asked.

"'One is a boy and one is a girl,' he explained.

"'That's great,' I said. 'How old are they?'

"'*Mom*,' he started to reply, 'that would be *rude* to ask.'

"I was puzzled by his response," Leinbaugh said, "but about an hour later, he came back.

"'*Mom*,' he shouted, 'I found out how old my new friends are. The girl is sixty-five and the boy is seventy.'"

Yes, good advice is given to both young and old in Psalm 119:9: "How can a young man keep his way pure? By living according to Your Word."

July 13 Giving Satan Exactly What He Wants?
Ephesians 6:12-18

A woman named Barb and her husband, Chuck, were youth leaders who had just arrived at a campground for a weekend retreat with their church's youth group. While Chuck unloaded the van, Barb handed out room assignments. On the bulletin board of the lobby in the main lodge was a poster declaring, "There are no problems, only opportunities."

One boy eventually came over to Barb and said, "Uh, Barb, I've got a problem."

Barb pointed to that sign and said, "Remember, Jeff, there are no problems, only opportunities."

"Well, if that's the way you want it," said Jeff, "but there's a girl in my room..."

The Bible doesn't hold back in explaining the challenge we have in facing the temptation to sin which is so prevalent all around us. In fact, the temptation to sin is so great and so dangerous, Scripture likens attempting to resist it like going into an actual military conflict or war. So from a variety of Bible versions, the passage for today comes from Ephesians 6:12–18: "For we wrestle not against flesh and blood, but against principalities, against powers, against the rulers of the darkness of this world, against spiritual wickedness in high places. So take up God's armor now! Then, when the evil day comes, you will be able to resist the enemy's attacks, and after fighting to the end, you will still hold your ground. Stand firm, then, with the belt of truth buckled around your waist, with the breastplate of righteousness in place, wearing for shoes on your feet the eagerness to spread the gospel of peace. above all, be sure you take faith as you shield, for it can quench every burning missile the enemy hurls at you. And then, you must accept salvation from G to be your helmet and receive the word of G from the Spirit to use as a sword. Pray all the time. Ask God for anything in line with the Holy Spirit's wishes.

Plead with him, reminding him of your needs, and keep praying earnestly for all Christians everywhere."

You see, as this passage so plainly puts it, the real battle in life is *not* between various individuals and groups of people, even though sometimes, it may seem like that. And it's not even between people and G, even though, once again, the main conflict and struggle in life is the one that takes place between our Creator (G) and his creation (that would be us). No, the real battle, the *true war* is the one that has been taking place since Lucifer's fall—the battle between G and Satan. That's why a fellow named Philip S. Watson once commented, "The fundamental biblical opposition is not between flesh and spirit, creature and Creator, but between the Creator of the flesh and it's destroyer, between G and the devil, between Christ and Satan, the Holy Spirit and the unholy."

So to give you some concrete examples of what I'm talking about, one of the ways in which we give Satan *exactly* what he wants is by allowing ourselves the opportunity to believe in a twisted, distorted version of the gospel truth. Now, of course, the easy answer to preventing a scenario like that from occurring to take the appropriate measure of studying and learning for ourselves the truth contained in the Bible, so that no one can fool or mislead us into believing false things about J. But when we neglect to at least read our Bible for a few minutes, on a daily basis, we open ourselves up to the distinct possibility of allowing one of the many false prophets of today to rob us of what could be a wonderful relationship with the Lord.

An example of that fact, then, is seen in the life of Christopher Edwards, who graduated from Yale University in the early summer of 1975. He enrolled at Berkeley with plans to pursue a master's degree. While there, he was approached by a stranger who offered him a "fun weekend" at a local farm. What Edwards didn't realize was that the farm he had been invited to visit was a front for the Sun Myung Moon's Unification Church in Berkeley. He went, and that "fun" weekend turned into seven and a half months of maddening brainwashing. Christopher was changed from a clear-thinking, brilliant, astute individual, into a completely subservient disciple of his new messiah, in his own words, "dependent on his leaders for every move, ready and willing to die or even kill to restore the world under the absolute rule of Rev. Moon."

He was kidnapped by his father and a team of trained professionals in January 1976, and not until he went through a full year of deprogramming and therapy under the direction of a specialist in cult-related problems did Christopher Edwards gain control over what he called "months of madness," as he explained in the book he wrote detailing his experience, entitled, *Crazy for G.* The lesson here, folks, is this: don't give the devil what he wants by allowing yourself to be ignorant of G's word and correct Christian doctrine.

Now, a second way in which people tend to give the devil what he wants is by being less than fully committed, dedicated, and devoted in living their life for J. I don't know if you've ever thought about it this way, but S just loves it whenever people in the church live in such a way as to demonstrate to the rest of the world that they really don't back up their saying that they're followers of Christ with corresponding and appropriate actions.

This is why the Bible says in Revelation 3:15–16, Romans 12:11, Hebrews 10:25, and Matthew 6:24, "I know all your ways; you are neither hot nor cold. How I wish you were either hot or cold! But because you are lukewarm, neither hot nor cold, I will spit you out of my mouth…Work hard and don't be lazy. Serve the Lord with a heart full of devotion…Let us not neglect our church meetings, as some people do, but encourage and warn each other, especially now that the day of his coming back again is drawing near…No one can cully serve two masters. He is bound to hate one and love the other, or be loyal to one and despise the other. You cannot serve both G and the power of money."

And if you want a New Testament example of the devotedness of the first followers of J, thus setting an example for others to follow, take a look at the New English Bible's version of Acts 2:42–47: "They met constantly to hear the apostles teach and to share the common life, to break bread and to pray. A sense of awe was everywhere, and many marvels and signs were brought about through the apostles. All whose faith had drawn them together held everything in common: they would sell their property and possessions and make a general distribution as they need of each required. W one mind, they kept up their daily attendance at the temple, and breaking bread in private houses, shared their meals with unaffected joy, as they praised G and enjoyed the favor of all the people. And day by day, the Lord added to their number those whom he was saving."

Walter Martin once wrote a sequel to C. S. Lewis's book *The Screwtape Letters*. In the second book, Screwtape, a demon in S's realm, writes his nephew, Wormwood, who is in training to be an emissary of the devil, to tell him how to handle the affairs of S and S's world, so that the Christians and the world will be confused and stay spiritually lost. Everything is opposite from Christianity. For example, the book closes, "Glory to Lucifer in the lowest, signed, Dragonslick." But there's one paragraph in the book that really stands out. Remember, everything in the book is in reverse to Christianity: J is the enemy, for instance, since, from the perspective of the devil, you know, everything is opposite.

So Screwtape, at one point, says to Wormwood, "If you can obscure these facts, there's a good chance that he will embrace what hell considers to be the perfect synonym for true religion—'churchianity.' In this marvelous imitation of the Enemy's church, everything looks and sounds right and good, but the Enemy's Spirit is conspicuously absent. You must arrange to make him a devout Methodist, Anglican, Baptist, or Presbyterian, or what have you. Make him THAT. He must come to accept the church as a type of religious social club where people congregate. Nothing more. In a word, Wormwood, help him to become more religious, but for hell's sake, not more Christian!"

So you see, by being less than fully and completely dedicated and devoted in our living for J, we are, in all honesty, giving the devil exactly what he wants.

Now, the third and final area in which people—even churchgoing people— often doing S's bidding is through the deliberate choice not to love all other people around them, as J most certainly commanded us to do. And that's exactly what he did, since the Bible records J saying in John 15:12, "My command is this: love each other as I have loved you." This is why, everybody, 1 John 2:9–11, 4:19–21, 3:10, and 4:8 flatly states, "Anyone who claims to be in the light and hates his brother is, in fact, still in complete darkness. The man who loves his brother lives in the light, and has no reason to stumble. But the man who hates his brother is shut off from the light and gropes his way in the dark without knowing where he is going. For the darkness has made him blind... We love, because G loved us first. If someone says, 'I love G,' but hates his brother, he is a liar. For he cannot love G, whom he has not seen, if he hates his brother, whom he has seen. This, then, is the command that Christ gave us: he who loves G, must love his brother also... Here is the clear difference between G's children and the devil's children: anyone who does not do what is right, or does not love his brother, is not G's child."

You see, one of the best things that you can do whenever you find yourselves in any kind of battle or war is to learn to know your enemy. what makes your enemy tick? How does he/she tend to think? Then, once we become wise to our enemy's tactics, it's then that we are most able to defend ourselves. That's why the Jerusalem Bible says in 1 Peter 5:8–9, "Be calm, but vigilant, because your enemy, the devil, is prowling around like a roaring lion, looking for someone to eat. Stand up to him, strong in faith and in the knowledge that your Christian brothers and sisters all over the world are suffering the same things," and also why the Phillips Modern English Translation of the Bible simply puts it in James 4:7, "Be humble, then, before g. resist the devil, and you'll find he'll flee from you."

The seaport of Aqaba, in 1917, then seemed impregnable. Any enemy vessel approaching the port would have to face the battery of huge naval guns above the town. Behind Aqaba in every direction lay barren, waterless, inhospitable desert. The Turks believed Aqaba to be safe from any attack, but they were wrong. Lawrence of Arabia led a force of irregular Arab cavalry across the area. They rallied support among the local people. On July 6, 1917, the Arab forces swept into Aqaba from the north, the blind side. A climactic moment of the magnificent film *Lawrence of Arabia* is the long, panning shot of the Arabs on their camels and horses, with Lawrence at their head, galloping past the gigantic naval guns that are completely powerless to stop them. The guns were facing the wrong direction. Aqaba fell, and the Turkish hold on Palestine was broken, to be replaced by the British mandate and eventually by the State of Israel. The Turks failed to defend Aqaba because they made two mistakes: (1) they didn't know their enemy, and (2) they didn't have the right weapons to fight with. We Christians need to make sure we don't make the same mistakes. Ephesians 6:12 makes it very clear who are enemy is: "Our struggle is not against flesh and blood, but against the rulers, against the authorities, against the powers of this dark world."

So one of the best weapons we have then, is to go to G in prayer, asking for protection from S not only for ourselves, but our loved ones as well. As J prayed, according to Matthew 6:13 and John 17:15, "Save us from the evil one…My prayer is not that you would take them out of the world, but that you would protect them from the evil one." That's why Paul also wrote in 2 Thessalonians 3:2–3, "Pray also that G will rescue us from wicked and evil men. For not all people believe the message. But the Lord is faithful. He will make you strong and keep you safe from the evil one." Ephesians 4:26 then advises, "Don't give the devil a foothold."

A lady named Amy Carmichael once wrote in an article she entitled "If," "If I belittle those whom I am called to serve, talk of their weak points in contrast perhaps with what I think of as my strong points; if I adopt a superior attitude, forgetting 'Who made thee to differ? And what do you have that was not given to you by the Lord?' then I know nothing of Calvary's love. If I take offense easily, if I am content to continue in a cool unfriendliness, though friendship be possible, then I know nothing of Calvary's love. If I feel bitterly towards those who condemn me, as it seems to me, unjustly, forgetting that if they knew me as I know myself, they would condemn me much more, then I know nothing of Calvary's love."

Yes, when we deliberately choose not to love others, we give the devil just exactly what he wants.

But as we've also been saying today, we also give the devil what he's after whenever we allow ourselves to remain ignorant of a proper understanding of what it means to be a Christian. When we don't understand true Christian doctrine for ourselves, we're once more doing more of the devil's work than G's. For example, one Sunday during Lent, a Sunday school teacher decided to ask her class what they knew regarding Easter.

One boy suggested, "Easter is when the family comes to the house, we eat turkey and watch football."

The teacher said, "You're thinking of Thanksgiving, not Easter."

Next, a little girl said, "Easter is when you come downstairs in the morning and you see all the beautiful presents under the tree."

Teacher was discouraged. After explaining to the girl she was thinking of Christmas, she called on a boy with his hand raised. Her spirits picked up when he said, "Easter is the time when J was crucified and buried." She felt she'd gotten through to at least one child, until he added, "Then, He comes out of the grave, and if He sees His shadow, he goes back in and we have six more weeks of winter."

Remember, everybody, don't allow yourselves to be uneducated about true Christian doctrine, don't be less than fully committed in your devotion to J, and don't let yourself have any feelings other than love for all other people. Otherwise, you'll be giving the devil exactly what he wants.

When You're on the Other Side of Gossip
Ecclesiastes 7:21-22, 10:20

I want to talk to you today about a common subject—that of gossip—but do so in an uncommon way—when you're the subject of it rather than a participant in the spreading of it. Many sermons have been written and preached throughout the centuries on the evils of the tongue and the dangerous product of it, gossip, and the basic message of those sermons has generally been, "Don't do it. Do not talk degradingly about other people." Okay, that's fine. Certainly, sermons like that are needed to be preached, unfortunately, quite often. However, I want to talk to you this morning about a much different angle. I want to address the issue of what happens when we find ourselves (or a loved one of ours) to be the object and target of gossip. That kind of thing has probably happened to everybody here at one time or another, to one extent or another. But when was the last time you had someone suggest to you, from a biblical standpoint, how you ought to properly handle such a situation? What is a person supposed to do when a less than complimentary story about them—or a loved one of theirs—is circulating throughout their local community? And maybe just as importantly, what are they not supposed to do about such a scenario? And to make this sermon on gossip even more unusual, I'm not even going to go near the usual Scripture passage that pastors use when preaching about it, namely James 3, which— among other things—describes the tongue as a restless evil, full of deadly poison. Instead, the Scripture passages I'll be using this morning are ones that, for the most part, don't get a whole lot of attention paid to during those typical types of sermons. So, hang on, and here we go.

The first thing I want to encourage you to do when you start to get an inkling of a vicious rumor that, apparently, is circulating about you through the community is this: don't listen to everything you hear other people say about one of your family members or friends (or even your preacher!). The Bible puts it in Ecclesiastes 7:21–22 like this: "Don't pay attention to every word people say, or you may hear your servant cursing you—for you know in your heart that many times, you yourself have cursed others."

So whenever someone in town comes up to you and says something like, "Guess what I heard about…" (whether it's about someone you know personally or not), don't automatically assume that this person before you knows precisely what they're talking about. Just because a person may make it sound like they are "well-informed," that's not always the case. How does the person speaking with you at the moment know, for certain, that what they're telling you is accurate? If you ask them how they know this bit of info to be true, and they say something like, "Well, that's what so-and-so told me," instead of saying that they know this to be true, firsthand, because they saw with their own eyes and/or heard with their own ears the subject their speaking about, there's probably little, if anything, to it. Don't listen to everything degrading or unflattering story that everybody else seems to be talking about.

Second, if the story circulating through town is about someone you yourself *know* to be honest and sincere and a person of integrity, again, don't automatically believe what you're hearing. Now, granted, anything is possible —"good" people sin and trespass against G's instructions all the time. No one is perfect, and history is full of examples of followers of J who "fell from grace" at some point through committing a blatant act of sin. But you know, until such an accusation is *proven* to be correct (and I'll talk to you more about that in a few minutes), don't automatically assume that that person is guilty. Yes, it's entirely possible that Satan at last seemed to find a crack in the spiritual armor of the person you know who's being spoken of and has succeeded into dragging them into a grievous act against G's will for them. But on the other hand, people who have demonstrated a life of integrity up to a certain point in their lives are often found completely innocent of charges which eventually turn out to be totally baseless.

Yes, as we've already said today, we *all* possess the potential to do all kinds of things contrary to the gospel message. But believe it or not, there *are* people who walk the earth who do a fantastic job of living exemplary lives in Christ. For instance, the Bible describes Caleb, in Numbers 14:24 and 32:12 in the following way: "My servant Caleb has a different spirit and follows me wholeheartedly." Nehemiah is mentioned in Nehemiah 2:7 as "a man of integrity who feared G more than most men do." Obadiah is spoken of, according to 1 Kings 18:3 as being "a devout believer in the Lord." Job is complimented in Job 1:1: "In the land of Uz, there lived a man named Job. This man was blameless and upright; he feared God and shunned evil." Then 2 Chronicles 22:9 tells us of Jehoshaphat, who sought the Lord with all his heart. And 2 Chronicles 29:2 informs us that Hezekiah did right in the eyes of the Lord, and Nehemiah 7:2 mentions Hanani, who was a man of integrity and who feared G more than most people do.

So when you catch wind of a rumor regarding someone you respect, whether it's a family member, coworker, neighbor, or even your preacher, give them the benefit of the doubt. Wait for them to be proven guilty, if that is the case. Conveniently enough, then, I want to talk to you next about that very aspect of when you catch wind of a rumor that's running rampant through the community about a loved one of yours: having proof that the person indeed committed the offense they're being accused of committing.

The Bible advises us on making sure that we have our unflattering story about someone else straight in the verses found in Matthew 18:15–16, 2 Corinthians 13:1, and 1 Timothy 5:19. It's in those places the Bible says, "If your brother sins against you, and show him his fault, just between the two of you. If he listens to you, you have won your brother over. But if he will not listen, take one or two others along, so that every matter may be established... Every matter must be established by 2 or 3 witnesses...Do not entertain an accusation against an elder unless it is brought by two or three witnesses."

What I'm suggesting to you, here, folks, is this: when someone comes up to you with a juicy bit of supposed information about someone in your local area (and you might know the person yourself, maybe you won't), say something like this to the person speaking with you at the moment: "Where did you get this information? Did you see/hear for yourself what you're telling me?" Chances are, the person will most likely admit that they don't know this information firsthand, but that it came to them by way of some other person in the community. Ask the person you're speaking with at that time how the person who told them knows this to be true and accurate information. If the person you're in discussion with says, "The person who told me this was there and saw/heard for themselves," that's what I would call fairly credible info. It's not perfectly credible, but it's pretty close. But if the person you're engaged in conversation looks at you and says something like, "Well, good old so-and-so told me, and somebody else told them…" most likely the "information" being given you is a bunch of "hooey."

This is what I would do, if someone came running up to me with a juicy piece of gossip that, if spread around enough, could have the potential for causing the person to be spoken of to lose their job, ruin their reputation, or cause undeserved stress for their family. I would look at the person telling this and say, "I'll believe you if you can provide me with any number of the following: a number of still photographs depicting the person in question committing the act they're accused of committing, a *video* depicting the person committing the act or an audiotape that clearly demonstrates the truth behind what you're telling me, then I want you to provide with three other people who can look me in the eye and tell me the exact same story you told me, three people who know firsthand what they're saying. And if you can't provide those things for me, then I'm not going to believe it."

Wow. Sounds pretty insistent, doesn't it? That's a bunch of pretty demanding requirements. But you know, if a person's reputation, their livelihood and the harmony of their family life are on the line, then we need to be as careful and as thorough as possible before we grab on to a juicy rumor we've had passed on to us and run with it to the nearest set of ears. A person should be considered innocent till proven guilty, not just in a court of law but also in matters of rumor or gossip.

But what are you supposed to do if the rumors are about *you*? How are you supposed to handle the trouble and difficulty that naturally seem to come along with having your good name dragged through the mud? How are you— according to biblical teaching and principles—supposed to deal with that kind of scenario? What do you do about it, and what don't you do?

Well, if you can honestly say that you have had no part in the activities of which you're being accused of participating in, then just simply continue to live out the life of honesty, sincerity, and integrity that you're used to living out, in J's name. Romans 12:9 tells us to hate what is evil and to cling to what is good. And Romans 16:19 advises for us to be innocent about what is evil. And likewise, 1 Thessalonians 5:22, KJV, tells us to avoid all appearance of evil. Let's face it—people don't need to actually see/hear someone like you or me actually say or do something contrary to Scriptural teaching. If they believe that they saw/heard us do anything close to such an offense, again, they'll take the ball and run with it. Let's not even give the slightest opportunity, then, for people to be able to come up with fodder for lies and rumors about us.

Second, if rumors and out and out lies begin to make the rounds in your community, don't let it get you down. Don't let it greatly discourage you, don't let it create a lot of division within your family, AND don't let it cause you to consider picking up and moving across to the other side of the country. Even if rumors about you or your loved one run rampant, hold your head up high, and continue to live the life of integrity that you're used to living. You see, it let it all bother us terribly, to allow the slander to cause us to go into depression and create strife and tension in our family is exactly what the devil wants to have happen. He wants us to suffer when a situation like this comes about. Let's not give him the satisfaction. It's at this point we might want to remind ourselves of passages from the Bible like Psalms 25:21 and 37:23–24, as well as Proverbs 10:9 and 28:18, when the Bible states in those places, "May integrity and uprightness protect me, because my hope is in you, God... If the Lord delights in a man's way, he makes his steps firm, though he stumble, he will not fall, for the Lord upholds him with his hand...The man of integrity walks securely...He whose walk is blameless is kept safe."

And at the same time, we need to pray that G will make it so that the person or people responsible for starting and continuing to promote this rumor will eventually be exposed for the liar that they are and come to experience the appropriate consequences. I'm not talking, now, of taking vengeance. We're to let God, after all, decide what kind of retribution that person/those people should suffer for their wrong and let G deliver it to them. But to help put a stop to the rumor-mongering and to help teach a lesson to the gossipers so that they might think twice about ever doing anything like this again to anyone else, I think it's very appropriate to go to G in prayer, asking that those who promoted these falsehoods to reap what they've sown. And I think if we ask that with a sincere heart, G will honor that request. As the Bible so eloquently points out together in Psalms 12:3–4 and 101:5; Proverbs 10:9, 10:14, and 13:3; and Matthew 12:36–37, "May the Lord cut off all flattering lips and every boastful tongue that says, 'We will triumph with our tongues; we own our lips— who is our master?'…Whoever slanders his neighbor in secret, him will I put to silence…The man of integrity walks securely, but he who takes crooked paths will be found out…the mouth of a fool invites ruin…He who guards his lips guards his life, but he who speaks rashly will come to ruin…But I tell you that men will have to give account on the day of judgment for every careless word they have spoken. For by your words, you will be acquitted, and by your words, you will be condemned."

You know, I've been told that when a rumor gets started about you, there will be no way to determine who started it, why and when. There's no way to track down the people responsible, it's been said. But you know, people who like to talk a lot—especially about other people—tend to talk a little too much. And if they *do* talk enough, eventually, they give themselves away. They eventually talk so much that they end up passing the rumor on to a close friend of the subject of the rumor, who then goes back to their friend and informs them, accurately, who has been slandering their good name. Or the gossiper winds up spreading the rumor within earshot of the person being gossiped about. Then, once the gossiper is discovered, their words come back to bite them, and bite them hard, one way or another.

So maybe the last remaining lesson we could take away for ourselves from this message this morning is to how to keep ourselves from getting caught up in the flurry of excitement that's produced when people gossip. If we ourselves don't ever want to be guilty of helping to create trouble for someone else due to what we've said, maybe a good thing to do is to follow the advice found in Ecclesiastes 10:20, when the Bible simply says there, "Don't revile the king, even in your thoughts, or curse the rich in your bedroom, because a bird of the air may carry your words, and a bird on the wing may report what you say."

There's No Crying in Happy Land
Revelation 21:1-4

It was last year when our youth group went to the annual Virginia Baptist YEC in Richmond, when we went that Saturday to Kings' Dominion. You know about KD—it's an amusement park, a place full of rides, shows and restaurants…a place of adventure, food and fun, a place where you'd think where everyone would have a smile on their face and laughter on their lips. Well, it was very interesting, being there that day. Yes, there were many people who were there, having a lot of fun. I saw a lot of people laughing and having fun with their families and friends, grinning from ear to ear. But I also saw something strange: a number of people who definitely were having anything but fun. There were kids crying and screaming because their parents wouldn't take them on the monstrous roller coaster for the fortieth time that day. There was the occasional episode where the boyfriend or girlfriend of a couple at the park seemed to be extremely perturbed at the behavior and remarks of their loved one. And there were also a number of people who just simply looked dog-tired over the course of the day, people who seemed like they were about to collapse. Ironically, there were people all over this place—this place I might have nicknamed Happy Land, in connection with its purpose and intention— who were anything but happy on that day.

Well, considering the earthly conditions we live in, there will always be some measure of disappointment, sadness and even anger, even when we go to places like KD, Carowinds, or Bush Gardens. But the reality of heaven will never disappoint those who end up there. Scripture relates to us what heaven will be like in Revelation 21:1–4 when the Bible states there, "Then, I saw a new heaven and a new earth, for the 1st heaven and the 1st earth had passed away, and there was no longer any sea. I saw the Holy City, the new Jerusalem, coming down out of heaven from God, prepared as a bride beautifully dressed for her husband. And I heard a loud voice from the throne saying, 'Now the dwelling of God is with men, and he will live with them. They will be his people, and God himself will be with them and be their God. He will wipe every tear from their eyes. There will be no more death or mourning or crying or pain, for the old order of things has passed away."

Likewise, Revelation 7:6–7 says when speaking of those in heaven, "Never again will they hunger; never again will they thirst. The sun will not beat upon them, nor any scorching heat. For the Lamb at the center of the throne will be their shepherd; he will lead them to springs of living water. And God will wipe away every tear from their eyes."

Yes, it is true that there are many enjoyable things about this life. Even with all the pain and suffering that humans typically endure, there's quite a bit about human life that does indeed add spice to it and make it worth experiencing. However, none of what human, earthly life has to offer can even come close to what heaven has in store for us. As Martin Luther once commented, "I would not give one moment of Heaven for all the joys and riches in the world."

But something else we need to keep in mind is that the amount of blessedness we'll receive in heaven is directly proportional to the kind of life we led here on earth. Our eternal reward reflects, then, the amount of God's glory that we allowed to shine through us. How much enjoyment do we want out of heaven? If the answer is, "As much as I can have," then we need to prepare and lay the ground work for that kind of reward.

Now, to be perfectly honest, there are a lot of questions the Bible does not answer regarding the hereafter. But I think one reason for that is illustrated by the story, told by Vance Havner, of a boy sitting down to a plate of spinach casserole, when at the same time, there's a chocolate cake at the other end of the table. He's going to have a hard-enough time just trying to eat the spinach casserole to begin with, but the task became even hard with that cake sitting there in full view at the opposite end of the table. Havner concluded his illustration by saying, "If G had explained everything to us about what's ours in Heaven to come (our dessert), then we'd have an even harder time 'eating our spinach' down here."

I'm sure you realize that even the Old Testament has a lot to say about heaven. For example, Isaiah 11:6–9 makes it plain and clear that there will be no chance for danger, sadness, or death, and that things there will be pretty much the opposite of the way they're here on earth when it says,

"The wolf will live with the lamb, the leopard will lie down with the goat, the calf and the lion and the yearling together; and a little child will lead them. The cow will feed with the bear, their young will lie down together, and the lion will eat straw like the ox. The infant will play near the hole of the cobra, and the young child will put his hand into the viper's nest. They will neither harm nor destroy on all my holy mountain, for the earth will be full of knowledge of the Lord as the water cover the sea."

And the Bible also lets us know that in Heaven, there will be no more "premature deaths," and that peace will come between former "natural enemies." Once again Isaiah 65:19–25 says, "I will rejoice over Jerusalem and take delight in my people; the sound of weeping and of crying will be heard in it no more. Never again will there be in it an infant who lives but a few days, or an old man who does not live out his years; he who dies at a hundred will be thought a mere youth; he who fails to reach a hundred will be considered cursed. They will build houses and dwell in them; they will plant vineyards and eat their fruit. No longer will they build houses and others live in them, or plant and others eat. For as the days of a tree, so will be the days of my people; my chosen ones will long enjoy the works of their hands. They will not toil in vain or bear children doomed to misfortune; for they will be a people blessed by the Lord, they and their descendants with them. Before they call, I will answer; while they are still speaking I will hear. The wolf and the lamb will feed together, and the lion will eat straw like the ox, but dust will be the serpent's food. They will neither harm nor destroy on my holy mountain."

Now, I'll admit to you that it's difficult to feel good about waiting to get to heaven, especially if one or more of our earthly love ones have died and gone on before us. But as Scripture relates to us, death does not permanently separate loved ones. That separation is only for a small time in all eternity. The story is told of a little girl who was upset that her older sister had moved out of the house after having gotten married. But the girl's mother explained to her that her sister had only moved to a house down the street from them and that they could go visit and see her sister—who was now in a home with just as much love and joy in it as their own—quite a bit. It just takes some patience getting to those times.

Now, another factor that will make heaven such a blessed place besides the absence of pain and suffering is that there will be all kinds of different people to share this blessedness with. An elderly Quaker once said to another, "Friend, does thee think there will be any others than Quakers in heaven?" His fellow Quaker replied, "Well, if there aren't, it would hardly pay to keep the place open!"

Yes, as unbelievable as it might sounds, heaven will be absent of threats to our life, and instead be a safe haven. It will be free from sadness but filled with joy instead. And death will not reside in heaven, only life. As Isaiah 35:1–10 pictures it, "The desert and the parched land will be glad; the wilderness will rejoice and blossom. Like the crocus, it will burst into bloom; it will rejoice greatly and shout for joy. The glory of Lebanon will be given to it, the splendor of Carmel and Sharon; they will see the glory of the Lord, the splendor of our God. Strengthen the feeble hands, steady the knees that give way; say to those with fearful hearts, 'Be strong, do not fear; your God will come, he will come with vengeance; with divine retribution he will come to save you.' Then will the eyes of the blind be opened and the ears of the deaf unstopped. Then will the lame leap like a deer, and the mute tongue shout for joy. Water will gush forth in the wilderness and streams in the desert. The burning sand will become a pool, the thirsty ground bubbling springs. In the haunts where jackals once lay, grass and reeds and papyrus will grow. And a highway will be there; it will be called the Way of Holiness. The unclean will not journey on it; it will be for those who walk in that Way; wicked fools will not go about on it. No lion will be there, nor will any ferocious beast get up on it; they will not be found there. But only the redeemed will walk there, and the ransomed of the Lord will return. They will enter Zion with singing; everlasting joy will crown their heads. Gladness and joy will overtake them, and sorrow and sighing will flee away."

Now, it's great to look forward to the blessedness of heaven. That's fine. But we need to realize that the amount of blessedness we will receive there will be reflected by the quality of Christian life that we led while alive. To illustrate that point, the story is told of a millionaire who once stood at heaven's entrance, waiting to be shown his heavenly home. He was led to a small cottage, located in the midst of other tiny, unpretentious homes.

He complained, "Can it be that I, who lived in a mansion on earth in luxury and comfort, must now live forever in this dinky, little house?"

The one who had been leading him replied, "We built this house out of the material you sent us while you were on earth! We could have built a palace for you, if you had sent us material with which to build it."

The point of that story is brought to light in the portion of the Jewish Talmud which states, "This world is only the vestibule to another world; you must prepare yourself in the vestibule so that you may enter the banquet hall."

Even Muslims—wrong as they are about the person and work of God—have a similar view of the blessedness of heaven. It is stated in the Koran, "Allah will reward the righteous with garments of silk. Reclining upon soft couches, they will feel neither the sun's burning heat, nor bitter cold. Trees will spread their shade over them, and bunches of fruit will hang low."

Once again, in heaven, G will care for us and there will be no more sorrow —especially since no one will need to grieve over the death of a loved one, there. In addition, the passage from the Koran that I just read apparently isn't that far from the reality of heaven according to the Bible, since we read in Isaiah 25:6–8, "On this mountain, the Lord will prepare a feast of rich food for all people, a banquet of aged wine—the best of meats and the finest of wines. On this mountain, he will destroy the shroud that enfolds all people, the sheet that covers all nations; he will swallow up death forever. The Sovereign Lord will wipe away tears from all faces."

Think about it. As Christians, we shouldn't be frightened of death. Instead, knowing what awaits us in heaven, we ought to look forward to the day of our demise. Joyously and confidently, David Livingstone exclaimed on his last birthday, "I am not old! You know I am not old! No man ever had a brighter hope, or a more inviting future!" This radiant, triumphant statement was made by Livingstone in response to a well-meaning friend who said to Livingstone that he was getting old. The prospects of all Christians are almost overwhelmingly bright. As 1 Corinthians 2:9 indicates, "Eye hath not seen nor ear heard, neither has entered into the heart of man, the things which God has prepared for them that love him." On the other hand, how dismally dark is the future of all who *reject* Christ. Their souls are wreathed in darkness and oftentimes paralyzed with fear as they face the coming day of reckoning. Thomas Hobbs, a blatant atheist, as his sinful soul was about to pass into eternity, said, "I am about to take a leap in the dark!"

Yes, as we just alluded to, maybe the best thing about heaven is that there, there will be no more death and dying. As 1 Corinthians 15:26 proclaims, "The last enemy to be destroyed is death." That every event, then, is described in Revelation 20:14–15, "Then death and Hell were thrown into the lake of fire. The lake of fire is the 2nd death. If anyone's name was not found written in the book of life, he was thrown into the lake of fire."

Consider this: a man who has a layover at an airport does not go into the bathroom, frown at its décor, and start redecorating! Why not? Because he *doesn't* live there. He has a home in another place. While he is away, he will get by with only what he absolutely needs, to have more money with which to furnish his permanent home. So, why do we Christians always work so hard at trying to make our life in *this* world more comfortable? This world is just the airport, and we are in the middle of our flights. We should spend our energy on enhancing our eternal reward and not worry so much about the bare walls in the airport restrooms!

License and Registration, Please
Revelation 13:11-18

How many of you have ever been in a car accident, before, in which you were behind the wheel and not just a passenger? Go ahead, raise your hands. How many of you have been driving and had an accident before? Well, after the policeman shows up to the scene, the *first* things he asks you is, "Are you hurt?" But what's the next thing he says to you? You know—those four magic words we all just love to hear in that situation: "License and registration, please." It's at that point that you start getting really nervous and your hands are shaking as your respond by saying, "Yes, *occifer*" (instead of officer). You then fumble through the glove compartment, trying to find the stupid registration, and then you spill the contents of your wallet as you attempt to get your license out of it. (Mockingly) License and registration, please. Why does the officer need your license and registration? Why can't you just tell him your name, address, phone number, what make and model your car is, etc. Well, he needs your license and registration as *official proof* that you are who you say you are. He can't just take *your* word for all that—he needs to have absolute US-government-approved identification that you're telling him is accurate.

Now, driver's licenses and registrations vary in appearance from state to state, but one day, everybody on the face of the earth will have the *exact same* kind of "government-approved" form of ID, and it will be known as "the mark of the beast," according to Revelation 13:11–18. In the Jerusalem Bible, this passage says, "Then I saw a second beast; it emerged from the ground; it had two horns like a lamb, but made a noise like a dragon. This second beast was servant to the first beast, and extended its authority everywhere, making the world and all its people worship the first beast, which had had the fatal wound and had been healed. And it worked great miracles, even to calling down fire from heaven on to the earth while people watched. Through the miracles which it was allowed

85

to do on behalf of the first beast, it was able to win over the people of the world and persuade them to put up a statue in honor of the beast that had been wounded by the sword and still lived. It was allowed to breathe life into this statue, so that the statue of the beast was able to speak, and to have anyone who refused to worship the statue of the beast put to death. He compelled everyone—small and great, rich and poor, slave and free—to be marked on the right hand or on the forehead, and made it illegal for anyone to buy or sell anything unless he had been marked with the name of the beast or with the number of its name. There is need for shrewdness here: if anyone is clever enough, he may interpret the number of the beast: it is the number of a man, the number is 666."

Now, the reason why I've tied the idea of a driver's license (or any proper form of ID) in with this passage which speaks of the mark of the beast is this. Notice what verses 16 and 17 say, once more: "He also forced everyone (small and great, rich and poor, slave and free) to receive a mark on his right hand or on his forehead, so that no one could buy or sell unless he had the mark, which is the name of the beast, or the number of his name." What this passage is saying then is this: no one anywhere in the world at that time will be able to conduct one iota of business unless they have the mark of the beast on their right hand or forehead—meaning of course, they won't be able to make a living in order to support themselves or their families. In other words, everyone on the face of the earth at that time will have to have the proper ID if they wish to survive.

Now, you need to understand something about this mark of the beast before we go any further, this morning. Many people are under the impression that the mark of the beast is a simple tattoo that people will have literally branded on their right hand or their forehead. You know, that would look pretty ridiculous—people walking around all over the place with a three-digit number written on their heads (or hands). But actually, the Greek word for our English word "mark" is "stigma," which is defined, according to Webster's, as "a scratch or a sticking under the skin." This has led biblical scholars to conclude then, that the mark of the beast will *not* be a tattoo or decal of the number 666 but instead something like a computer chip implanted just beneath the surface of the skin. Now, I don't know if you're aware of this, but for several years now, they've had the capacity to implant a particular type of computer chip, called the VeriChip, inside the body, and for some reason, those who have developed this chip have determined that the best places on the body to implant them are (1) the forehead (just below the hairline) and (2) the back of the hand.

The purpose of these chips, then, is basically twofold. In today's society where there is so much crime and lawless (and, as you know, it's only getting worse), criminals and perpetrators of crime can be tracked down by using the homing device like signal that these chips give out, and second, when the person who is being looked for his located, a scanner will be able to read the chip implanted in that person and will identify, for certain, that this person is indeed the one being searched for, by disclosing all kinds of information stored on the chip. There will be no need, then, for the police or those in authority to require that a person come up with their "license and registration, please," since everything that will be required to know of that person will be able to be read, instantly, by a chip scanner/reader. The mark of the beast, then, will be the "universal i.d." at that time. Mexican officials have even gone as far as having the chip implanted in numerous citizens of Mexico, in order to help them track down/locate future kidnap victims.

Now, here's where it really starts to get creepy. We said a minute ago that the Greek word for "mark" was "stigma." Well, when the word "stigma" is looked up in Strong's Concordance of the Bible, the number 666 is given. In addition, then, when the actual English word "mark" (taken from Revelation 13:16) is looked up in Strong's Concordance, it's defined by Strong's as "a badge of servitude." So, anyone who has the mark implanted in them will be considered a servant or a slave to the antichrist—they will be *owned* by him.

You know, a lot of people look at this area of Scripture and assume that this idea of an identifying mark is something that Satan will have come up with on is own. After all, even many non-Christians know of this "mark of the beast on the right hand or forehead thing." The problem is that many people don't know that the idea of an identifying mark on the right hand or forehead in the Bible ISN'T exclusive to Satan's use, as depicted here in Revelation. There are other places in the Bible where God himself makes use of such a thing. It's true. I didn't even realize that this was the case until I read through the Bible in its entirety. Work with me here and take your Bibles (there are some in the pews in front of you if you didn't happen to bring one) and follow along with me. (Wow! Christians using their Bibles in church—imagine that!)

Anyway, turn with me if you will to Exodus 13:6–9. Here the Bible says, "For seven days eat bread made without yeast and on the 7th day, hold a festival to the Lord. East unleavened bread during those 7 days; nothing with yeast in it is to be seen among you, nor shall any yeast be seen anywhere within your borders. On that day, tell your son, 'I do this because of what the Lord did for me when I came out of Egypt.' This observance will be for you like a sign or your hand and a reminder on your forehead that the law of the Lord is to be on your lips." Okay, do you see that? Now, skip down to verses 14–16: "In days to come, when your son asks you, 'What does this mean?' say to him, 'With a mighty had, the Lord brought us out of Egypt, out of the land of slavery. When Pharaoh stubbornly refused to let us go, the Lord killed every 1st born in Egypt, both man and animal. This is why I sacrifice to the Lord the 1st male offspring of every womb and redeem each of my 1st born sons' and it will be like a sign on your hand and a symbol on your forehead that the Lord brought us out of Egypt with his mighty hand."

Interesting, huh? But those aren't the only examples in the Bible where God chose to use the idea of sign/symbol on the right hand or forehead to have people be in connection with him. Turn with me, again, in your Bibles to Deuteronomy 6:4–9. It's here the Bible says, "Hear O Israel, the Lord our G, the Lord is one. Love the Lord your G with all your heart and with all your soul and with all your strength. These commandments I give you today are to be upon your hearts. Impress them on your children. Talk about hem when you sit at home and when you walk along the road, when you lie down and when you get up. Tie them as symbols on your hands and bind them on your foreheads. Write them on the doorframes of your houses and on your gates." Now, turn just a few chapters over to Deuteronomy 11:18: "Fix these words of mine in your hearts and minds; tie them as symbols on your hands and bind them on your foreheads." Isaiah 44:5 states, "One will say, 'I belong to the Lord'; another will call himself by the name of Jacob; still another will write on his hand, the Lord's."

Now, all that those Scriptures have been interesting in that they've shown us that G has used the idea of the forehead/right hand sign and symbol to identify those who follow him. We saw earlier that the beast of Revelation will employ that idea in that whoever has the mark of the beast will be protected from being persecuted, since it's assumed that those who will take the mark of the beast will *not* be Christians. But once again, God used the exact same scenario well-before Satan will have a chance to, according to Ezekiel 9:3–6. Once more, turn with me in your Bibles to Ezekiel 9:3–6 and follow along with me: "Now the glory of the G of Israel went up from above the cherubim, where it had been, and moved to the threshold of the temple. Then the Lord called to the man clothed in linen who had the writing kit at his side and said to him, 'Go throughout the city of Jerusalem and put a mark on the foreheads of those who grieve and lament over all the detestable things that are done in it.' As I listened, he said to the others, 'Follow him through the city and kill, without showing mercy or compassion. Slaughter old men, young men and maidens, women and children, but do not touch anyone who has the mark.'"

You see, folks, what all this teaches us, in part, is that Satan doesn't do anything original—he's not a creator of things. Satan doesn't do anything on his own, creatively. He specializes in two other areas. He either attempts to destroy what G has already created, or he copies, mimics, apes, and imitates what G has created. Of course, when Satan does choose to copy something G has already done, he does it from an evil perspective and for evil purposes.

The question for us, this morning, is "Whose mark do we bear at this point in our hearts and minds?" We might not have a physical tattoo or decal *on* us, and we might not have a mini-computer chip implanted *in* us, but all of us are either living for G in Christ, or we're living for Satan. A lot of people might respond to a statement like that and say, "Actually, I don't pay either one—G or Satan—much attention. I live my *own* life, according to the way I want to live it, for me, and I'm doing just fine, just like that." Well, you know everyone, I can't say for certain of course, but I can't imagine that all the people who will be living on earth when the beast of Revelation takes over will willing give their lives in service to him. I'm sure that there will be many people who would rather have nothing to do with him—not because they're devoted followers of Christ but simply because they want to live life their own way and do their own thing. But do you know what? All those people will have to give their allegiance to the beast—they won't have a choice—other than to proclaim J as their Savior, and then face execution.

If some sort of "theological policeman" were to approach you someday and required that you produce your "license and registration, please," meaning that he'd want to see evidence of the mark of the beast on your person, how would you respond? When it comes to the person of JC, who are we? Do we have a real connection with him? If the day should come when we actually found ourselves in that kind of situation, how would it turn out for us?

Tell the Bully, "Have a Nice Day"
Matthew 5:44; Romans 12:14-21

On the topic of hold a grudge, a man by the name of William H. Walton was once quoted as saying, "To carry a grudge is like being stung to death by one bee." Okay, that brings to mind an interesting visual. No, carrying a grudge and wanting revenge are definitely not the things we ought to focus on in life, but unfortunately, such an attitude and mindset seem to come to us all too naturally. For instance, there was once a newspaper cartoon that showed a tiny baby, only seconds after his birth. The doctor was pictured holding the kid up by the feet, upside down, and slapping his rear end. But instead of crying, the child was shown to angrily be screaming, "I want a lawyer!"

Shortly after 9/11, a rock group that's been popular now for the last couple of decades, named Bon Jovi, came out with a song in which they described how the world seems to keep getting uglier, nastier, and more self-centered. But the main message of the song is summed up in the last two lines of the chorus, "So when the world gets in my face, I say, 'Have a nice day.'" The singer seems to be saying that when the world treats him in a nasty way, he will "retaliate with kindness rather than with vengeance." Well you know, that's exactly what J instructed us to do in Matthew 5:43–48 and what the apostle Paul laid out as part of a set of guidelines for Christians to follow in Romans 12:14–21: "You have learned how it was said: 'You must love your neighbor and hate your enemy.' But I say this to you: love your enemies 7 pray for those who persecute you; in this way, you will be sons of your Father Heaven, for he causes his sun to rise on bad men as well as good, and his rain to fall on honest and dishonest men alike. For if you love only those who love you, what right have you to claim any credit? Even the tax collectors do as much, do they not? And if you save your greetings for your brothers, are you doing anything exceptional? Even the pagans do as much, don't they? You must therefore be perfect, just as your heavenly Father is perfect."

Ask G to bless those who persecute you; yes, ask him to bless, not to curse. Be happy with those who are happy, weep with those who weep. Have the same concern for all alike. Do not be proud but accept humble duties. Do not think of yourselves as wise. If someone does evil to you, do not pay him back with evil. Try to do what all men consider to be good. Do everything possible, on your part, to live at peace with all men. Never take revenge my friends, but instead, let G's wrath do it. For the Scripture says, "I will take revenge, I will pay back, says the Lord." Instead, as the scripture says, "If your enemy is hungry, feed him; if he is thirsty, give him a drink; for by doing this, you will heap burning coals on his head. Do not let evil defeat you; instead, conquer evil with good."

A certain college student needed a small two-hour course to fill out his schedule, and the only class offered that would fit was one in wildlife zoology. The student had some reservations about taking this class, since he had heard that the course was hard and that the teacher was a bit "different." But as it was the only option, he signed up. After one week and one chapter, the professor passed out a test for the class to take. It was a sheet of paper divided into squares, and in each square was a carefully drawn picture of some bird legs. No bodies, no feet, just different birds' legs. The test simply asked the students to identify the birds from the picture of their legs. Well, this particular student was absolutely floored. He didn't have a clue, so he sat, staring at the test, getting madder and madder.

Finally, reaching a boiling point, he stomped up to the front of the classroom and threw the test on the teacher's desk, exclaiming, "This is the worst test I have ever seen, and this is the dumbest course I've ever taken!"

The teacher looked at him and replied, "Young man, you just flunked the test." Then the teacher picked up the young man's test paper, noticed that the student hadn't even written his name anywhere on the test, and said, "By the way, young man, what's your name?"

At that, the student leaned over, rolled up his pants legs, and said, "Go ahead…identify me."

You see, as that story illustrates, "fighting fire with fire" really doesn't accomplish anything. It doesn't make our situation any better, and it certainly doesn't help to put things the way G would have them.

Now, though there are plenty of examples of people in the Bible who did indeed strike back and take revenge on their enemy, there are fortunately numerous instances of people who took the high road and expressed love/compassion—if not at least tolerance—toward their enemies. You know the story of Joseph from Genesis—Joseph's brothers had become insanely jealous of him, attacked him and sold him into slavery. But through events directed by the providence of G, Joseph went from being a slave to having a position of authority in Egypt. It was at that point that Jo had the perfect opportunity to take the authority he had and really let his brothers have it, for all they had done to him. But he didn't.

This is how the Bible explains how Jo handled the situation, according to Genesis 50:15–21: "When Jo's bros saw that their father was dead, they said, 'What if Joe holds a grudge against us and pays us back for all the wrongs we did to him?' So they sent word to Jo, saying, 'Your father left these instructions before he died: "This is what you are to say to Joseph—I ask you to forgive your brothers the sins and the wrongs they committed in treating you so badly." Now please forgive the sins of the servants of the G of your father.' When their message came to him, Jo wept.

"His brothers then came and threw themselves down before him. 'We are your slaves,' they said. But Jo said to them, 'Don't be afraid. Am I in the place of G? You intended to harm me, but G intended it for good to accomplish what is now being done, the saving of many lives. So then, don't be afraid. I will provide for you and your children. And he reassured them and spoke kindly to them.'"

David did the same kind of thing, in restraining himself from taking revenge on Saul, who had been trying to kill him. Scripture says in 1 Samuel 26:5–11, "Then David set out and went to the place where Saul had camped. He saw where Saul and Abner had lain down. Saul was lying inside the camp with the army encamped around him. David then asked Ahimelech and Abishai, 'Who will go down into the camp with me to Saul?'

"'I'll go with you,' said Abishai. So David and Abishai went to the army by night, and there was Saul, lying asleep inside the camp with his spear stuck in the ground hear his head. Abner and the soldiers were lying around him. "Abishai said to David, 'Today G has delivered your enemy into your hands. Now let me pin him to the ground with one thrust of my spear; I won't strike him twice.'

"But David said to Abishai, 'Don't destroy him! Who can lay a hand on the Lord's anointed and be guiltless? As surely as the Lord lives, the Lord will strike him; either his time will come and he will die, or he will go into battle and perish. But the Lord forbid that I should lay a hand on the Lord's anointed.'"

You see, in both of these biblical examples, the man of G involved took the high road and decided not to strike back at the one(s) who had given them trouble. Some people, however, just can't seem to refrain from retaliating whenever they're given the opportunity. For instance, there's the story of a rancher's daughter, who had just broken off her engagement with a young doctor. "Do you mean to tell me," exclaimed a friend of hers, "that he actually asked you to return all the presents he gave you?"

The rancher's daughter nodded. "Not only that, but he also sent me a bill for forty-four house calls."

Now that was an instance where someone took advantage of their social standing/profession and used it in their favor to strike back at someone whom they'd had a falling out with. But, everybody, that's exactly how Christians are *not* to behave, even when they have the perfect chance (and supposed reason) to do so.

The thing to do, then, is to take on the same attitude that J had, according to what's explained to us in the Good News Bible's version of Philippians 2:3– 11: "Don't do anything from selfish ambition, or from a cheap desire to boast; but be humble toward each other, never thinking you are better than others. And look out for each other's interests, not just for your own. The attitude you should have is the one that Christ J had: He always had the very nature of G, but he did not think that by force he should try to become equal with G. Instead, of his own free will, he gave it all up, and took the nature of a servant. He became like man and appeared in human likeness. He was humble and walked the path of obedience to death—his death on a cross. For this reason G raised him to the highest place above, and gave him the name that is greater than any other name. And so, in honor of the name of J, all being in heaven, on earth, and in the world below will fall on their knees, and all will openly proclaim that J Christ is Lord, to the glory of God the Father."

Three heavyset and leather-jacketed clad fellows on huge motorcycles pulled up to a highway café where a truck driver, just a little guy, was perched on a stool quietly eating his lunch. As the three fellows came in, they spotted him, grabbed his food away from him and laughed in his face. The truck driver said nothing. He got up, paid for his food, and walked out.

One of the three cyclists, unhappy that they hadn't succeeded in provoking the little man into a fight, commented to the waitress: "Boy, he sure wasn't much of a tough guy, was he?"

The waitress replied, as she looked out the restaurant window, "Well, I guess not, but apparently, he's not much of a truck driver, either, because he just ran over three motorcycles in the parking lot."

You know, I realize that in times like that, it's really easy to cheer on the person who succeeds in giving back to someone what apparently that other person deserves. But we need to because careful, since, remember, our scripture passage for today includes the statement, "I will take revenge; I will pay back, says the Lord." And, as the Bible states in Proverbs. 24:29, "Don't say 'I'll do to him as he has done to me; I'll pay that man back for what he did.'"

Now, an additional problem with the want for revenge is that it not only does spiritual damage to the person who has those feelings, but if that person is charismatic or influential enough, those spiritually warped feelings and attitudes can spread to other people around them, like a cancer, with disastrous effects. Baseball great Mickey Mantle once had a friend who would let him hunt on his ranch. One day, the two of them went to the ranch to hunt along with teammate Billy Martin. When they arrived, Billy stayed in the car while Mickey went into the main building to check in with his friend. Mickey was indeed given permission to hunt, but the rancher friend asked a favor of him. The rancher's old mule was going blind and had become crippled, but the rancher didn't have the heart to put the animal out of its misery—so he asked Mickey if he would shoot the old mule for him, as a favor. When Mickey got back to the car, he decided to play a trick on Billy and pretended to be angry.

"What's wrong?" Billy asked.

"My friend told me—no hunting!" Mickey then pounded the dashboard with his fist, feigning anger and said, "Why that guy has got me so mad, I'm going to go to his barn and shoot one of his mules."

With that, Mickey jumped out of the car and heads for the barn. In quick order, he took care of the mule and started back to the car in order to inform his friend that it was all a joke. Just then, Mickey heard two shots fired, ran toward the direction of the noise and found Billy standing over two dead cows.

"What are you doing?!" he asked Billy.

Martin replied, "Well, I saw how mad you were, I wanted to let your rancher buddy know that he couldn't mess with me either!"

Now, this next thing is easier said than done, but what we really need to do is to let G take care of exacting justice for us. For example, G spoke through Moses, In Deuteronomy 32:35, when the Bible records him saying there, "It is mine to avenge, I will repay." In addition, Proverbs 20:22 states, "Do not say, "I'll pay back for this wrong! Wait for the Lord, and he will deliver you." So what we probably need to do, then, when faced with the opportunity to take revenge on someone, is to do anything else but take revenge. Do whatever it takes—within the bounds of biblical teaching—to avoid getting in that type of spiritual trouble. Thomas Jefferson, for instance, believed, "When angry, count to ten; if very angry, count to a hundred." Mark Twain once said, "When angry, count to four. If you're very angry, swear." All right, that's not such a great suggestion, obviously, for a churchgoing Christian. But I think you know what I'm getting at.

You know, sometimes, enemies serve a purpose and can be quite helpful, in a way. Charles Spurgeon once advised, "Get your friends to tell you your faults, or better still, welcome an enemy who will watch you keenly and sting you savagely. What a blessing such an irritating critic will be to a wise man, what an intolerable nuisance to a fool!" Yes, we can learn, constructively, from our enemies. Maybe that's partly the reason why Exodus 23:4 instructs us, "If you come across your enemy's ox or donkey wondering off, be sure to take it back to him. If you see a donkey of someone who hates you fallen down under its load, do not leave it there, be sure you help him with it."

It's been pointed out that it's a very easy thing to get mixed up when you're four years old and in church. For instance, one particular four-year-old once erroneously prayed, "Forgive us our trash baskets as we forgive those who put trash in our baskets." I don't know. Maybe that kid wasn't so far off the real meaning of "forgive us our sins as we forgive those who sin against us."

Once more, J speaks on the topic from Luke 6:27–35: "Love your enemies and do good to those who hate you. Pray for the happiness of those who curse you; implore G's blessing on those who hurt you. If someone slaps you on one cheek, let him slap the other, too. If someone demands you coat, give him your shirt besides. Give what you have to anyone who asks you for it; and when things are taken away from you, don't worry about getting them back. Treat others as you want them to treat you. Do you think you deserve credit for merely loving those who love you? Even the godless do that! And if you do good only to those who do you good—is that so wonderful? Even sinners do that much! And if you lend money only to those who can repay you, what good is that? Even the most wicked will lend to their own kind for full return! Love you enemies! Do good to them! Lend to them! And don't be concerned about the fact that they won't repay. Then, your reward from heaven will be very great, and you will truly be acting as sons of G."

A sign once appeared on a convent, reading, "Absolutely no trespassing. Violators will be prosecuted to the fullest extent of the law. Signed, the Sisters of Mercy."

Have You Still Not Found What You're Looking For?
Deuteronomy 4:29; Matthew 9:14-27

(Start by playing a recording of "I Still Haven't Found What I'm Looking For," by U2.)

Sherlock Holmes and Dr. Watson went on a camping trip. As they lay down for night, Holmes said, "Watson, look up into the sky and tell me what you see."

Watson looked up and said, "I see millions and millions of stars."

Holmes then asked, "And what does that tell you?"

Watson then thoughtfully answered, "Astronomically, it tells me that there are millions of galaxies and potentially billions of planets. Theologically, it tells me that G is great and that we are small and insignificant. Meteorologically, it tells me that we will have a beautiful day, tomorrow. What does it tell you, Holmes?"

Holmes then deduced, "Someone stole our tent!"

That's the problem with our world, today. There are a lot of people out there who do indeed recognize that there is some sort of truth and wisdom to be found all around them that they've observed, but they miss the big picture in that they misunderstand the real truth of who G is and what he's all about. Yes, they've correctly come to realize that there is some sort of spiritual reality in life —something beyond the physical world in which we live—but they still have discovered what exactly that truth is: they still haven't found what they're looking for. But the Good News Bible encourages us along those lines, in Deuteronomy 4:29: "There, you will look for the Lord your G, and if you search for him with all your heart, you will find him."

Heck, there are even times in life where people who aren't necessarily seeking and searching for G come to know him personally for themselves anyway, as the Bible indicates in Isaiah 65:1 and Romans 10:20: "I revealed myself to those who did not ask for me; I was found by those who did not seek me."

But for those who have looked and searched for G and who have come to have a measure of truth in their minds and hearts, these folks need to understand that some truth, a little of the truth, is not enough. Chuck Swindoll said that he once walked into a church where in it were huge pictures, portraits of people, great people all around the inside of the church's circumference. There were pictures of Mahatma Gandhi, Abe Lincoln, Socrates, and former president Eisenhower, as well as a portrait of J. Above all these pictures on a massive bronze engraving were the words, "You are all sons of G..." The ellipses mean, "This quote isn't complete, but here's enough of it for you to read." Galatians. 3:26 was the reference from the Bible, from where that quote came. Swindoll later turned to that very passage of Scripture and read it in its complete form: "You are all the sons of G, by faith in JC." They weren't all sons of G unless they had placed their faith in J, excluding on one, Swindoll said to himself. We need the whole truth.

Speaking of Abe Lincoln, he indicated at one point that understood that human wisdom is extremely limited, when he once stated, "I have been driven many times to my knees by the overwhelming conviction that I had nowhere else to go. My wisdom, and that of all about me, seemed insufficient for the day." The problem, though, is that though there are people like Lincoln who recognize the limitedness of their wisdom, there are those who think they have all truth, knowledge, and wisdom in their hearts and minds, even though that may not be the case at all. Think of it this way: Children seem to know all the questions, but teenagers always seem to have all the answers.

So the thing that we need to do, then, if we've been looking for G and not yet found him for ourselves is to still keep at it, not give up and keep searching and seeking until we do indeed find him, and we will. The Bible promises us as much when it states in 1 Chronicles. 28:9 and in 2 Chronicles. 15:2, "If you seek the Lord, He will be found by you." So we're instructed, then, in 1 Chronicles 22:19 to "devote our heart and soul to seeking the Lord our G," and as Isaiah 55:6 puts it, "to seek the Lord while he may be found; to call on him while he is near."

Unfortunately, though, many people don't take that advice. So, the situation for a lot of people today is lots of knowledge but little understanding, lots of means but little meaning, lots of know-how but little know-*why*, and lots of sight but little *in-sight*.

Yes, I know, we humans have come a long way in many respects. There's a lot that we can do now that we couldn't one hundred years ago, but as an article in *Time* magazine once pointed out, "The experts don't know for sure how old or how big the universe is. They don't know what most of it is made of. They don't know in any detail how it began or how it will end." The Bible, however, tells us these things. Yes, a lot of people would like to think that the meaning of life can be found anywhere else than in the record of G's word, but as Flannery O'Conner once said, "The truth does not change according to our ability to stomach it."

Well, if J is the Way, the Truth, and the Life, like he himself claimed to be according to John 14:6, then how can we settle that truth in our minds for ourselves? For those of us here this morning who are seeking and search for ultimate truth and meaning in our lives, how can we find them? I'd like to suggest to you this morning that the thing to do is to go to G in prayer, asking him to give us faith in J. Asking G to help us have faith in him is partly what he's all about, as demonstrated in the Living Bible's version of Mark 9:17–27: "A man in the crowd said to J, 'Teacher, I brought my son to you, because he has an evil spirit in him and cannot talk. Whenever the spirit attacks him, it throws him to the ground, and he foams at the mouth, grits his teeth, and becomes stiff all over. I asked your disciples to drive the spirit out, but they could not.'

"J said to them 'How unbelieving you people are! How long must I stay with you? How long do I have to put up with you? Bring the boy to me.' So, they brought him to J.

"As soon as the spirit saw J, it threw the boy into a fit, so that he fell on the ground and rolled around, foaming at the mouth. 'How long has he been like this?' J asked the father.

"'Ever since he was a child,' he replied. 'Many times, it has tried to kill him by throwing him in the fire and in the water. Have pity on us and help us if you can.'

"'What do you mean "if I can,"' asked J. Everything is possible for the person who has faith.'"

Now, hear carefully what comes next: "The father at once cried out, 'I do have faith, but not enough. Help me to have more!'

"J noticed that the crowd was closing in on them, so he gave a command to the evil spirit. 'Deaf and dumb spirit,' he said, 'I order you to come out of the boy and never go into him again!' The spirit screamed, threw the boy into a bad fit, and came out.

"The boy looked like a corpse, so that everyone said, 'He is dead.'

"But J took the boy by the hand and helped him rise, and the boy stood up."

You know everyone, I personally believe that in most Christian churches around the world every Sunday, there are people who are a lot like the father in this biblical account. They believe in G—to an extent. They know that G is out there, somewhere, but they "just haven't found what they're looking for." It's not that they're trying to "make their own G," trying to find a theology that will naturally fit the sinful way they like to live. They honestly want to know who the true G of the universe really is and what he's all about, but they'll honestly admit to you that they haven't satisfactorily concluded their search yet. And if you're here today, already knowing J as your savior for yourself, you have to know that there are people out there in that situation who are just waiting to run in to someone like you, just so they can say, "You know, I do believe that there is an all-powerful, all-loving G out there somewhere…I just haven't found him yet. I now need you, a professing Christian, to help me find G for myself…"

In other words, there are a lot of people out there, who are a lot like the father in that story who could just as easily walk up to us and proclaim, "I do have faith, but not enough—help me to have more."

Still, one of the problems of someone going on a search for G is the potential danger of them beginning to listen to the words of a false prophet, someone who would lead them further away from J, rather than closer to him. If you happen to be here today, on a search for ultimate truth, just let me give you a friendly piece of advice—be careful who you listen to on regards of this subject. Sometimes what people will tell you about G couldn't be further from the truth. What they say, then, might turn out to be a lot like some statements you hear people in the world make all the time, such as (1) "The check is in the mail," (2) "Of course I'll respect you in the morning," and (3) "I'm from the government, and I'm here to help you."

After a morning church service, a man stopped the evangelist Chuck Swindoll and said, "I've got a question, and it might take a while for you to answer, but here it goes. I want you to tell me 'What is truth?' I've heard you talk and preach. What do you mean when you refer to the truth?"

The man was standing there, holding his Bible, so Swindoll pointed to the book and answered, "Everything within the covers of that book and nothing else." Swindoll later noted that he didn't think he'd ever answer a question like that before.

Swindoll then added, "This man expected a long answer, but to his surprise, and a little to mine, it wasn't very long at all. Scriptural truth is all we need."

Yes, maybe there's someone in here today who has been, for a long time, struggling between believing in Christianity and some other major world religion or popular philosophy. Well, the famed evangelist D. L. Moody was once quoted by Geo Sweeting in the book *Great Quotes/Illustrations* as having said, "The best way to show that a stick is crooked is not to argue about it or spend time denouncing it, but to lay a straight stick next to it."

In other words, I think what Moody was getting at was that if you're presently thinking about devoting your life to following a certain religion or philosophy, take the text of that teaching/mindset, and put it up against what the Bible has to say. Then judge for yourself which is correct. I think that you'll find that the Bible will win out.

But see, there's a real problem, here, and that problem is that many people— when confronted with the truth of the Bible, don't want to accept it, because of what is says and what it will mean to them if they should decide to make it their life's guide. It would require too much sacrifice on their part to follow the teachings of the Bible rather than to follow a much easier set of standards that the world or some other religious faith might hand them. In other words, it's kind of like the old saying, "The truth hurts!" Now, that phrase "the truth hurts" is reminiscent of a fourth-grade teacher who once received a get-well card from her fourth-grade class. She opened it up, and it read, "Dear Mrs. Fisher, your fourth-grade class wishes you a speedy recovery by a vote of 15– 14." Yes, at times for many of us, the truth found in the Bible may hurt a bit. But the thing is, the pay-off, the sacrifice is worth it! J lives, he loves, and there are rewards for us to receive if we place our faith and trust in him, instead of some other false religion.

Yes, it's a wonderful thing to "go on a search for truth and to earnestly seek G" for oneself. But whenever we attempt to do that, we need to be careful that we don't make the mistake of following our own intuition where we should not let us go. Being humans, we have fallible minds and mindsets that can lead us in the wrong direction, even if we're truly trying to do something as noble as to get close to G. There's the story of a man's plane that crashed in the heart of the darkest jungle of Africa. He pried himself from the wreckage and began to work his way through the dense jungle. As he entered a clearing, he found himself face-to-face with what looked like a hunting party of cannibals.

His response was immediate: "I'm a dead man now."

Then he heard a voice saying, "You're not a dead man. There is a spear at your feet. Pick it up and thrust it though the heart of the chief of this tribe."

The man did as the voice instructed him. He looked down at the ground, and indeed, there was a spear. He picked it up and thrust it through the heart of the tribal chief.

Then the voice spoke to him once more: "*Now*, you're a dead man, it said."

In Acts 26, the apostle Paul is witnessing the truth about J to King Agrippa. Now Agrippa was like the type of person we've been talking about, today. He was someone who had some knowledge about spiritual things, but he was no full-blown believer in J—yet. So in Acts 26:25–29, the Bible says, "Paul said to Agrippa, 'I'm not insane, your Majesty. What I'm saying is true and reasonable. King Agrippa, I can speak to you with all boldness, because you know about these things. I'm sure that you have taken notice of every one of them, for this thing has not happened hidden away in a corner. King Agrippa, do you believe the prophets? I know that you do.'

"Agrippa said to Paul, 'In this short time, do you think that you will make me a Christian?'

"'Whether short time or long time,' Paul answered, 'my prayer to G is that you and all the rest of you here who are listening to me today might become what I am, except for these chains.'"

If there's anyone in here who hasn't yet come to make J their Lord and their Savior, if there's anyone in the room this morning who has not yet made J their God and their guide, the highest priority in their life, *now* is the time for them to go on a spiritual journey toward the truth.

How Many Close Shaves Have You Had?
2 Corinthians 11:21-29

It's on the schedule, every Monday evening at Capon Springs (which is the hotel/resort that my extended family operates in Hampshire County of West Virginia) that that evening's main course for dinner is BBQ chicken, which is prepared and served in the pavilion building just off the 1st fairway of the golf course. About nine on Monday nights, then, they hold a hayride for the teenagers who are there at the hotel with their families on vacation, and part of that hayride takes a path that cuts through a portion of the golf course.

One Monday night, back when I was in my teens, we took the usual hayride through the woods and by the GC. On this particular night, it happened to be during the Fourth of July week of that summer, and one of the kids on the hayride had brought along some firecrackers that he had bought for that week. As this guy began to take some firecrackers out of his pocket and proceed to light them and throw them out of the wagon, my first thought was, "Oh my gosh! We're all gonna die!" As sparks from the firecrackers started falling into the hay wagon, I'm thinking to myself, "Great—we just had BBQ chicken for dinner here on the golf course, and now, we're about to have BBQ teenager here on the golf course!"

Now, maybe I'm blowing things out of proportion, and maybe it takes quite a bit for hay to catch on fire, more than just a spark landing on it. But I'm under the impression that dry hay plus a fire source plus a dozen or so live bodies equals disaster, almost certainly. I consider it only by the grace and providence of G that we did not die on that night. That fact that we got out of the wagon without a scratch after the ride was over that evening is what I like to call a close shave.

The apostle Paul talked about some of the close shaves that he, himself, had experienced, in 2 Corinthians 11:21–28: "What anyone else dares to boast about, I also dare to boast about. Are they Hebrews? So am I. Are they Israelites? So am I. Are they Abraham's descendants? So am

I. Are they servants of Christ? I am more. I have worked much harder, been in prison more frequently, been flogged more severely, and been exposed to death again and again. 5 times I received from the Jews the 40 lashes—1. 3 times I was beaten with rods, once I was stoned, 3 times I was shipwrecked, I spent a night and a day in the open sea, I have been constantly on the move. I have been in danger from rivers, in danger from bandits, in danger from my own countrymen, in danger from Gentiles; in danger in the city, in danger in the country, in danger at sea; and in danger from false brothers. I have labored and toiled and have often gone without sleep; I have known hunger and thirst, and have often gone without food; I have been cold and naked. Besides everything else, I face the daily pressure of my concern for all the churches."

Yes, it sounds like the apostle Paul had a few close shaves of his own, doesn't it? how about you? How many close shaves have you had throughout your life? Obviously, I'm not talking about one of these (stroke chin and side of face with hand). You know the kind of thing that I'm getting at. We've all had at least a few of those instances in our lives where we just narrowly avoided having a serious car accident. Maybe we miraculously survived a massive heart attack that—by all rights—should have killed us. Or maybe G chose to heal us of a terminal disease with which we'd been diagnosed. I think you know the kind of thing I'm talking about. How many times have you—only by the grace of G —cheated death. Some of you, I know, are sitting there thinking, "Oh, yeah... I forgot about that near-fatal car wreck that I had back after I 1st got my license. Man, I was lucky there—I was almost decapitated in that one!"

I want to suggest to you good folks, this morning, to reflect on as many of those instances as you have indeed had in your life, and never forget about them. No, I'm not suggesting that we ought to think about those times all throughout every day of our lives after each one of them occurs. But I do think that when we actually experience episodes like that along the course of our lifetimes, they ought to change us—they ought to instill in us the realization that from that point on, we are living on borrowed time. I believe learning lessons from our experiences as we go along in life, taking what we can to learn from present circumstances so that we can be better prepared to face—and deal with—the future. But the problem is, many people have those types of experiences that Paul faced (physical abuse at the hands of others, being exposed to the elements without protection, being deprived of food and water for a time), and yet shortly thereafter, they forget all about those "close shaves" and continue on living their lives as if nothing unusual had taken place. In other words, many people do indeed have—from time to time—those potentially life-changing experiences in their lives, but they don't let those experiences give them new perspective that they might so desperately need to have.

The first major point that I want to suggest to you this morning is that for all of us who presently enjoy strong, solid mental and physical health (while we still have all of that), we should take advantage of, and use, that mental and physical agility for G's glory. You know, this sermon you're hearing would make a great Thanksgiving sermon—e.g., "be thankful and appreciative to God for all that you have, including your health in every aspect." But the point for today, folks, is much more than simply being thankful to God for all of our health and well-being. The message for today is, while we are thankful and appreciative to G for our strong, healthy bodies and minds, we then do something with those abilities in order to serve him. And we need to do whatever it is we think that G is leading you to do for him now before it's too late.

Along those lines, Romans 12:1 encourages in Today's English Version, "And so, dear brothers, I plead with you to give your bodies to God. Let them be a living sacrifice, holy—the kind of sacrifice that He can accept. When you think of what he had done for you, is this too much to ask?" You know, I hope and pray that none of us in this room today ever gets to the point in the deterioration of our health that we can no longer fend for ourselves, let alone go about on our own, independently working for Christ. But we see that such things do happen to people. Such an example from the Bible is seen in the instance of Eli, from 1 Samuel 3:2. It's here that the Bible states, "One night, Eli, whose eyes were becoming so weak that he could barely see, was lying down in his usual place." None of us likes to think that that might be us, someday. But that could happen someday, and all it would take would be to have one "BBQ teenager on the golf course" experience for that to happen.

From another angle, it might be that, one day, we could find ourselves more mentally incapacitated than physically. That would be another instance where we would no longer be able to serve G as much or as thoroughly as we once did. I have recovered splendidly, thank the Lord, from my fall in which I broke my back. I'm fine, now, physically. But if it had been my head that I had hit— if I had suffered major brain damage, I probably would have been pretty much severely handicapped for the rest of my life. Romans 7:25 states, "I serve God with my mind." So let's commit ourselves to doing just that instead of putting such an activity off for a more convenient time. That's because you just never know when you might have one of those experiences that eventually makes the fulfillment of such plans next to impossible.

Next, I think it's important for us to realize that while each of us still enjoys the gifts of human life and health, we need to value/treasure our family relationships. And once again, we need to value and treasure our loved ones before it gets too late before something "life-ending" occurs either to them or ourselves. Scripture teaches us that we are to definitely love, honor, respect, treasure, and value each other within the family structure. You're familiar with the assorted verses. Ephesians 5:25, 28, and 33 and 6:1–4 have these things to say on the subject: "Husbands, love your wives, just as Christ loved the church and gave himself up for her… In this same way, husbands ought to love their wives as their bodies. He who loves his wife loves himself… However, each one of you also must love his wife as he loves himself, and the wife must respect her husband. Children obey your parents in the Lord, for this is right. 'Honor your father and mother' which is the 1st commandment with a promise— 'that it may go well with you and that you may enjoy long life on earth.' Fathers, do not exasperate you children; instead, bring them up in the training and instruction of the Lord."

You see, the point of that passage is that every relationship in the family— spouse to spouse, parent to child, child to parent—was covered, and they are all to love and honor each other and treat each other with respect.

So before you have another one of those "close shaves" that's just a little bit too close, begin to get close to your family, if you haven't already done so, before it's too late. If you're old enough to remember the 1970, you'll probably remember the TV show *The Love Boat*. It centered on a cruise ship, and every week, new couples (married or dating) would board this ship to go on a cruise together. But in each case at the beginning of the show, there was a problem in each couple's relationship. One storyline that they used over and over again on the show was the scenario where the big-time successful business man was going on a cruise with his neglected wife/girlfriend. At the beginning of these episodes, it was obvious that the fellow was spending too much time at the office, and that the lady was being very much ignored. But as the show progressed in each of these cases, the man in the couple somehow always woke up to how much of a jerk he'd been, they fall madly in love with each other all over again, and exit the cruise at the end of the show to live happily ever after. It was a really corny show, but that often-repeated story line made an important point. while you still have time, make time to spend time with your estranged loved one, because one day soon, it might be too late.

One evening a few weeks ago, Candace asked me at dinner if, after dinner, the two of us could go outside and I pitch the softball to her to practice hitting. I agreed, so we went to do just that after we finished eating. Now, I warned Candace when we got outside what a lousy pitcher I was, but I don't think she believed me until we actually got started. After my first couple of pitches, she looked at me and said, "Dad, you can't pitch. you just cannot pitch." I told her that I had warned her just a moment before, but that I'd try to do better. Well, after a few more pitches, she looked at me and stated, "Dad, you are definitely a bad pitcher. You are so bad."

"Sorry, Candace," I said, "I'm trying to work on it. Just be patient."

Unfortunately, I digressed even further, because shortly after that, her comment was, "Dad, you stink at pitching. Boy, do you stink at pitching." (Each time, of course, she was good-natured about it.)

Now, you know that I could have chosen to do anything else at that time of day. I could have decided to go make some visits. I could have come over to my church office and worked on a sermon. I could have decided to park myself on the couch and read the day's paper. But playing softball with my daughter was something that I didn't want to miss—no matter how frustrating it might have become for either of us. That's a memory that I will always treasure—a memory that either of us might not ever have had to keep if I had decided "I have something better to do," and then one or the other of us had had "one close shave too many," if you know what I mean.

Finally, besides appreciating our mental and physical health along with their accompanying abilities and our family/loved ones, let's make sure that we're careful to always do God's will for us through each and every step of our lives, each and every day, each and every moment of the day. The proper and careful usage of our time is stressed in Proverbs 10:5, which effectively points out, "He who gathers crops in summer is a wise son, but he who sleeps during harvest is a disgraceful son." Face it, there are times in the life of each Christian where it is the opportune time to do something in J's name. But to not even be paying attention to the "time of our life," in effect allowing those times to slip by us, brings us disgrace, as far as G is concerned.

Now, many people will try to excuse themselves from doing what they know deep, down inside G is trying to get them to do for him by saying that they are not nor ever will be fully equipped and prepared to do this particular work. "I feel that G is calling me to go into the mission field," they begin to say, "but I'm not the person for the job." Well, figure it out, folks. G—having made us who we are—is not going to direct us to go in a direction he's not equipped us to undertake. After all, as 2 Corinthians. 8:10–12 points out, "And here is my advice to you: Last year, you were the 1st, not only to act, but also to have the desire to do so. Now finish the work, so that your eager willingness to do it may be matched by your completion of it, according to your means. For if the willingness is there, the gift is acceptable based on what one has, not on what he does not have." It would seem very fitting, then, that we begin to close today's message from the New Testament letter of James 4:17, which says, "Anyone, then, who knows the good that he ought to do, and doesn't do it, sins."

Maybe there's someone here, today, who knows that G has been prompting them to do a particular task for him. Please don't put off doing it. Before you have one close shave too many, before you wind up like a "teenage BBQ on the golf course," won't you start taking G's will seriously and start doing it today?

I Used to Be Judge and Jury
Matthew 7:1-5; Luke 6:41-42; Romans 14:10

A twenty-five-year-old pastor had been at his first church as a pastor for only a short time, when he noticed that one of his church members, an elderly lady, had missed attending services several Sundays in a row. So he decided to go visit her and find out what the problem was. Well, after she greeted him at the door and the two of them engaged in some small talk, he got around to asking her if there was a particular problem that was causing her to not come to church on Sundays. In a very straight forward manner, then, she answered him firmly, "Young man, you aren't old enough to have sinned enough to have repented enough to be able to preach about it."

You see, this elderly lady was passing spiritual judgment on her pastor, saying that he wasn't too sinful to be able to preach about sin and judgment. Quite the opposite—she was saying that he was not sinful enough to have the personal experience to know what he was talking about whenever he decided to preach regarding sin and judgment.

Don't we wish that this was a problem in our churches, that people would think so highly of each other spiritually that they would never think of passing judgment on each other, accusing each other of various sins and misdeeds. But unfortunately, that is exactly the problem that so many people have—the habit of looking at the sins and vices in other people's lives and then acting as G's "agent of judgment and justice," even though they themselves are *far* from spiritual perfection. What makes people think, feel, and believe that they have a God-given right to pass judgment on others around them?

Well, that is exactly one of the spiritual issues that J dealt with in the Sermon on the Mount, as recorded specifically in Matthew 7:1–5. The Phillips Modern English Translation of the Bible records J as saying here, "Don't criticize people, and you will not be criticized. For you will be judged by the way you criticize others, and the measure you give will be the measure you receive. Why do you look at the speck of sawdust in your brother's eye, and fail to notice the plank in your own eye? How can you say to your brother, 'Let me get the speck out of your eye,' when there is a plank in your own eye? You hypocrite! Take the plank out of your own eye, first, and then you can see clearly enough to remove the speck of dust from your brother's eye."

But it's because of the fact that we, ourselves, have our own sins, faults and spiritual weaknesses that, like our sinful neighbor, we, too, will be judged by G someday. G's judgment won't just fall on the person next to us who we might be aware of as participating in sinful behavior. We, too, will fall far enough to come into judgment by G, if we're not careful, as Romans 14:10, when it's there that the Living Bible admonishes, "You have not right to criticize your brother or to look down on him. Remember, each of us will personally stand before the judgment seat of G."

Now, if you were with us last week, you know we spent time look at the conversion of Johnny Lee Clary, a former Grand Dragon of the Ku Klux Clan, who came under conviction of G and changed his views from being an outright racist to someone who actually preached against the ugly mindset. Well, I wish that I could have found the example of someone else who had, at one point in their lives, been in the practice of personally passing judgment on other people around them, but then who had a similar instance of conviction and conversion, and thus came to be much less self-righteous in dealing with people who differed from them spiritually. Well, it's sad to say, but I wasn't able to come across any such examples. But what I did discover was the example of someone who used to carry on a personal war against people who participated in a couple of sinful practices, and in doing so, this person went to such extremes that he's presently serving time in prison for having committed numerous crimes against such people. Maybe you'll recognize his name, Eric Rudolph.

For a long time, Mr. Rudolph has held strong anti-government views. This former itinerate carpenter from Murphy, North Carolina, ultimately responsible for a total of four bombings that killed two people and injured a total of 150 between 1996 and 1998, was not the kind of person you might expect, having a long criminal rap sheet. Nor was he ever a member of a radical group of militiamen or of a specific hate group. No, he pretty much just kind of a regular guy. But as we'll see as the message unfolds, this morning, Eric had a real problem in that the people he targeted in his hatred for his sins in vices became the victims of violence from him himself. In 1981, when he was thirteen years old, Eric father died of cancer. His mother, then, moved with all of her children near a man named Tom Brham, who had a hatred for the federal government and who also had been convicted of federal weapons charges. Patty, shortly after making this residential move, began to get herself and the kids involved in a local branch of what's called the Church of Israel, which teaches and promotes racial segregation and leeriness of big government. But the Church of Israel also railed against the practices of abortion and homosexuality, tenants of the Catholic faith that Patty had grown up with and held to. This branch of the church allowed their family to stay—rent-free—in a church-owned trailer, and the members of the church saw to it that they had plenty to eat. Eric, however, struck the church members as being a loner and someone who was very hard to get to know.

You see, that's a large part of the problem when Christian judge each other or other people outside the church. Many times, as ironic as it might sound, those very people have, precisely, the same kind of evil that fills their own hearts and minds (thus leading them to commit the same kind of sins) as the people who become targets of their self-righteous judgments. As the Living Bible almost comically puts the verse found in Romans 2:1, "'Well,' you may be saying, 'what terrible people you have been talking about!' but wait a minute! You are just as bad. When you say they are wicked and should be punished, you are talking about yourselves, for you do these very same things."

Well, Eric and his family didn't hang around the Church of Israel for long, since his mother decided for them to leave the church just after the pastor delivered a "God is wrathful" type of sermon. Eric then soon thereafter acquires his GED, then joins the army but is eventually discharged from the army for unclear reasons. Now, here's where the clues about Eric's future begin to fall into place. Sometime after he was discharged from the military, he "ran into" his sister's ex-husband, Joel, and this chance encounter took place just a few short weeks before the first bombing that Eric carried out. Joel discussed about, and disagreed with, Eric's violent antigovernment views, and later on with a conversation with

Eric's sister, Joel said that he didn't think he could let himself carry on any more conversations with Eric, because everything with him was "hate, hate, hate."

All right, so Eric Rudolph had formed a humongous bone to pick with the government. Kiddingly, I can identify. But it sounds to me like Rudolph was a little more than just upset with the US government—he wanted to do it harm. What Christians need to remind themselves then, whenever they start to have similar feelings and thoughts, is to consider the Scripture found in James 4:11– 12, as given in the Philips Modern English translation: "Never pull each other to pieces, my brothers. If you criticize your brother and judge him, you have become, in fact, a critic and judge of the Law. Yet, if you start to criticize Law instead of obeying it, you are setting yourself up as a judge. There is only one judge, the One Who gave the Law, to whom belongs absolute power of life and death. How can you then be your neighbor's judge?"

So in order to understand the mindset of such a person and thus help prevent ourselves and/or someone else we know from getting to that same point, I think we have to ask the question, "How did Eric Rudolph get from being a middle-class kid to a serial bomber of abortion clinics and gay nightclubs? What was he trying to say?"

"He never said much of anything," recalled the family's pastor in Missouri.

"He was sort of a loner…really hard to get to know. He called himself a 'warrior' against abortion and the government that permits it."

Eventually, as you might already know, if you're familiar with his story, he was indeed arrested. It was after his arrest then, that Rudolph explained that stopping abortion was his main motive for the bombings, and that any agent of the government that allows the practice was an enemy that deserved death. Rebutting claims that his antigovernment views were shaped by racism, family members, or cult-like churches, Rudolph referred to himself as a "Catholic at war over abortion."

All right. To be honest, this is the part of Rudolph's life that I just don't get. You say you're against abortion, because you believe that it's tantamount to murder, because you believe that it's the immoral taking of an innocent human life. Okay, fine. So you say you want to help put an end to that practice. Okay, fine. But even though you're opposed to the taking of innocent human life, you're going to bomb the buildings in which such things happen, and in doing so, end up taking the lives of the people therein. I don't get it. It's like the people who rant and rave about a certain topic, even though they really don't know what in the world they're talking about. It's kind of like when the pastor of a rural church in the Ozarks suggested to the congregation that they purchase a chandelier. It was put to a vote, and all the church members voted against the idea.

"Why do you guys oppose buying a chandelier for the church?" the pastor questioned.

"Well," one of the church members began, "first, we can't spell it, so how are we gonna order it? Second, even if we did get it, no one could play it, and third, what we really need in this church is more light."

Oh boy. King David must have been having one of those times in his walk through life where he "just didn't get it," when he committed adultery with Bathsheba, then arranged to have her husband, Uriah, killed in battle, just so he could have her all to himself. When Nathan confronted David about this, by first giving David an imagined scenario about a rich man who unfairly took and killed a poor man's one and only lamb for his own use, 2 Samuel 12:5 and 7 say that David burned with anger against that man and said to Nathan, "As surely as the Lord lives, the man who did this deserves to die!" Then, Nathan said to David, "You are that man!" As the Living Bible puts it in James 5:9, "Don't grumble about each other, brothers. Are you yourselves above criticism? For see! The great Judge is coming. He is almost here."

Eric Rudolph eventually got to testify in order to defend himself in court. "Because I believe abortion is murder, I also believe that force is justified in attempt to stop it." Emily Lyons, who lost an eye and almost her life, in the Birmingham Alabama bombing attack, wept as she watched in court. "He just sounded so proud of it—that's what really hurt," she later stated. While railing against homosexuality, Rudolph also blasted what he called the government's acceptance of the biblically condemned behavior. So he said that the two bombs planted at a certain gay nightclub actually targeted law-enforcement officials, and not the club's patrons. He denied allegiance to any racist, anti- Semitic, anti-gay church-type movements, stating, "I was born a Catholic, and with forgiveness, I hope to die one."

Get that? He hopes to die a Catholic, with forgiveness. Now, far be it for me to pass judgment on Eric Rudolph. But from my understanding of what it means to be a true Christian, he really needs to come to have a proper understanding of the faith, recognizing that Christianity's second greatest commandment is to love our neighbor as ourselves, with no exclusions, exceptions, or omissions.

If you ask me, the Scripture makes it pretty plain and clear just exactly who our judge in this life is, and it's not Eric Rudolph. As Isaiah 33:22 plainly states, "For the Lord is our judge, the Lord is our Lawgiver." So if it is indeed God who is our judge, then we can, should, and need to stop attempting to pass judgment on one another. Unless there's someone walking the earth today who wants to go around proclaiming that they, themselves, are the second coming of Christ—and as you know, there have been many people who've done such a thing throughout the centuries, unfortunately—then none of us has the right to look at anyone else and personally condemn them. This is why Romans 14:13 encourages us to "stop passing judgment on one another."

Yes, on the day we're judged, it will be Jesus who sums up the value of how we spent our life on earth, and no one else. The Bible reiterates that fact in 1 Peter 4:5, when it's there the Bible explains, "But those people will have to give account to him who is ready to judge the living and the dead."

And yes, everybody sins and is thus disqualified on that account from being able to judge others—even us ministers. For example, there's a story from the life of Rev. Hector Hanks, a chaplain at Mills Hospital. Rev. Hanks was on his way home, one evening, when, as he neared his house, he saw a group of little boys sitting in a circle with a dog in the middle. He asked them what they were doing with the dog. Little Joey Bateson spoke up then and said, "We ain't doing nuthin' to the dog...we're just tellin' lies, and the one who tells the biggest lie gets to keep the dog."

The chaplain told them, "I'm shocked, fellas. When I was a little boy, I never would have thought about telling a lie."

Immediately, Joey looked at his friends and ordered, "Give him the dog, fellas."

I Used to Be Prejudiced
Luke 10:30-37; Acts 10:34

A woman testified to the transformation in her life that had taken place due to her having accepted Christ as her Savior. She declared to a friend, "I'm SO glad I've become a Christian. I have an uncle I used to hate so much that I vowed that I'd not go to his funeral. But now, why, I'd be happy to go to it anytime!"

Now, I don't know what the issue was that caused this lady to hate her uncle so much, but regardless, as a Christian, she should have realized that there's no good excuse for hating anybody. Everyone in here is probably familiar with the J's parable of the Good Samaritan from Luke 10: 25–37—the story of a man who had been attacked and left for dead by robbers. As he lay there by the side of the road, injured, he was dismissed for the opportunity to receive help from both a priest and a Levite. It's a Samaritan, then, who comes along, sees the man, and goes to great lengths to do what he can to help.

This is how the Living Bible's version of Luke 10:34–35 puts it: "Kneeling beside him, the Samaritan soothed his wounds with medicine and bandaged them. Then, he put the man on his donkey and walked along beside him till they came to an inn, where he nursed him through the night. The next day, he handed the innkeeper two $20 bills and told him to take care of the man. 'If his bill runs higher than that,' he said, 'I'll pay the difference next time I'm here.'"

Now, besides the point that followers of Christ are to express the love of Christ, in part, by helping others who are in need, there's the lesson in the realm of race relations here. After all, the parable isn't called "The Good Jew." You see, tensions between two races of people had never been higher than those between Jews and Samaritans. J told Jews that Samaritans who help in self-giving love make the best neighbors. Self-giving love, then, helps to overcome racial barriers. And it would make sense, then, that J would make a point like this, since Acts 10:34 states in the Good News

Bible, "Peter began to speak: 'I now realize that it is true that G treats all men on the same basis. Whoever fears him and does what is right is acceptable to him, no matter what race he belongs to.'"

Well, fortunately, there are not only Christians who realize this truth, but there are also those instances where someone who used to be prejudiced toward people of other races have come to realize, through the truth of the gospel, that they were wrong in feeling and thinking that way. I'd like to begin to share with you the story of a Mr. Johnny Lee Clary as an example. We begin with the time that Mr. Clary was waiting at a local radio station for his verbal opponent, Rev. Wade Watts, a civil rights activist. Clary expected the reverend to hate whites as much as Clary hated black people. But then Watts stunned Clary by walking into the broadcast booth, smiling and telling the then Grand Dragon of the KKK that he loved him.

Clary couldn't believe this—he had set a fire that damaged Watts's church— a crime for which he was never prosecuted. Still, he couldn't help but shake the pastor's extended hand, despite the KKK rule against touching African Americans. That night, Clary first began to doubt his racist convictions. In another decade, he left the Klan as Imperial Wizard, and a couple of years after that, he began is itinerate ministry against racism. He now draws crowds around the world who come to hear his story of failure and redemption, of overcoming racism in one of hits ugliest forms.

Clary's path to the KKK began when he was raised in a house filled with hatred in Del City, Oklahoma, where everyone was one color, his color. His father, an alcoholic, and his uncle would tell stories filled with racial slurs. Then, at age eleven, Clary said he watched his father kill himself. "He took a .45 caliber pistol and blew his brains out right in front of me," Clary said. After that, Clary's mother sent him to live with his sister in LA. He said his sister's boyfriend beat him. "The more he hit me, the more I hated," Clary stated. The seed of hatred was planted.

Now, as we've just seen, hatred toward people of other races often is instilled in a person through the "training to hate" they receive from other people. But it also may come from just simply looking at and judging someone and deciding to then hate them based on what we see on the outside. It's kind of like when the judge glared down from his bench at a prospective juror, asking, "And just why is it that you don't want to serve on this jury?"

The man replied, "Well, Your Honor, I'm biased. One look at that man, over there, convinced me he is guilty."

The judge then scowled and replied, "That man over there isn't the defendant...he's the district attorney."

In connection, then, with the problems arising from judging people from what we see on the outside, Peter Marshall, former chaplain of the US Senate, once wrote the following poem: "We have the nicest garbage man / He empties out our garbage can / He's just as nice as he can be / He always stops and talks to me / My mother doesn't like his smell / But my mother doesn't know him well."

The Good News Bible puts it in James 2:1, "My brothers, as believers in our Lord Jesus Christ, you must never treat people in different ways, according to their outward appearance."

So it was after Johnny Lee Clary had begun to be mistreated by his aunt's boyfriend that, one day, he spotted David Duke on TV, and Duke's message appealed to Clary. The seed of hatred started to grow. Duke reminded Clary of his dad, and he commanded respect. Clary wanted a part of that respect, so he reached out to the KKK, and it welcomed him. So he joined the Klan youth corps, becoming an adult member at seventeen and quickly rising through the ranks. Returning to Oklahoma, he became the Grand Dragon there and later the Imperial Wizard, a rank similar to a national spokesman.

Well, time passed, and for more than a decade, Rev. Wade Watts led the Oklahoma branch of the NAACP. In 1979, Watts and Clary met on that national radio program. They had a debate that even Clary admits Watts won. No matter how much bile Clary threw at Watts, the preacher responded with love. When Watts tried to shake Clary's hand, Clary recoiled, but then Watts shook it anyway. "Don't worry, Johnny," Watts encouraged Clary. "It don't come off." Clary said Watts then introduced to him his adapted daughter, a half-white, half-black girl named Tia. Watts asked how Clary could hate a child, and Clary just turned away.

Now, we've been talking about how people shouldn't play favorites. Well, the Bible makes it plain and clear that God certainly doesn't do this either, as 2 Chronicles 19:7 states, "Now let the fear of the Lord be on you.

Judge carefully, for with the Lord our G, there is no injustice or partiality or bribery." Likewise, Deuteronomy 10:17 points out that "the Lord your G is God of gods and Lord of lords, the great G, might and awesome, who shows no partiality and accepts no bribes." In addition, Romans 2:11 just plainly and simply states, "For G does not show favoritism."

You know, it's interesting. While we Christians should plainly see that racism and prejudiced are absolutely out of step with the teaching of Scripture and very wrong, for someone like the way Johnny Lee Clary used to be, the way they see things is the way it is, and that's that. But what people need to do in such cases is recognize these biases for what they are. There was once a driver of a tour bus in Nashville, Tennessee. The driver was one day pointing out the sights of the Civil War Battle of Nashville, saying, "Right over there, a small group of Confederate soldiers held off a whole Yankee brigade."

A little farther along, he stated, "Over here, a young Confederate boy fought off a Yankee platoon, all by himself."

This kind of thing went on and on until a member of the tour group questioned, "Didn't the *Yankees* win anything in the battle of Nashville?"

The bus driver then replied, "Not as long as I'm driving this bus, they didn't."

Well, as strongly as Clary once believed in the cause of the KKK, once he had met with Watts, he began to question his devotion to the Klan. "When I heard the Klan and skinheads say they wanted to kill all African Americans, I used to think of Rev. Watts, and think, 'Do you really want to see this man hurt?'"

Clary said, "He was such a good man that I started doubting all these things I was supposed to teach." The change in him didn't come all of a sudden, but one day, Clary said, he found himself at a loss. His friends were routinely being hauled down to the police station for questioning, and so was he. He also found out that his girlfriend was an FBI informant.

"Deep down inside, I didn't like myself," he explained. Clary said he was drinking and suicidal. He was going to follow in his father's footsteps. He went to his fellow Klansmen, but he said they turned on him. "They were like a bunch of rattlesnakes," he said.

At a loss, Clary started reading the Bible. After Clary came to Christ, he went looking for Rev. Watts.

In 1989, Clary called the Klan's Grand Council and told them he was quitting. A few years later, he said he felt God calling him to preach. He soon called Watts and asked for forgiveness. The pastor, in turn, asked *him* to deliver a sermon to his all-black church, the one that Clary had set on fire.

You know, as terrible as the outward expressions of prejudice and racism can be, when they are exhibited, such displays have a way of creating good out of something bad by actually bringing people together. A little girl went on to her first day of first grade in a newly integrated school at the height of the segregation storm. An anxious mother met her daughter at the door after the girl got off the bus at the end of the day.

"How did everything go, honey?"

"Oh, Mom! You know what? A little black girl sat next to me!"

In fear and trepidation, the mother expected trauma but tried to ask calmly, "So what happened?"

"We were both so scared, we held hands all day!"

Well, I have to say that something good came out of J. L. Clary's visit to Watt's church. When Clary got to the church, he was nervous to think about the last time he had been there. Reporters gathered for his first public appearance since leaving the KKK. Watts had warned his church members the week before that the former KKK leader was coming. Many stayed home. The worshippers in the worn wooden pews crossed their arms and stared at Clary with lowered brows. He got no hallelujahs or amens, when he told the congregation about his reformation. Finally, he asked if anyone there wanted to know J as their Savior, and a teenage girl started crying and ran to the pulpit to give him a hug. The ice had been broken. It wasn't long after that service took place that Watts and Clary become good friends, traveling the country together, preaching about G and against racism. Before Watts died in 1998, Clary promised his former enemy that he would carry on his ministry. Clary then ended up being a pallbearer at Watts' funeral.

You see, regardless of what the Klan, neo-Nazis and others may teach, believe and preach, G loves us all, and he loves us all equally. He loves no one race or segment of society any more or any less than any of the others. And besides, no matter what segment of human race our ancestors might have come from, none of them can claim to be "tighter with G more so than others," since we're all sinners and fall short of G's glory.

Galatians 2:6, 1 Samuel 16:7, and Colossians 3:25 together explain, "As for those who seemed to be important—whatever they were makes no difference to me, God does not judge by external appearance—those men added nothing to my message...The Lord doesn't look at the things man looks at. Man looks at the outward appearance, but the lord looks at the heart...anyone who does wrong will be repaid in kind, and G does not favor one person more than another." Mark 12:13 finally records that some Pharisees came to J and recognized that J paid no attention to any one's particular status in life, but instead taught the truth about G's will for man.

In 1963, George C. Wallace, governor of Alabama, literally stood in the door of the University of Alabama, preventing Vivian Malone Jones, a young African American woman, for enrolling as a student, there. Thirty-five years later, Wallace awarded Jones the first Lurleen B. Wallace Award of Courage. The award, named in honor of Wallace's wife, recognizes women who have made outstanding contributions to the state of Alabama. Wallace publicly apologized to Jones for the 1963 controversy; Jones, in turn, forgave Wallace. Robert F. Kennedy Jr., on hand for the event, said, "This event really is a moment of reconciliation and redemption."

Very fortunately, there *are* those people, like Johnny Lee Clary now who do what they can to take a positive attitude toward those who are different from themselves in various ways and, therefore, do their best to get along with everyone. Making a sharp right turn off the main road onto a narrow two-lane road, a Caucasian man skidded on the gravel and wound up just short of hitting a parked car. He immediately expected a testy reaction from the car's occupants—a group of African American laborers, just getting ready to leave a nearby construction job site. But the driver's comment to the man was goodhumored: "Man, we do want to integrate, but not quite that fast!"

I Used to Hate the Rich or the Poor
Job 31:13-15; Proverbs 22:2

A pastor was talking to the eight-year-old's Sunday School class about things money can't buy. "It can't buy laughter," he told them. "That comes from deep, down inside of our soul. And it can't buy love, certainly, either." Summing up his point, he questioned, "What would you do if I offered you a thousand dollars not to love your mother and father?" A couple of seconds of silence followed while the kids mulled over potential responses. Then from within the group, one of the boys asked, "How much would you give me not to love my big sister?"

Those of you who've been with us long enough know that I like to take the month of February, the Valentine's month, to focus on the Christian characteristic of *love* in each Sunday's message. So today, I'd like to focus on the fact that J's command to us to love each other includes loving those other people who might be quite a bit richer or poorer than ourselves. You might not think that it would be so hard, especially for a Christian, to commit themselves to love, honor, and respect someone who is considerably more or less wealthy than themselves, but if we were all honest with ourselves, we'd probably have to say that it can be a lot harder than we'd like to admit. This is where "class struggles" throughout the centuries come in to play.

Well, as you might imagine, the Bible has numerous places in which the issues of the contrast between the rich and the poor are dealt with, and two of those passages come from Job 31:13–15 and Proverbs 22:2. It's in these two passages that together explain that God is the one who is responsible for having brought both the rich and the poor into existence, when the Bible plainly states, "If I have denied justice to my menservants and maidservants when they had a grievance against me, what will I do when G confronts me? What will I answer when called to account? Did not he who made me in the womb also make them? Did not the same one form both of us within our mother's wombs?...The rich and the poor have this in common—The Lord is the Maker of them all."

In addition, Proverbs 29:13 stresses the fact that once they do enter this life that G gave them, G blesses them both throughout their time on earth, as when there, the Bible points out, "The poor man and his oppressor have this in common: The Lord gives sight to the eyes of both."

Now, I original idea for this message, this morning, was to find at least one example of someone who used to really "have it out" for wealthy people, and someone else who used to truly detest poorer folks, but who do so no longer and share with you their testimony of how they came to have a change of heart toward people whose economic health and well-being differed greatly from their own. Unfortunately, I wasn't able to find any true stories from people along those lines. What I did find, however, was a fascinating exchange on an Internet message board between several individuals—all of whom, I'm assuming, were in their young adulthood at the time these statements were posted. I'd like to share with you, now, portions of this running conversation, piece by piece throughout the rest of the message, to help us understand what people's perceptions—both good and bad—of the rich and the poor often are. By the way, the people who made these postings used their online nicknames, not surprisingly.

To begin with, an unnamed person posed the question, "Why do poor people and rich people often hate each other?" Excellent question. The first response, then, comes from a participant calling himself "Filipino," and he says, "Most poor people gripe and moan about rich people and do nothing with their lives to get a ton of money. So why are they complaining so much? Jealousy?"

Someone with a French-sounding name then responded, "Sounds like your parents are rich. Hopefully, you're not as clueless as you sound."

"Charlie" then answered, "Well, the hardworking people hate the rich people because some rich people don't deserve to be where they are."

"College Boy '89" chimes in, "Most people don't complain, and if they do, it's human nature. Why would you ask such an oblivious question?"

"Fed-up" then entered the conversation. "I would say it's the other way around. The rich don't have any time for the poor and would rather blow them off and ignore them than to have anything to do with them."

"Bonny," then, winds up this portion of the exchange by flatly stating, "You lack character. It's not about hating anyone—it's about letting everyone have the chance to live their American Dream. When 80% of the wealth is held by 20% of the population, you might 'hate' them too. The rich corporations are firing the working-class Americans and sending work overseas to be done for pennies to make their fat pockets even fatter. Rich people, one average, are stingy, obnoxious, and disassociated from the real world and callous. Grow up!"

Okay. So much for friendly, polite conversation. Well, as we can see from this exchange, the Bible is absolutely correct in pointing out that envy and jealousy are powerful forces in people's lives, as much of it as coming from the rich to the poor as it often goes from the poor to the rich. That's why the Bible points out in Proverbs 27:4, "Anger is cruel, and fury is overwhelming, but who can stand before jealousy?"

Now, of course, an important part of today's message is that someone can manage to be envious and jealous of somebody else, with the elements of money and material possessions not even being a part of the scenario. We can be envious and jealous of other people due to the talents and abilities or other resources they have and that are at their disposal, or we can simply feel that way toward them due to all the attention and acclaim they receive from other people, when we ourselves remain for the most part unnoticed. Such was the case with other various other people envying J, as indicated by Matthew 27:15–18, where the Living Bible explains, "Now the governor's custom was to release one Jewish prisoner each year during the Passover celebration—anyone they wanted. This year, there was a particularly notorious criminal in jail named Barabbas, and as the crowds gathered before Pilate's house that morning, he asked them, 'Which shall I release to you—Barabbas or J your Messiah?' For he knew very well that the Jewish leaders had arrested J out of envy because of his popularity with the people."

But J wasn't the first person mentioned in the Bible who suffered abuse at the hands of someone else who was jealous. In his speech to the Sanhedrin, recorded in Acts 7:9, Stephen mentions the fact that it was because of the fact that Joseph's brothers were jealous of him that they sold him into slavery. And as the apostle Paul was preaching in Antioch, the Bible mentions in Acts 13:44–45, "One the next Sabbath, almost the whole city gathered to hear the word of the Lord. When the Jews saw the crowds, they were filled with jealousy, and talked abusively against what Paul was saying."

You know, when you think about it, it's a pretty ridiculous thing to be envious or jealous of someone. Some would even say it's somewhat childish. Maybe that's why the Bible points out in Job 5:2, "Resentment kills a fool, and envy slays the simple." Heck, I especially don't like to admit this, but even preachers can fall victim to the temptations of envy and jealousy, as indicated by Paul and Timothy to the church in Philippians 1:15, when there, they wrote, "It's true that some preach Christ out of envy and rivalry, but others out of goodwill."

Shakespeare called envy the green sickness. Francis Bacon admitted that envy "has no holidays." Horace declared that "tyrants never invented a greater torment." Barrie said it "is the most corroding of the vices." Sheridan referred to it in his play, "The Critic," when he wrote, "There is not a passion so strongly rooted in the human heart as this." Phillip Bailey, the eloquent English poet of yesteryear, vividly described it as "a coal that comes hissing hot from hell." And when connecting envy with hell, maybe no one has done a better job of portraying envy than Dante. In his play, "Purgatory," the envious sit like blind beggars by a wall. Their eyelids are sewn shut. The symbolism is appropriate, showing the reader that it is one of the blindest of sins—partly because it is unreasonable, partly because the envious person is sewed up in himself and swollen with poisonous thoughts in a dark constricting world of almost unendurable self-imposed anguish.

Well, let me give you another snippet from the message board conversation I found on the internet on this topic. Someone named Matokah wrote, "As a poor student, I guess I get annoyed with rich people who were born that way and do nothing to earn or deserve the money they've got (like Paris Hilton and Nicole Ritchie). Life's not fair, though, so I don't dwell on it too much. Besides," Matokah began to conclude, "if I end up passing the bar, maybe they'll need my legal services in 3 years, and then I can charge them through the nose and become rich, too."

Now, a possible hint as to how we can keep ourselves from getting caught up in the attitudes of envy and jealousy toward others is by making sure we often focus on putting our money where G would have us put it, and do so willingly, rather than begrudgingly. A circus strong man earned his living by displaying amazing feats of physical strength. His show would normally conclude with a demonstration of him squeezing an orange dry! After accomplishing this feat, he would then typically ask if there was anyone in the audience who could manage to extract just one more drop of juice from the already crushed piece of fruit.

One day, a little man in the crowd volunteered. He was so small that his appearance raised a laugh from the crowd. Ignoring their taunts, the man walked up on the stage and took from the strongman the shriveled-up piece of fruit. He firmly compressed his hand around the rind, and to everyone's amazement, a drop of orange juice formed and fell into the glass below. As the cheers subsided, the strongman invited the little guy to tell how he managed to develop such amazing powers. "Nothin' to it," the little fellow began to reply with a grin. "I happen to be the treasurer of the Baptist church here in town." In all seriousness, when we give back to G a portion of what he's given us, we don't have the time or the presence of mine to get caught up in the ugly game of envy and jealousy of others.

Allow me, next, to continue to share with you some of the running internet dialogue I've related to you throughout the message today. To the person who posed the original question of "Why do the rich and the poor hate each other?" a person calling himself Felix D blasted, "You're ignorant. [No subtlety, there, huh?] Poor people are too busy struggling to feed their families. They don't have time to worry about rich people. FYI, rich people get rich by exploiting the poor, so go read a book before you ask another offensive question like this."

Someone referring to themselves as Jess H then comically bragged, "I totally know what you mean. Yeah, I'd say they're jealous. Like, last week, I went to school, and I came out of the limo, and all these poor girls were giving me dirty looks, calling me a 'show-off.' I'm sorry, but, like, my dad won't let me take the bus to school, sooo, I don't blame them."

BBQ then chimed in, "I don't hate rich people. I love Bill Gates."

Windows then said, "Poor people hate rich people, because rich people are snobby, stuck-up, rude and selfish."

Another person participated, saying, "But I believe the more money you have, the more probs you have as well. Even the rich hate on each other—the old money hates the new money."

St. Louis typed in, "I used to be poor—I'm more like middle class, now—but I just hate rich kids, 'cause their parents spoil them and they get what they want whenever they whine—it's sooo immature and annoying."

Queenie then contributed to the conversation: "Your assumption that all the poor people hate the rich isn't true. It's the minority that's the loudest, but that doesn't mean that all of them feel that way. Plus, selfish and ignorant rich people—like Britney Spears, Paris Hilton, and others—are far worse off than true, honest, loving poor people."

From the mouths of babes. Now, I seriously doubt that these people are in their childhood. But still, you can see from their various comments and viewpoints just what kinds of attitudes—good or bad—are out there in the world toward rich and poor people alike.

Ephesians 6:9 pretty well begins to sum it all up, this morning, as Paul is addressing the issue of slavery: "And you slave owners must treat your slaves right, just as I have told them to treat you. Do not threaten them, since you know that he who is both their master and yours is in heaven, and there is no favoritism with him." It might also do us well to remember the message of Ezekiel 35:11, where G stated, "Therefore, I will treat you in accordance with the anger and jealousy you showed in your hatred of them."

To conclude the running internet dialogue, then, someone named Funpurple reminded the poster of the original question, "Remember, you can't take all you money and worldly possessions with you when you die. All these rich people answering with their superior attitudes ought to have something more to substantiate their existence than only their wealth."

It sounds like to me that Fun-purple understood the message of Job 21:23– 6: "One man dies in full vigor, completely secure and at ease, his body wellnourished, his bones rich with marrow. Another man dies in bitterness of soul, never having enjoyed anything good. Side by side, they lie in the dust and worms cover them both."

Old Cyrus Baker was the richest man in town. When he became terminally ill, there was much speculation among the villagers concerning the extent of his wealth. So when he died, one of the town's busybodies made it his business to run to Mr. Baker's lawyer and asked, "How much money did ol' Cyrus leave, anyway?"

The lawyer said, "All of it, my friend."

I Used to Want Revenge
Matthew 5:44; Luke 6:27-31, 23:34

Two little brothers, Harry and James, had just finished supper and were playing until bedtime. Somehow, Harry hit James with a stick, and tears and bitter words followed. Charges and accusations were still being exchanged as their mother prepared them for bed.

She then instructed, "Now, James, before you go to bed, you're going to have to forgive your bother."

James was thoughtful for a minute, and then he replied, "Well, okay, I'll forgive him tonight, but if I don't die before I wake up, he'd better look out in the morning."

Possibly, some of you here, this morning, have heard about the man who was told by his doctor, "Yes, indeed, you do have rabies."

Upon hearing this, the patient immediately pulled out a pad and pencil and began to write something down. Thinking that his patient was beginning to make out his will, the doctor said, "Listen, this doesn't mean that you're going to die. There is a cure for rabies, you know."

"I know that," the man responded. "I'm making out a list of people I want to go around and bite."

Yes, sadly, these two stories demonstrate the mindset that a lot of people have toward people they consider to be their enemies. But what did J say, specifically regarding how we should treat the people we consider to be our foes, our adversaries? Well, the scripture passages taken from J's own words on this topic, together, come from Matthew 5:44, Luke 6:27–31, and Luke 23:34, the second Luke reference being at the point of when J was being crucified. It's in these verses the Bible states, "But what I tell you is this: Love your enemies and pray for your persecutors...As for the man who hits you on one cheek, offer him the other one as well! And if a man is taking away your coat, do not stop him from taking your shirt as well. Give to everyone who asks you, and when a man has taken what belongs to you, don't demand it back. Treat men exactly as you would like them to treat you... 'Father, forgive these people,' J said, 'for they don't know what they're doing.'"

Well, let me continue by giving you an actual contemporary example of someone who took that kind of attitude, just as J instructed us to. Martha Henry prays each day for a particular prisoner close to her heart. She has worked and waited for his freedom ever since she met him thirteen years ago— after he killed her son. Strange as it might seem, friendship has blossomed between a mother and the man who robbed her son of life, a bond they say is built on faith and forgiveness. "If a person has done something wrong and proven he's sorry, he should be given another chance," she said. "He can't undo it. He can't bring him back. Why should another life be wasted?" Mrs. Henry said she always accepted Edward Henderson's explanation that her son's death was an accident.

Parole officials say it is unique to have a member of a victim's family plead for—rather than protest—a prisoner's release from prison. "We've never had anything like this happen before," said Lewis Gregory, parole board chairman.

Chuck Swindoll tells the story of when he once drove his car into a busy shopping center, and there was a small parking space just big enough for the compact car he was driving. He knew it would be a tight squeeze to get his ample frame in and out of the car without bumping the car next to him, but he was willing to try. After, parking spaces are usually pretty scarce. Well, Swindoll's son, who was then pretty little, was with him. The boy slipped out of his side with no problem, but Swindoll accidentally bumped the car on his side just a little bit. It bothered him that he did this, so he wiped off the side of the car just to make sure it was okay, even though there wasn't a visible mark on it.

When Swindoll straightened up after having done this, he noticed that the man sitting inside this other car wasn't smiling. Swindoll smiled and said, "I'm sorry, but there's no damage." The other man still wasn't smiling, so Swindoll closed his car door, and his son and he started to walk on into the store. Something told Swindoll to turn around and look at his car, before they got into the store. He did, just in time to see the fellow from the other car get out, open a door of his car and deliberately hit it up against the side of Swindoll's car.

Swindoll's first reaction was to go over and separate the man's head from his body! But then he thought, "Man, what a scandal *that* would create…Pastor kills man in parking lot." Swindoll then noticed how big the man was and thought, "How much worse to read, 'Man kills pastor in parking lot.'" So needless to say, Swindoll chose not to do anything. His little boy put his hand in his dad's, and Swindoll then thought to himself, "Boy, it would just foul everything up if he saw his daddy out there getting smeared all over the parking." So he didn't do anything. But then, he did do something, Swindoll later recalled. He applied patience, a rare virtue in his life, he says, and he walked away. Swindoll says that he looks back at that instance with fondness, since that day, he actually exhibited within himself being able to walk away from people's natural tendency toward revenge.

Yes, it's not only possible for a Christian to determine not to give in to the want to take revenge, but it's a command to us to refrain from taking revenge in both the Old and New Testaments. For example, the scripture instructs us from both Leviticus 19:18 and Romans 12:14–21, "Don't seek revenge or bear a grudge against one of your people, but love your neighbor as yourself. I am the Lord…Bless those who persecute you, bless and do not curse. Rejoice with those who rejoice; weep with those who weep. Live in harmony with one another. Don't be proud, but be willing to associate with people of low position. Do not be conceited … Do not repay anyone evil for evil. Be careful to do what is right in the eyes of everybody. If it is possible, as far as it depends on you, live at peace with everyone. Do not take revenge, my friends, but leave room for G's wrath, for it is written, 'It is mine to avenge; I will repay,' says the Lord. On the contrary: 'If your enemy is hungry, feed him; if he is thirsty, give him something to drink. In doing this, you will heap burning coals on his head.' Do not be overcome by evil, but overcome evil with good."

But the Bible doesn't just command us to forgive and love our enemies. The Bible also gives us some great examples of people throughout time who have had to face these very kinds of situations we've been talking about this morning, and who have triumphed by gathering up the faith within themselves to do just that—to forgive and love their adversaries. There's the story of Joseph, whose brothers beat him up and sold him into slavery, having done so out of jealousy. But after all the ups and downs

Joseph was to later go through, he was able to forgive them for what they had done, as we see from Genesis 50:19–21, when there the Bible relates, "Joseph said to them, 'Don't be afraid. Am I in the place of G? You intended to harm me, but G intended it for good to accomplish what is now being done, the saving of many lives. So then, don't be afraid. I will provide for you and your children.' And he reassured them and spoke kindly to them."

And yes, David could have decided to strike back at Saul for all the pain and grief Saul had dished out to him, but David expressed the attitude (when he penned what he wrote in Psalm 94:1–2) of waiting and letting God take vengeance, instead of taking that role for himself, when there the Bible says, "O Lord, the G who avenges, O God who avenges, shine forth. Rise up, O Judge of the earth; pay back to the proud what they deserve."

And finally, in this set of biblical examples, Stephen is seen in Acts 7:54–60 having the same mindset in regards to those who are about to take his life. There, the Bible tells this story: "When they heard this, they were furious and gnashed their teeth at him. But Stephen, full of the HS, looked up to heaven and saw the glory of G, and J standing at the right hand of G. 'Look,' he said, 'I see heaven open and the Son of Man standing at the right hand of G.' At this, they covered their ears and, yelling at the top of their voices, they all rushed at him, dragged him out of the city and began to stone him. Meanwhile, the witnesses laid their clothes at the feet of a young man named Saul.

"While they were stoning him, Stephen prayed, 'Lord J, receive my spirit.' Then he fell on his knees and cried out, 'Lord, do not hold this sin against them.' When he had said this, he died."

Well, for just a few minutes, let's look back at the story we began earlier with Martha Henry, whose son was murdered. Mrs. Henry says that she isn't discouraged and won't rest until Edward Henderson, her son's killer, is freed from prison. She's hoping that this will take place soon. "I've been praying and praying that it will be all over," she said.

Their friendship began in July 1973. Henderson said that he had been harassed regularly by the brother of a woman he was dating. The night of the shooting, he said, the man threatened him and used his car to block a building entrance Henderson used when he left his girlfriend. Scared,

Henderson said he ran to his car, grabbed a rifle, and shot at the car. Two men were inside, and Mrs. Henry's son was one of them. Henderson did not know him. "If I could get into a time machine and turn my life back, I never would have done it," Henderson has stated, adding that he never intended to kill anyone and had no prior record. Henderson then fled, not realizing that he had wounded anyone.

But it's still unfortunately true that for all those wonderful stories of forgiveness that exist today, there are many people who hold intense resentment in their heart toward people who've offended them. Many of these people are Christians, many of them are not, but still, either way, it doesn't matter. It's just as wrong and sinful no matter who holds that mindset. Take, for example, the following classified ad once run in a local newspaper: "Wedding dress for sale, never worn. Will trade for .38 pistol."

Sir Francis Bacon once pointed out that "Revenge is a kind of wild justice; which the more man's nature runs to, the more the law should weed it out... certainly, in taking revenge, a man might get even with his enemy; but in passing it over, he is superior, for it is a prince's part to pardon."

I remember reading about an eagle that swooped to the ground, one day, catching a weasel in its powerful talons. But when it began to fly away, its wings inexplicably went limp, and the majestic bird dropped to the ground like a lifeless doll. As it turned out, the weasel had bitten its attacker in midflight, killing the proud eagle as it flew high in the atmosphere. If we cling to an attitude of anger or resentment, it will, like the weasel, sink its teeth into us when we least expect it and do us a world of harm.

A lady named Jan Vajnar once explained that the four sons of one of her friends were young and bursting with energy, especially in church. But the sermon that her minister preached on Sunday on turning the other cheek got their undivided attention. The minister stressed that no matter what others do to us, we should never try to get even. That afternoon, the youngest boy came into the house, crying. Between sobs, he told mother that he had kicked one of his brothers, who had kicked him in return.

"I'm sorry that you're hurt," his mother consoled. "But you shouldn't go around kicking people."

The tearful child then replied, "But the preacher said he wasn't supposed to kick me back!"

Everyone, let's not try to use the biblical command to not take revenge as an excuse to "make a first strike" against a fellow Christian and then expect them to follow J's instructions, while all the time, we avoid them.

Instead of retaliating against our enemies, then, let's do good to them. After all, Exodus 23:4 states, "If you come upon your enemy's ox that has strayed, take it back to its owner. If you see the donkey of someone who hates you struggling beneath a heavy load, do not walk by. Instead, stop and offer help." And as both Proverbs 25:21 and Romans 12:20 say, "If you enemy is hungry, feed him. If he his thirsty, give him something to drink. Then, he will be ashamed of what he has done to you. And when we involve ourselves in forgiving our enemies, we need to do it completely. After all, it's been pointed out that those who say they will forgive but can't forget are actually burying the hatchet, but leave the handle out for immediate use."

Once again, the Bible gives testimony to how J handled this issue of the want for revenge. 1 Peter 2:23 states, "He never answered back when insulted; when he suffered, he did not threaten to get even; he left his case in the hands of G who always judges fairly." And, for guidance for ourselves on this matter, 1 Corinthians 4:12 and 13:5 together instruct, "When we are cursed, we bless; when we are persecuted, we endure; when we are insulted, we answer back with kind words...love is not rude, it is not self-seeking. Love is not easily angered; it keeps no record of wrongs."

When once asked about her feelings toward Edward Henderson, the man who killed her son, Martha Henry simply stated, "I had no intention of holding anything in my heart against Edward. I just had emptiness. My son had been killed." It was the second family tragedy for her, because in 1968, her son Larry had been killed in Vietnam. A deeply religious woman, Mrs. Henry said it was G's will Calvin died.

"Edward was the executioner," she said, adding that Calvin had been using drugs. Mrs. Henry attended Henderson's trial, but didn't start lobbying for his release until they came to know each other. Henderson said this special relationship will not end once he's free.

"This isn't something that's going to be over when I get out," he said. "I feel she's my mom and I'm her son."

If Christians Went on Strike
James 2:14-26

Countless people facing persecution have reason to thank British lawyer Peter Benenson, the founder of Amnesty International. It was his inspiration in the 1960s that launched a worldwide citizens' movement to expose and confront government injustices.

His flair for controversy emerged early on, when his complaint to the school headmaster about the poor quality of the school's food prompted a letter to his mother, warning of her son's "revolutionary tendencies." At age sixteen, he launched his first campaign: to get school support for the Spanish Relief Committee, which was helping orphans in the Spanish civil war. He himself "adopted" one of the babies, helping to pay for its support. He then turned his attention to the plight of Jews who were fleeing Hitler's Germany. Despite some opposition, he got his school friends and their families to raise $4,000 to bring two young German Jews to Britain, probably saving their lives.

So it was in the 1950s that the Trades Union Congress sent Benenson to Spain to observe trials of Trade Unionists. Benenson was appalled by what he saw and drew up a list of complaints with which he confronted the judge. The trials ended in acquittals, a rarity in fascist Spain. It was through such activities that he began to acquire an international reputation. In Cyprus, he helped and advised Greek Cypriot lawyers whose clients had fallen foul of their British rulers. He persuaded Labor, Liberal, and Conservative lawyers to send observers to Hungary during the 1956 uprising and ensuing trials and to South Africa, where a major treason trial was due to take place. The relative success of these schemes led to the formation of the organization Justice, a UKbased legal and human rights organization.

It was this constant activity that laid the groundwork for his main endeavor, the 1961 launching of Amnesty International. Benenson was outraged after reading a news item about the arrest and imprisonment of two students in a Portuguese café, who had raised their glasses in a toast to liberty. With the publication of a front-page appeal in The Observer newspaper entitled, "The Forgotten Prisoners," Amnesty International was born. The term "prisoner of conscience" soon became commonplace, and AI's logo, a candle surrounded by barbed wire, became a worldwide symbol of hope and freedom.

Now, I have no idea whether Peter Benenson was a Christian or not. But even if we could determine that he was not, it seemed like he fully understood our main passage of Scripture for this morning, taken from the Living Bible's version of James 2:14–26: "Dear brothers, what's the use of saying that you have faith and are Christians, if you aren't proving it by helping others? Will that kind of faith save anyone? If you have friend who is in need of food and clothing, and you say to him, 'Well, good-bye and G bless you; stay warm and eat heartily,' and then don't give him clothes or food, what good does that do? So you see, it isn't enough to just have faith. You must also do good to prove that you have it. Faith that doesn't show itself by good works is no faith at all —it is dead and useless."

But someone may argue, "You say the way to G is by faith alone, plus nothing"; well, I say that good works are important also; for without good works, you can't prove whether you have faith or not; but anyone can see that I have faith by the way I act. Are there still some among you who hold that "only believing" is enough? Believing in one G? Well, just remember that the demons believe in G, too—so strongly, in fact, that they tremble in terror! Fool! When will you ever learn that "believing" is useless without doing what G wants you to do? Faith that doesn't result in good deeds is not real faith.

Don't you remember that even Abraham was declared good because of what he did, when he was willing to obey G, even if it meant offering his son Isaac to die on the altar! You see, he was trusting G so much that he was willing to do whatever G told him to do; his faith was made complete by what he did, by his actions and his good deeds. And so it happened, just as the Scriptures say, that Abraham trusted G, and the Lord declared him good in G's sight, and he was even called "the friend of G." So you see, a man is saved by what he does, as well as by what he believes. Rahab, the prostitute, is another example of this. She was saved because of what she did when she hid those messengers and sent them safely away by a different road. Just as the body is dead when there is no spirit in it, so faith is dead if it is not the kind that results in good deeds.

You see, I think the type of person who believes great things about G but then never does anything about those beliefs is one of the types of people J was talking about in Matthew 7:26–27, when he said there, according to the Good News Bible, "But everyone who hears these words of mine and does not obey them will be like a foolish man who built his house on the sand. The rain poured down, the rivers flooded over, the winds blew hard against that house, and it fell. What a terrible fall that was!"

For the first few years, Mr. Benenson worked tirelessly for the new, burgeoning movement, supplying much of the vital financial resources, going on research missions to various countries and playing a part in all areas of the organization. "At that time, we were still putting our toes in the water and learning as we went on," Benenson later reflected. "We tried every technique of publicity, and we were very grateful to the widespread help of journalists and television crews throughout the world who not only sent us information about the names of prisoners, but also, whenever they could, gave space to stories about prisoners."

Peter Benenson never gave up campaigning for a better world. He founded a society for people with celiac disease, a condition from which he himself suffered. In the 1980s, he became the chair of the newly created Association of Christians Against Torture, and in the early 1990s, he organized help for the orphans of the repressive government of Romania.

When I first heard of Mr. Benenson's story, it hit me just what a tremendous difference one simple person can make. Amazing, isn't it? Just one person created a fantastic positive difference in the lives of thousands of people. But the example from his life isn't a lot different from that of a Mrs. Betty Williams, from Northern Ireland. A Roman Catholic married to a Protestant, Mrs. Williams decided that she had had enough of the carnage when, in August 1976, she witnessed three children accidentally killed by a car whose terrorist driver had been shot by a British soldier. Despite threats on her life, she organized peace marches and toured the US, appealing to Americans to stop sending money to the Irish combatants.

Ms. Mairead Corrigan, a Roman Catholic from Belfast, was the aunt of the three children whose deaths had been witnessed by Mrs. Williams. During a demonstration in Belfast a week later, Corrigan joined forces with Williams and began organizing peace marches throughout Ireland and England. She helped persuade Sen. Edward Kennedy and other prominent Irish Americans to speak out against violence in Northern Ireland. Williams and Corrigan, then, were the first women to win the Nobel Peace Prize since 1946.

You see, the message that we're getting here, today, is that to be a *real* follower of J, we need not only to believe, but also *act* on that belief that we claim to have. After all, as the Good News Bible explains in Hebrews 11:4–9: "It was by faith that made Abel offer to G a better sacrifice than Cain's. Through his faith, he won G's approval as a righteous man, because G himself approved of his gifts. By means of his faith, Abel still speaks, even though he is dead. It was faith that kept Enoch from dying. Instead, he was taken up to G, and nobody could find him, because G had taken him up. The scripture says that before Enoch was taken up, he had pleased G. No man can please G without faith. For whoever comes to G must have faith that G exists and rewards those who seek him.

"It was faith that made Noah hear G's warnings about the future he could not see. He obeyed G and built an ark in which he and his family were saved. In this way, he condemned the world, and received from G the righteousness that comes by faith. It was faith that made Abraham obey when G called him and go out to a country which G had promised to give him. He left his own country without knowing where he was going. By faith, he lived in the country that G had promised him, as though he were a foreigner."

Now, I know what some of you are thinking. "Well, all of this is great, Roger, and yes, maybe I ought to try to do something more in my life for Christ and accomplish something great for him, but I'm just 'little old me.' I'm just from Podunk Broadway, Virginia. I myself am not rich, influential, and powerful, and I don't even know anybody like that, so where am I going to get the resources to start a worldwide organization that will make a serious dent in global problems like starvation, poverty, oppression, crime, pollution, and the like?"

Well, I'm sure there were a lot of people told of in the record of Scripture, who, when they first received G's call thought that there was no way they could do whatever it was he was calling them to do. But now listen to this Bible passage from the other end of Hebrews 11:32–35: "Is there any need to say anymore? There is not time for me to give an account of Gideon, Barak, Samson, Jephthah, or of David, Samuel and the prophets. These were men who, through faith, conquered kingdoms, did what is right and earned the promises. They could keep a lion's mouth shut, put out blazing fires and emerge unscathed from battle. They were weak people who were given strength, to be brave in war and drive back foreign invaders. Some received back their dead raised to life."

Still, another contemporary example of what we're talking about today comes from the life of Bob Geldof. If you're old enough to remember the Live Aid concert, held on July 13, 1985, you know what I'm talking about. After watching a BBC documentary on the famine in Ethiopia, Geldof decided that something had to be done about it. So he almost single-handedly organized every aspect of writing, producing and releasing of the song, "Do They Know It's Christmas?" a song addressing the plight of those effected by the famine, with the proceeds from the sale of the song going to famine relief efforts. He oversaw everything from the donating of the studio time to contacting all the people involved from musicians to engineers—all at his expense.

July 13, 1985, then, was one of those days that everyone who was alive then and is still with us should always remember. It's hard to talk to someone who didn't see at least part of Live Aid. Unlike Woodstock, which was for hippies, Live Aid had no demographic market. It was estimated that over $100 million was donated to the Live Aid Trust.

As he sang "Do They Know It's Christmas" during the concert, everyone in the world watching knew what he had done. Because of his efforts, millions of dollars were going to fight starvation and disease in Ethiopia. He had pulled off the greatest concert of all time, and there was no disputing that. He did it because he cared about humanity. He didn't do it for the money or the fame or career advancement. At that point, Bob Geldof showed everyone that one person can make a difference in the world.

Now, everybody, I can't tell you about where any of the people we've looked at this morning stand in a relationship with JC. I have no idea whether Peter Benenson, Betty Williams, Mairead Corrigan, and Bob Geldof are Christians. As far as I know, they either weren't or aren't. But you have to admit, they've done a heck of a lot to help put a serious dent in the effects of injustice, war and poverty. If only all people who call themselves Christians would at least attempt to make their corner of the world as blessed as possible, for those who suffer for whatever reason. Maybe G doesn't have it within his will for us to create a protest march that turns out hundreds of participants, to start a worldwide organization or a charitable entertainment program that's seen around the world. But maybe there's at least a little something that each of us can do—in J's name—to make this a better world for someone. After all, the Bible says in James 3:13, "Is there someone among you who is wise and understanding? He is to prove it by his good life, by his good deeds performed with humility and wisdom." As well, John the Baptist is recorded in Luke 3:11 as saying, "If you have two coats, give one to the poor. If you have extra food, give it away to those who are hungry." And the Bible records in 1 John 3:17, "If someone who is supposed to be a Christian has money enough to live well, and sees a brother in need, and won't help him—how can G's love be within him?"

You know, people are often remembered through history—long after their deaths—for the incredible positive contributions they made in this life to reduce the suffering of others. Along those lines, 1 Thessalonians 1:2–3 says, "We always thank G for you all, and always remember you in our prayers, for we remember before our God and Father how you put your faith into practice, how your love made you work so hard, and how your hope in our Lord JC is firm." When I hear that verse, I think of Oscar Schindler, on whom the movie Schindler's List is based—the guy who worked so hard to see that so many Jews were kept safe during World War II.

As Galatians 5:6 points out, "The only thing that counts is faith expressing itself through love."

Is That You, Jesus?
John 10:1-14

When I was a kid, it often happened that I'd walk in a room at home, where my brother, Glenn, was at the time. Well, I'd come into the room, and Glenn would inevitably look at me and ask, "Is that you, Roger?" He did this every time I'd walk in wherever he was.

So I got to the point where every time he'd ask me that, I'd say to him, "Well, duh! It's not Clint Eastwood. I'm not Geo Bush. It's not Arnold Schwarzenegger. The lights are on, I'm standing right here and you're looking right at me, Glenn. Who in the world do you think it is!"

It got to be a real joke within my family—so much so that anytime I appear on the scene where any of my siblings or even cousins are, I get asked—to this very day—"Is that you, Roger?" It's kind of ridiculous for my loved ones to have to ask me that. After all, they know me, they recognize me when they see me, and they know who I am.

Well, what's really scary is that there are people in the world today who claim to be followers of J. But even though they know of J to an extent, they must not be close enough to recognize when an imposter of Christ, a false J appears to them, since they follow people like this without reservation. For example, there's actually a group of people who belong to a new movement devoted to a man who calls himself the Second Coming of J and who also claims the title of antichrist," which, to him, is the next incarnation of J on earth, not an evil being. To show their devotion, some of the followers of this man literally INK themselves with the figure of "666" on their hand. One follower of this man said, "I just want to make sure it's visible, that everyone knows my life belongs to this man."

They and others like them are sincerely devoted to a sixty-year-old Puerto Rican whose legal name is Jose de Jesus, or Jose of Jesus. He counts his followers in more than thirty countries. So where does this man live? He lives with his wife in a suburban community just outside Houston, Texas.

140

Well, J explained that his true followers wouldn't have any real difficulty in telling the difference between him and anybody else claiming to be him, in John 10:11–14. "I tell you the truth, the man who does not enter the sheep pen by the gate, but climbs in by some other way, is a thief and a robber. The man who enters by the gate is the shepherd of his sheep. The watchman opens the gate for him, and the sheep listen to his voice. He calls his own sheep by name and leads them out. When he has brought out all his own, he goes on ahead of them, and his sheep follow him because they know his voice. But they will never follow a stranger; in fact, they will run away from him because they don't recognize a stranger's voice." J used this figure of speech, but they did not understand what he was telling them.

So J said again, "I tell you the truth, I am the gate for the sheep. All who ever came before me were thieves and robbers, but the sheep didn't listen to them. I am the gate; whoever enters through me will be saved. He will come in and go out, and find pasture. The thief comes only to steal, kill and destroy; I have come that they may have life and have it to the full. I am the good shepherd. The good shepherd lays down his life for the sheep. The hired hand is not the shepherd who owns the sheep. So, when he sees the wolf coming, he abandons the sheep and runs away. Then the wolf attacks the flock and scatters it. The man runs away, because he is a hired hand and cares nothing for the sheep. I am the good shepherd; I know my sheep, and my sheep know me…"

You see, what we Christians in the church need to do is to train ourselves, each other and others around us to be able to tell the difference between the real J and anyone else claiming to be Him. Now that might sound pretty easy, but think for a moment about the people I described when I opened up the message a moment ago. Those people really believe that this guy, who lives, today, outside Houston is the one and only Son of God. This is why, everybody, that (together) Ezekiel 44:23 and Leviticus 10:10 say, "They are to teach my people the difference between the holy and the profane and show them how to tell the difference between the clean and the unclean… You must distinguish between the holy and the common, between the unclean and the clean."

Well, to get back to this Jose of Jesus for a second, when asked to explain who he is, he answers, "JC, man, the second manifestation, the

Second Coming of Christ." He acknowledges that it "bothers a lot of people" that he calls himself J. Born in Puerto Rico, this fellow grew up poor, living in government housing. He stole for a living to pay for his teenage heroin addiction and admits to eight felony charges that put him in jail for nine months. Like many people, he claims that he was born again while in prison. From there, he moved to the US, where he became involved in church youth groups, and eventually a vision, he says, that turned him from a man of G to being G. "That same spirit that was in J of Nazareth is in me," De Jesus says. "He came to me and integrated with my person in 1973." De Jesus says this happened when two angels came to him in a vision, and while he admits there's no real way for him to prove that he's Christ, he says his followers aren't asking for proof.

Now, I don't mean to be making fun of anyone here, this morning. You see, being able to tell the real J from a false one could possibly be a little harder than what we might think. That's why, I think, J is recorded as having said in Matthew 7:15–16 and 24:24, "Watch out for false prophets; they come to you looking like sheep on the outside, while they are really like wild wolves on the inside. You will know them by the way they act…for false Christs and false prophets will arise, and will do wonderful miracles, so that if it were possible, even G's chosen ones would be deceived. See, I have warned you."

All right. Fair enough…we've been warned. So how are we supposed to guard ourselves against such a danger? Well, I think the answer is twofold: (1) always be on guard and be suspect of every new "teacher" of scripture that comes along, and (2) read and study the Bible enough so that you can use it proficiently to help defend your knowledge of the truth against false teaching. 1 John 4:1–3 instructs us, in fact, to do just this when, there, in the Living Bible, it says, "Dearly loved friends, don't always believe everything you hear just because someone says it is a message from G: test it first, to see if it really is. For there are many false teachers around, and the way to find out if their message is from the Holy Spirit is to ask: Does it really agree that JC, G's Son, actually became man with a human body? If so, then the message is from G. If not, the message is not from G, but from one who is against Christ, like the anti-Christ you have heard about who is going to come…" And a perfect biblical example of people actually following that kind of advice—to test the spirits to see if they are really from G—is seen in Acts 17:11, which reads, "The Bereans were of more noble character than the Thessalonians, for they received the message with great eagerness and examined the scriptures every day to see if what Paul said was true."

Yes, the followers of this Jose of Jesus fellow really do seem happy. They greet him with mariachi bands at airports and often collapse in tears when they hear him preach. But when he speaks to them, it's without theatrics. No "holyrolling," no miraculous healings—it's a pretty straight forward lesson in the fundamentals of what he believes. But it's an overly upbeat, no-fault, sin-free message. That's right. This self-proclaimed Jesus doesn't believe in sin, hell, the devil, or damnation or any kind. "Before the presence of G, there's no more sin," he says. And with no sin, there's no devil and no need for prayer, because after J of Nazareth die and was resurrected, one can literally do no wrong in G's eyes. He says things like murder and theft are crimes, but not sins, and that people are punished for these crimes on earth. "Heaven doesn't have anything to do with your behavior," he says.

This self-appointed reincarnation of Christ doesn't mind that his ministry often gathers in the corner tavern. "Like my former, J of Nazareth, he used to go to places like this and the religious people used to criticize him…I'm just doing the same kind of thing." But he does draw the line: no drugs and no getting drunk. "J never got drunk, and I never get drunk. I just enjoy life. I enjoy everything I do."

It sounds to me like Jose of Jesus enjoys taking a lot from others— their admiration, devotion, and service—but he's not much for giving of himself. He's not an exemplary servant like the real J was when he walked the earth. Considering that aspect of this contemporary religious leader, I'm reminded of scripture passages like Ezekiel 34:1–10 and Jeremiah 23:1–2. Together, these verses say, "The word of the Lord came to me: 'Son of man, prophesy against the shepherds of Israel; prophesy and say to them: "This is what the Lord says: Woe to the shepherds of Israel who only take care of themselves! Should not shepherds take care of the flock? You eat the curds, clothe yourselves with wool and slaughter the choice animals, but you do not take care of the flock. You have not strengthened the weak or healed the sick or bound up the injured. You have not brought back the strays or searched for the lost. You have ruled them harshly and brutally. So they were scattered because there was no shepherd, and when they were scattered, they became food for all the wild animals. My sheep wandered over all the mountains and on every high hill. They were scattered over the whole earth, and no one searched or looked for them.

"Therefore, you shepherds, hear the world of the Lord: As surely as I live, declares the Lord, because my flock lacks a shepherd and so has been plundered and has become food for all the wild animals, and because my shepherds did not search for my flock but cared for themselves rather than for my flock, therefore, O shepherds, hear the word of the Lord. This is what the Lord says: I am against the shepherds and will hold them accountable for my flock. I will remove them from tending the flock so that the shepherds can no longer feed themselves. I will rescue my flock from their mouths, and it will no longer be food for them... Woe to the shepherds who are destroying and scattering the sheep of my pasture! Therefore, this is what the Lord says to the shepherds who tend my people: 'Because you have scattered my flock and driven them away and have not bestowed care on them, I will bestow punishment on you for the evil you have done.'"

But the True Shepherd, J, is prophesied about, also in these Old Testament books. It's in Isaiah 40:11 and Ezekiel 34:11–16 and 23 that the true shepherd is described: "He tends the flock like a shepherd: He gathers the lambs in his arms and carries them close to his heart; he gently leads those that have young...For this is what the Lord says: I will search for my sheep and look after them. As a shepherd looks after his scattered flock when he is with them, so I will look after my sheep. I will rescue them from all the places where they were scattered on a day of clouds and darkness. I will bring them out from the nations and gather them from the countries, and I will bring them into their own land. I will pasture them on the mountains of Israel, in the ravines and in all the settlements in the land. I will tend them in good pasture, and the mountain heights of Israel will be their grazing land, and there, they will feed in a rich pasture on the mountains of Israel. I myself will tend my sheep and have them lie down. I will search for the lost and bring back the strays. I will bind up the injured and strengthen the weak, but the sleek and the strong I will destroy. I will shepherd the flock with justice."

Jose of J has come a long way from Puerto Rico and the tough times there. Today, his believers freely give him money. And WHERE does all this money GO? His daughter, Joanne, who is the accountant for his ministry, says, "What you see as luxuries are gifts members have given him. They're just very grateful, and they want to give him gifts." But what about the children who grow up in his church, believing that their Savior is actually walking around on earth today, leading the very individual church they're a part of? Well, he calls those children the Super Raza, or Super Race, because they are being brought up pure without stain of false religion on them. Unfortunately, the ministry of Jose of J is growing, with big followings in Venezuela, Columbia, and even Cuba, and the man who believes that he's the Second Coming of Christ is now turning his attention to America. "Miami is the bridge for all nations," he says, "and that's where Hispanics are, and then eventually, I'm going to find a lot of beautiful English-speaking people who will want to believe in me and I'm going to have millions of them." Just remember, everybody, it's the J of the Bible—not suburbia—of which Hebrews 13:20 speaks when there the Bible describes him as "that great Shepherd of the sheep." Just as Paul warned the Ephesian elders in Acts 20:29–31, "I know that after I leave, savage wolves will come in among you and will not spare the flock. Even from your own number, men will arise and distort the truth in order to draw away disciples after them. So be on your guard! Remember that for 3 years, I never stopped warning each of you day and night with tears."

Of all the cons we can fall prey to, one of the worst is being duped by a religious phony. These cons aren't always done for the benefit of some leaders whose name you can't spell. No, every week, lies dressed up in their Sunday best receive nodding approval in mainline churches everywhere. Warren Wiersbe once commented, "False teachers use our vocabulary, but they don't use our dictionary. They talk about 'salvation,' 'inspiration,' and other Christian terms, but they don't mean what we mean."

How can we keep from being deceived, ourselves? (1) Stop. Refuse to blindly accept someone's teaching just because others have been "blessed by it." Stop long enough to compare what they say with what the Bible says. (2) Look closely at the main spokesperson. Don't be wowed just because of their charisma or because they talk so smooth. And (3) Listen. Pay attention to the terms a person uses and how they're defined. Also, listen to what's not being said. Don't judge supposed truth just by how you feel; think and make your judgments according to what the Bible teaches.

My brother, Glenn, and my cousins back at Capon Springs all *know* me very well. They know who I am, even in the dark. They really don't need to ask, when they seem me, "Is that you, Roger?" But if we should ever meet someone claiming to be J, and we feel as though we have to ask them, "Is that you, Jesus?" then I dare say that we really don't know J as well as what we might like to think. Maybe it's time for us to clear away the confusion. Maybe it's time to get to know J for ourselves, without a doubt.

It Should Be a Silent Night, Holy Night
Luke 2:8-20

A lady had a circle of friends for whom she really wanted to buy Christmas presents. Time slipped away and it was so busy at work for her that she just wasn't able to get to the store to purchase those gifts. Time was running out, so not too many days before Christmas, she decided to give up on the gift idea and just buy everybody the same beautiful Christmas card. She went to the local gift store and hurriedly went through the now picked over a tack of cards and found a box of fifty, just exactly what she wanted. She didn't take time to read the message, she just noticed a beautiful cover on it, and there was gold around it and a floral appearance on the front of the card. "That's perfect," she thought, as she simply signed all of them, "With all my love."

As New Year's came and she had time to go back to two or three cards that she had not sent out from the stack that she bought and sent out, she was shocked to read the message inside. It said in a little rhyme, "This little Christmas card is just to say, a little gift is on the way."

Now, the hurriedness that this lady was apparently feeling, to me, seems to have been felt by the shepherds on that first Christmas night. Let me explain that by first reading the main passage for this morning, Luke 2:8–20, in the NIV. "There were shepherds living out in the fields nearby, keeping watch over the flocks at night. An angel of the Lord appeared to them, and the glory of the Lord shone around them, and they were terrified. But the angel said to them, 'Do not be afraid. I bring you good news of great joy that will be for all the people. Today in the town of David a Savior has been born to you; he is Christ the Lord. This will be a sign to you: You will find a baby wrapped in strips of cloth, lying in a manger.' Suddenly a great company of the heavenly host appeared with the angel, praising G and saying, 'Glory to G in the highest, and on earth peace to men on whom his favor rests.' When the angels had left them and gone into heaven, the shepherds said to one another, 'Let's go to

Bethlehem and see this thing that has happened, which the Lord has told us about.'

"So, they hurried off and found Mary and Joseph, and the baby, who was lying in the manger. When they had seen him, they spread the word concerning what had been told them about his child, and all who heard it were amazed at what the shepherds said to them. But Mary treasured up all these things and pondered them in her mind. The shepherds returned, glorifying and praising G for all the things they had heard and seen, which were just as they had been told."

Now, the one verse that I really want us to take note of for today, out of that entire passage, is verse 16, where the gospel proclaims (again, in the NIV, as does the Good News Bible and the Jerusalem Bible), "So they hurried off and found Mary and Joseph and the baby, who was lying in the manger." The Living Bible says that the shepherds "ran to the village," the RSV says "they went with haste," the New English Bible says "they went with all speed," and the Phillips Modern English Version of the Bible states that they went as fast as they could."

Now of course, there was an excellent reason why the shepherds were in such a hurry, that first Christmas night—the Savior of the world had been born. But do we really need the stress/tension of running around like chickens with our heads cut off at Christmas, trying to buy and do everything? Is that what the reason for the season is all about? What I'm starting to suggest this morning, folks, is this: If we are starting out the Christmas season this year with the mindset of those shepherds—always being in an absolute hurry to accomplish everything we think we need to do this Christmas season—we might want to take a piece of advice from Steven J. Cole, who once noted, "God's Word often refers to the Christian experience as a walk, seldom as a run, and never a mad dash." Two times, I like that.

It's interesting. We often run around like crazy, this time of year, with one thousand things to get done, and when it's all over (a month from now), we will have forgotten all about all that we felt like we needed to get done/accomplish in that short time period. We might even look back on it and say, "You know, I really didn't need to break my neck to do all that stuff," not even being able to recall half of all the tasks we threw ourselves into. We honestly do tend to forget, eventually, all about much of the stuff in life that gets us upset and bent out of shape at certain times in our life. After all, Rebekah wisely pointed out to Esau that he would eventually calm down, forgetting all about the fact that his brother, Jacob, stole his birthright from their father, Isaac, according to Genesis, 27:44–45, and he did do just that, eventually. And as J pointed out, while talking about the disciples eventually forgetting about his crucifixion and eventually being filled with joy, he observed, in John 16:20 that "a woman giving birth to a child indeed has pain because her time has come; but when her baby is born, she forgets the anguish because of her joy that a child is born into the world." In addition, the Bible reminds us in Psalm 85:8 that "G promises peace to his saints;" and we're all familiar with J's own words, according to John 14:27: "Peace I leave with you; my peace I give you. I do not give to you as the world gives. Do not let your hearts be troubled and do not be afraid."

Now, although she wasn't necessarily addressing the issue of stress/tension at Christmastime, a woman named Evelyn Underhill did speak to the topics of self-reliance and stress—which, of course, can be applied to any time of year— when she said, "G always works in tranquility. Fuss and feverishness, anxiety, intensity, intolerance, instability, pessimism and wobble, and every kind of worry and hurry—these, even on the highest levels, are signs of the self-made and self-acting soul; the person who relies on themselves for spiritual growth and success. The saints are never like that. They share the quiet and noble qualities of the great family to which they belong."

Yes, the person who doesn't trust in G—but only in themselves—often has a reason to worry, because they recognize that no matter how good they are in certain skilled areas in life, they have no ultimate source of help, guidance, and strength to truly be successful in life.

So if we're having trouble getting through Christmastime due to inner pain and suffering, the idea is not to rely on our own strength to help us deal with the pain, but rather to look to G for help. Always remember of what the Bible tells us in Philippians 4:7: "The peace of G, which transcends all understanding, will guard your hearts and minds in Christ Jesus." I've always felt that what this passage of Scripture was saying to us was that we need to place all of our burdens on G, and then do our best to forget all about them as we go on our way, facing the future. I know that

that can seem like a tough thing to do, but as John Oxenham once stated, "Thanks be to G for a life fullpacked with things that matter, crying to be done…a life, thank G, of neverending strife against the odds—Just enough time to do one's best, and then pass on, leaving the rest to him."

Remember, as Christians, we're called to live lives full of peace, as Colossians 3:15 and 1 Corinthians 7:15 together say, "Let the peace of heart that comes from Christ be always present in your hearts and lives, for this is your responsibility and privilege as members of his body. And always be thankful… for G wants his children to live in peace and harmony." But it's not just a serene feeling that we get to have in our own minds that G gives us when we come to live with the peace of G in our hearts and minds. Doing so also means that we do our best to "get along with other people." Combining the passages found in Hebrews 12:14 and Romans 12:18, it's in those two places that G's word proclaims, "Make every effort to live in peace with all men and to be holy; without holiness, no one will see the Lord…be at peace with everyone, just as much as possible."

So our part in helping to create this sense of peace for ourselves and in others around us is seen in taking the initiative to promote that kind of feeling all around us. Along those lines, the Bible states in Romans 14:19, "So then, we must always aim at those things that bring peace, and that help strengthen one another." And, in agreement, Psalm 34:14 instructs us to "Turn from evil and do good; seek peace and pursue it."

In his book entitled *Stress Fractures*, famed Christian author/speaker Chuck Swindoll wrote, "I vividly remember some time back being caught up in the undertow of too many commitments in too few days. It wasn't long before I was snapping at my wife and our children, choking down my food at mealtimes, and feeling irritated at those unexpected interruptions through the day. Before long, things around our home started reflecting the patter of my hurry-up style. It was becoming unbearable.

I distinctly recall after dinner one evening the words of our youngest daughter, Colleen. She wanted to tell me about something important that had happened to her at school that day. She hurriedly began, "Daddy-I-wanna-tellyou- something-and-I'll-tell-you-really-fast."

Suddenly realizing her frustration, I answered, "Honey, you can tell me… and you don't have to tell me really fast. Say it SLOWLY."

Swindoll then said he'd never forget her response: "Then listen slowly."

You know, as important as a mission that the wise men who came to see the baby J were on, they didn't appear to let the enormity of their task to stress them out at all. You know the story according to Matthew 2:1–12: "After J was born in Bethlehem in Judea, during the time of King Herod, Magi from the east came to Jerusalem and asked, 'Where is the one who has been born king of the Jews? We saw his star in the east and have come to worship him.' When King Herod heard this, he was disturbed, and all Jerusalem with him. When he had called together all the people's chief priests and teachers of the law, he asked them where the Christ was to be born. 'In Bethlehem in Judea,' they replied, 'for this is what the prophet has written: "But you, Bethlehem, in the land of Judah, are by no means least among the rulers of Judah; for out of you will come a ruler who will be the shepherd of my people Israel."'

"Then Herod called the Magi secretly and found out form them the exact time the star had appeared. He sent them to Bethlehem and said, 'Go and make a careful search for the child. As soon as you find him, report to me, so that I, too, may go and worship him.' After they had heard the king, they went on their way, and the star they had seen in the east when ahead of them until it stopped over the place where the child was. When they saw the star, they were overjoyed. On coming to the house, they saw the child with his mother Mary, and they bowed down and worshipped him. Then, they opened their treasures and presented him with gifts of gold and of incense and of myrrh. And having been warned in a dream not to go back to Herod, they returned to their country by another route."

Yes, even though the wise men had to have felt pressure due to Herod's attempt to find and kill the Christ child, they nevertheless continued in their pursuit of finding the Christ child, and when they did, verse 10 there says that they were overjoyed.

But even after all we've said this morning about having inward peace being the real meaning of Christmas, many people still don't get it—thinking and feeling that materialism is the real "reason for the season." Many people take for themselves the view apparently shared by one of the characters in Louise May Alcott's story *Little Women*, when one of those characters is quoted as saying, "Christmas just won't be Christmas without any presents." So when we're faced with attitudes like that from the world, what we need to do is to take J's advice from John 16:33, when he proclaimed and encouraged, "I have told you these things so that in me you may have peace. In this world, you will have trouble. But take heart! I have overcome the world."

Yes, we *can*, I believe, take heart in knowing that J has overcome the world. In agreement with that proclamation of Christ's, a man named Bruce Thielemann once was quoted as having said, "Good Friday came after Christmas, but the angels still sang at the manger. In the midst of the harshest reality of life, there is always a welcome for tenderness and beauty."

You know, when we get all stressed and bent out of shape about various things, they can cause us to miss out on a lot during any time of year, but maybe especially at Christmas, as exemplified in the following story. It seems that late one Christmas Day, a resident of the posh community of Hillsborough, California, accompanied by his wife/children set out to sing carols for the neighbors. As they were tuning up outside their first stop, the woman of the house came to the door, looking distraught.

"Look, buddy," she began, "I'm just too busy to fool with this, right now. The plumbing's falling apart, I can't get anybody to fix it, and there's a mob of family members coming for dinner. If you really feel like singing Christmas carols for us, come back around nine, okay?"

"Yes, ma'am," replied Bing Crosby respectfully, as he herded his troupe elsewhere.

Have you experienced true Christmas peace this season?

Jesus Had Nothing to Do with It
John 3:27; Psalm 100:4

Back in early September, during the Creative Arts Emmy Awards, Comic Kathy Griffin made a provocative comment as she took the stage of the Shrine Auditorium to collect her Emmy for best reality program for her Bravo Channel show, *My Life on the D-List*.

"A lot of people come up here and thank Jesus for this award. I want you to know that no one had less to do with this award than Jesus," an exultant Griffin stated, holding up her statuette. "Suck it, Jesus. This award is my god, now." Asked about her speech backstage a short time later, an unrepentant Griffin added, "I hope I offended some people. I didn't want to win the Emmy for nothing."

As you might expect, her speech drew fire from, among others, a leading Roman Catholic group, the Catholic League for Religious and Civil Rights, which condemned Griffin's remarks as "obscene and blasphemous." "It's a sure bet that if Griffin had said, 'Suck it, Muhammad,' there would have been a very different reaction," Catholic League president Bill Donohue said in a statement posted on the group's website. He called on TV academy president Dick Askin to denounce Griffin's remarks and on Griffin to apologize. Griffin's reaction to the controversy, according to a statement issued by her publicist: "Am I the only Catholic left with a sense of humor?"

Now, first of all, I want to apologize for having quoted, verbatim, that statement. I hope I didn't unnecessarily offend anyone here today by having related that story to you. It actually made me squeamish to repeat it. And second, although there are several spiritual issues that could be easily addressed within the next half hour, due to that statement (blasphemy and idolatry obviously among them), I want to specifically address the portion of the statement where Griffin touted, "I want you to know that no one had less to do with this award than Jesus."

Well, I'd like all of you to know, during this season of Thanksgiving, that Miss Kathy Griffin couldn't have been more wrong. The basis of this morning message, in fact, comes from an extremely short—but nevertheless powerful— verse found in John 3:7. It's in this short piece of wisdom-filled truth that John the Baptist says in conversation with some of his disciples in the Good News Bible, "No one can have anything unless God gives it to him." That's your memory verse for this week, by the way—short, sweet, and to the point but yet very powerful: No one can have anything unless God gives it to him. By the way, that includes Emmy Awards.

You know, my experience has been that at T-giving time, we tend to focus on giving thanks mostly for the necessities of life (food, clothing, and shelter) and the love of family and friends. But I think we often forget to thank G for things like our talents and abilities—things that we never would have (things that help us to achieve things in the world, like honors at the Emmys) if G had not given them to us to begin with. No, Miss Griffin, I have to tell you that J had everything to do with your winning that award. Maybe what you should do, then, Miss Griffin, is to take the advice of Psalm 100:4 and "Enter into his gates with thanksgiving and into his courts with praise."

The Masai tribe in West Africa has an unusual way of saying "Thank you." Translators tell us that when the Masai express thanks, they bow, put their foreheads on the ground, and say, "My head is in the dirt." When members of another African tribe want to express gratitude, they sit for a long time in front of the hut of a person who did the favor and literally say, "I sit on the ground before you." These Africans definitely understand, then, what thanksgiving is all about and why it's oftentimes so difficult for us: at the core of Thanksgiving is an act of humility, obviously very much unlike the attitude exhibited by one Kathy Griffin.

So besides thanking G for our abilities, what else do we have that we can offer thanks to G for? Well, for one thing, we can begin by thanking G for our church, as the ancient Israelites did, according to Ezra 3:10–11, when it's there the Bible states, "When the builders laid the foundation of the Temple of the Lord, the priests in their vestments and with their trumpets, and the Levites with cymbals, took their places to praise the Lord, as prescribed by David, king of Israel. With praise and thanksgiving, they sang to the Lord: 'He is good; His love to Israel endures forever.' And all the people gave a great shout to the Lord because the foundation of the temple had been laid."

After thanking G for our church, we can thank him for being with those who carry on the work of the ministry. Along those lines, the apostle Paul writes in 2 Corinthians 2:14, "Thanks be to G who, wherever he goes, makes us in Christ partners in his triumph, and through us is spreading the knowledge of Himself, like a sweet smell everywhere."

We can (and should) thank G for giving us victorious living in J, as Paul did in 1 Corinthians 15:56–57, when we penned the words, "Death gets is power to hurt from sin, and sin gets its power from the Law. But thanks be to G, who gives us the victory through our Lord Jesus Christ!"

2 Corinthians 9:15 instructs us to "give thanks to G for His indescribable gift!" And in another portion of Scripture where Paul is giving thanks to G, Paul writes in 2 Corinthians 1:11, "So it will be that the many prayers for us will be answered, and G will bless us; and many will raise their voices to him in thanksgiving for us."

And yet, there are still more things that we can be thankful for, not just at this time of year, but through every season of our lives. While researching for this sermon, I came across the following list, entitled Sampler on Thanks: "Things to be thankful for: (1) Only you and G know all the facts about you. (2) Even if you can't pay your bills, at least you don't have to be one of your creditors. (3) In case your job is a little harder than you'd like, it's worth remembering that you can't sharpen a razor on velvet. (4) The doors of opportunity that lay before you and for the friends who oil the hinges of those doors."

Maybe good old Dennis the Menace hit the nail on the head as he was talking with his friend Joey. As the two of them, in the month of December, were looking into a store window that was all decorated for Christmas, Dennis remarked, "Last month was our giving thanks holiday, and Christmas is G's 'You're welcome.'"

Yes, we all have things in our lives we can be thankful and grateful for. Sometimes, more than one person can be grateful for something, even though each person involved may choose to be thankful in that situation for various reasons. Let me give you an example. It seems that one Sunday in church, members of this particular church were listing praises for what the Lord had done in their lives over the previous week. Mr. Stanley said that the roof of his house had caught fire, but thankfully, a next-door neighbor had seen the fire in the early stages, took the appropriate actions, and the potential disaster was averted with only relatively minor damage. A few seconds later, a woman stood up in the congregation. "I have a praise, too," she began to announce. "I'm Mr. Stanley's insurance agent."

An attitude of proper thanksgiving is important in church, because it's only when we come to the Lord for worship with grateful and thankful hearts that we can truly worship G as he should be worshipped. That truth is demonstrated in the scripture passages located in 1 Chronicles 16:4 and 16:7– 36 as well as 2 Chronicles 7:3. Together, those passages say, "David appointed some of the Levites to minister before the ark of the Lord, to make petition, to give thanks, and to praise the Lord, the God of Israel…That day, David committed to Asaph and his associates this psalm of thanks to the Lord: 'Give thanks to the Lord, call on his name; make known among the nations what he has done. Sing to him, sing praise to him; tell of all his wonderful acts. Glory in his holy name; let the hearts of those who seek the Lord rejoice. Look to the Lord and his strength; seek his face always. Remember the wonders he has done, his miracles and the judgments he pronounced, O descendants of Israel his servant, O sons of Jacob, his chosen ones.

"He is the Lord our G; his judgments are in all the earth. He remembers his covenant forever, the word he commanded for a thousand generations—the covenant he made with Abraham, the oath he swore to Isaac. He confirmed it to Jacob as a decree, to Israel as an everlasting covenant: To you I will give the land of Canaan as the portion you will inherit. When they were but few in number, few indeed, and strangers in it, they wandered from nation to nation, from one kingdom to another. He allowed no man to oppress them; for their sake he rebuked kings: 'Do not touch my anointed ones; do my prophets no harm.'

"Sing to the lord, all the earth; proclaim his salvation day after day. Declare his glory among the nations, his marvelous deeds among all peoples. For great is the Lord and greatly to be praised; he is to be feared above all gods, for all the gods of the nations are idols, but the Lord made the heavens. Splendor and majesty are before him; strength and joy in his dwelling place. Ascribe to the Lord, O families of nations, ascribe to the

Lord glory and strength, ascribe to the Lord the glory due his name. Bring an offering and come before him; worship the Lord in the splendor of his holiness. Tremble before him, all the earth.

"The world is firmly established; it cannot be moved. Let the heavens rejoice, let the earth be glad; let them say among the nations, 'The Lord reigns!' Let the sea resound, and all that is in it; let the fields be jubilant, and everything in them! Then the trees of the forest will sing, they will sing for joy before the Lord, for he comes to judge the earth. Give thanks to the Lord, for he is good; his love endures forever. Cry out, 'Save us, O God our Savior; gather us and deliver us from the nations, that we may give thanks to your holy name, that we may glory in your praise.' Praise be to the Lord, the G of Israel, from everlasting to everlasting. Then, all the people said 'Amen' and 'Praise the Lord.'

"When all the Israelites saw the fire coming down and the glory of the Lord above the Temple, they knelt on the pavement with their faces to the ground, and they worshipped and gave thanks to the Lord, saying, 'He is good; his love endures forever.'"

You see, as these verses indicate, true worship of G comes from grateful hearts. Feelings such as bitterness, envy, hostility, and in the case of Miss Kathy Griffin, pride disqualifies someone from genuine worship. Thanksgiving opens up the door of the heart toward G in such a way that the individual is freed for true worship of God. Everywhere in Scripture, this spirit of thanksgiving is revealed as vital to our worship experience. Yes, thanksgiving and worship are inevitably bound together. Thanksgiving, then, should be expressed from a position of humility and reverence. The worshippers here of ancient Israel bowed their faces to the pavement leading to the temple. In the Hebrew language, the term "worship" means to bow down to pay homage to the person with superior rank or position. The basic definition of worship includes giving homage to God because he is superior to us by nature—a truth obviously not believed by Kathy Griffin and her many Hollywood buddies.

Now, those of us who are so inclined might want to occasionally give G thanks through the avenue of our singing voices. Nehemiah 12:27–31 states, "At the dedication of the wall of Jerusalem, the Levites were sought out from where they lived and were brought to Jerusalem to celebrate joyfully the dedication with songs of thanksgiving and with the music of cymbals, harps and lyres. The singers were also brought together, for they had built villages for themselves around Jerusalem...Two large choirs were also assigned to give thanks."

And in the New Testament, the well-known passage comes from Ephesians 5:19–20: "Speak to one another in the words of psalms, hymns, and sacred songs; sing hymns and psalms to the Lord, with praise in your hearts. Always give thanks for everything to G, the Father, in the name of our Lord JC." Still, Scripture goes on to say in 1 Thessalonians 5:17 (in the Phillips Modern English version of the Bible), "Be thankful, whatever the circumstances might be." The Bible also indicates that by our demonstration of generosity, those who are on the receptive end of our generosity will give thanks to G for it, when 2 Corinthians 9:11 states, "Yes, G will give you much so you can give away much, and when we take your gifts to those who need them, they will break into praise and thanksgiving to G for your help." And finally, Psalm 95:2 encourages us to "come before Him with thanksgiving and extol him with music and song."

You know, I can imagine that if I had been present at the Shrine Auditorium to personally see the Emmy Awards, and Kathy Griffin had said what she had said from the podium, I don't think I would have protested right then and there. I don't think I would have shouted to her to stop it or even loudly moan "boo!" No, instead, I think I would have hightailed it out of the building. Why? Because it's usually after someone makes a statement like this that people often envision a bolt of lightning coming down from out of the sky and frying the person who said it on the spot. Yes, contrary to Miss Griffin's beliefs, J had everything to do with allowing her to receive that award. He gave her the talent and ability to earn it. Remember, we don't have a thing that hasn't come from G.

Jesus the Divider
Acts 13:49-52, and 14:1-4

A teetotalling mother was very vocal from time to time about her theory that only grape juice—not wine—was served at the Last Supper. During one of these discussions, her daughter said, "But, Mom, don't you remember that a Cana, J turned the water into wine?"

Her mother, eyes blazing, then, snapped back, "Yes, and he never should have done it, either!"

You know, what that story illustrate for me is that many people will argue— and do so many times ridiculously—about J. It actually struck me hard, a couple of years ago, as I read through the Bible in its entirety, of how much J was a divider among the people that he appeared to and was preached about to. There are at least nine different places—interestingly enough all located in the gospel of John and in the book of Acts—in which people who J interacted with, or were told about him, either clung to him, or were repelled by him. There didn't seem to be any middle stance taken by people on J in those instances.

The first two examples I'll give this morning come from Acts 13:49–52 and 14:1–4. It's here together that these verses read, "And the word of the Lord spread throughout all the region. But the Jews incited the devout women of high standing and the leading men of the city, and stirred up persecution against Paul and Barnabas, and drove them out of their district. But they shook off the dust from their feet against them and went on to Iconium. And the disciples were filled with joy and with the HS… At Iconium, Paul and Barnabas went as usual into the Jewish synagogue. There, they spoke so effectively that a great number of Jews and Gentiles believed. But the Jews who refused to believe stirred up the Gentiles and poisoned their minds against the brothers. Paul and Barnabas spent considerable time there, speaking boldly for the Lord, who confirmed the message of his grace by enabling them to do miraculous signs and wonders. The people of the city were divided; some sided with the Jews, others with the apostles."

You see, as these two passages begin to show, proclaiming the gospel brings one of two responses from people: some will accept the gospel with faith and repentance, and others will respond with rejection and rebellion. When Simeon spoke of Jesus in the temple, shortly after J had been born on earth, he pointed out those two possible results, as indicated in Luke 2:34, which reads, "Then Simeon blessed them and said to Mary, his mother, 'This child is destined to cause the falling and rising of many in Israel, and to be a sign that will be spoken against, so that the thoughts of many hearts will be revealed. And a sword will pierce your own soul, too.'" The results, then, belong to G. Our assignment is to simply preach the gospel so that all people will be brought either to receive him or reject him.

So what exactly was J saying and doing that was ticking so many people off that, at the same time, was getting many other people to wholeheartedly follow him? Well, he was simply telling the truth about himself, about who he really was—explaining it to the people. An example of him doing just that and then getting another "mixed reaction" from the crowd is seen in the Jerusalem Bible's version of John 10:7–21: "So J spoke to them again: 'I tell you most solemnly, I am the gate of the sheepfold. All others who have come are thieves and robbers; but the sheep took no notice of them. I am the gate. Anyone who enters through me will be safe and will go freely in and out and be sure of finding pasture. The thief comes only to steal and kill and destroy. I have come so that they may have life and have it to the full. I am the good shepherd; the good shepherd is on who lays down his life for his sheep. The hired man, since he is not the shepherd, and the sheep do not belong to him, abandons the sheep and runs away as soon as he sees a wolf coming, and then the wolf attacks and scatters the sheep; this is because he is only a hired man and has no concern for the sheep. I am the good shepherd; I know my own and my own know me, just as the Father knows me and I know the Father; and I am willing to die for my sheep. And there are other sheep I have that are not of this fold and these I have to lead as well. They, too, will listen to my voice, and there will be only one flock, and one shepherd. The Father loves me, because I lay down my life in order to take it up again.

No one takes it from me, I lay it down of my own free will, and as it is in my power to lay it down, so it is in my power to take it up again; and this is the command I have been given by My Father.' These words caused disagreement among the Jews. Many said, 'He is possessed, he is raving, why bother to listen to him?' Others said, 'These are not the words of a man possessed by a devil: could a devil open up the eyes of the blind?'"

And if it isn't the person of J that has and continues to cause division, then another prevalent source of conflict among people is the differences of interpretation people have over just exactly what the Bible is saying. One of those instances is seen in John 7:37–43: "On the last day, the climax of the holidays, J said in a loud voice to the crowds, 'If anyone is thirsty, let him come to me and drink. For the Scriptures declare that rivers of living water shall flow from the inmost being of anyone who believes in Me.' He was speaking of the HS, who would be given to everyone believing in him; but the Spirit had not been given yet, because J had not yet returned to his glory in Heaven.

"When the crowds heard him say this, some of them declared, 'This man surely is the prophet who will come just before the Messiah.' Others said, 'He is the Messiah.' Still, others insisted, 'But he can't be! Will the Messiah come from Galilee? For the Scriptures clearly state that the Messiah will be born of the royal line of David, in Bethlehem, the village where David was born.' So the crowd was divided about him."

Still, another example from John 9:13–16. It's in the New English Version that the Bible says here, "The man who had been born blind was brought before the Pharisees. As it was a Sabbath day when J made the paste and opened his eyes, the Pharisees now asked him by what means he had gained his sight. The man told them, 'He spread a paste on my eyes; the I washed, and now I can see.' Some of the Pharisees said, 'This fellow is no man of G; he does not keep the Sabbath.' Others said, 'How could such signs come from a sinful man?' So they took different sides."

I guess what all these biblical examples go to show is that even when everybody in the same immediately space is confronted with the exact, same presentation of the gospel message (in other words, the truth), there will always be those who will refuse to believe in that truth, insisting that "they know better." They remind me of the professor in the old Alfred Hitchcock movie *The Lady Vanishes*. Upon being confronted with the rock-solid evidence that proves his theory wrong, the professor emphatically replies, "Nonsense. My theory is perfectly correct. It's the facts that are misleading."

And you know, it would be bad enough if there were to be only those who believed the gospel message when they heard it, and those who simply didn't. But often, the problem is that those who choose not to accept the message then set out to do whatever they can to stop the furtherance of the gospel. Think about it. Just as many of us feel called to do what we can to spread the gospel, there are those who do everything within their power to prevent it from going forward. And still further, there are those who honestly don't care, one way or another, about the gospel story who, if the conditions are right, can eventually find themselves right, smack dab in the middle of a battle in the spiritual war we all find ourselves in. Such was the case as explained in The Good News Bible's version of Acts 17:2–5: "According to his usual habit, Paul went to the synagogue. There during three Sabbath days, he argued with the people from the Scriptures, explaining them and proving from them that the Messiah had to suffer, and rise form death. "This J whom I announce to you," Paul said, "is the Messiah." Some of them were convinced and joined Paul and Silas; so did a large group of Greeks who worshipped G, and many of the leading women.

But the Jews were jealous and gathered some of the worthless loafers from the streets and formed a mob. They set the whole city in an uproar and attacked the home of Jason, trying to find Paul and Silas and bring them out to the people." You see, as this passage points out, it can be a dangerous thing to be a "worthless spiritual loafer," since we could then get caught up fighting on the wrong side of earth's ongoing spiritual war.

Now, another thing to consider is that if we ourselves are serious about being an active part in the spiritual war that takes place all around us, we have to expect that there will be people who will not play by the rules when engaging in this spiritual conflict with us. There will be people who, working for Satan's causes, will lie to us and try their best to deceive us in any way they deem necessary. And these people aren't by any means beyond using physical force/violence to keep the gospel from spreading.

An example along those lines is seen in the Living Bible's version of Acts 23:6–10: "Then, Paul thought of something. Part of the Council were Sadducees, and part were Pharisees! So he shouted, 'Brothers, I am a Pharisee, as were all my ancestors! And I am being tried here today because I believe in the resurrection of the dead!'"

This divided the council right down the middle—the Pharisees against the Sadducees—since the Sadducees say there is no resurrection, angels, or eternal spirit within us, but the Pharisees believe in all of these. So a great clamor arose. Some of the Jewish leaders jumped up to argue that Paul was correct.

"We see nothing wrong with him," they shouted. "Perhaps a spirit or angel did speak to him."

The shouting grew louder and louder, and the men were tugging at Paul from both sides, pulling him this way and that way. Finally, the commander, fearing they would tear him apart, ordered his soldiers to take him away from there by force and bring him back to the armory."

A lady who was hurried and frustrated with her shopping experience up to the present moment approached the perfume counter and asked the busy sales clerk, "Do you still have Elizabeth Taylor's Passion?"

The clerk then quickly replied, "If I did, honey, would I be working here?"

Yes, for whatever reason, there are many people who just don't seem to have any enthusiasm/excitement about anything. But the gospel often helps people to make up their minds whether they're going to be on fire for or against J. If people don't make up their minds one way or another on the Son of God, that's their fault, not the fault of the gospel.

Now, a final scriptural example of what we've been talking about, today, comes from Acts 28:23–28: They arranged to meet Paul on a certain day, and came in even larger numbers to the place where he was staying. From morning till evening, he explained and declared to them the kingdom of G and tried to convince them about J from the Law of Moses and from the Prophets. Some were convinced by what he said, but others would not believe. They disagreed among themselves and began to leave, after Paul had made this final statement: "The HS spoke the truth to your ancestors when he said through Isaiah the prophet: 'Go to this people and say, You will be ever hearing but never understanding; you will be ever seeing, but never perceiving. For this people's heart has become calloused; they hardly hear with their ears, and they have closed their eyes. Otherwise, they might see with their eyes, hear with their ears, understand with their hearts, and turn and I would heal them.' Therefore, I want you to know that God's salvation has been sent to the Gentiles, and they will listen." Some were convinced by what he said, but others would not believe. That's just the way it goes. Which one of these describes us best?

Clarence E. McCartney writes in his book *Preaching Without Notes* that when Geo Whitfield was getting the people of Edinburgh out of their beds at 5:00 a.m. to hear his preaching, a man on his way to the church met up with David Hume, the famed Scottish philosopher and skeptic, a definite nonbeliever in the Christian faith. Surprised to see Hume on his way to listen to Whitfield, the man said, "I thought you didn't believe in the gospel."

Hume then replied, "I don't, but he does!"

You see, though we've been talking this morning about people who don't believe in J verses people who do believe, there is always that chance that a believer in J can help turn someone from a mindset of unbelief in Christ, to having a heart full of devotion toward him.

Just as in the Days of Noah
Genesis 6:5-13; Revelation 13:3-4, 8, 12

It's been stated that "We don't really become more ethical or moral as we grow older—we just choose our sins more carefully." When I was ministering in Hot Springs, whenever the topic of the sad spiritual state of the world came up, one of our church members would shake his head and exclaim, "Just as in the days of Noah...just like the Bible says regarding the end times." Well, what does the Bible say about the early earth's history in regard to the overwhelming prevalence of sin in the world? Although specific sins (such as drunkenness, theft, murder, and sexual immorality, except for violence) are not listed in connection with the sins of the people in Noah's day, we definitely get a sense of the thoroughness of the general sinfulness of the people in Genesis 6:5–13: "The Lord saw how great man's wickedness on the earth had become, and that every inclination of the thoughts of his heart was only evil all the time. The Lord was grieved that he had made man on the earth, and his heart was filled with pain. So the Lord said, 'I will wipe mankind, whom I have created, form the face of the earth—men and animals, and creatures that move along the ground, and birds of the air—for I am grieved that I have made them.' But Noah found favor in the eyes of the Lord.

"Noah was a righteous man, blameless among the people of his time, and he walked with G. Noah had 3 sons: Shem, Ham and Japheth. Now the earth was corrupt in g's sight and full of violence. G saw how corrupt the earth had become, for all the people on earth had corrupted their ways. So G said to Noah, 'I am going to put an end to all people, for the earth is filled with violence because of them. I am surely going to destroy both them and the earth.'"

"Wow!" we say. "That's pretty bad if all the people except for Noah and his family had "gone the wrong way, spiritually." Let's hope it never gets to that point again." Well, I hate to tell you, but I believe it's certain to happen. If not well before then, the time of the future depicted in

Revelation 13 seems to indicate that this is the way it will certainly go. Together, verses 3, 4, 8, 11, and 12 of that chapter say this: "One of the heads of the beast seemed to have a fatal wound, but the fatal wound had been healed. The whole world followed the beast. Men worshipped the dragon because he had given authority to the beast, and they also worshipped the beast and asked, 'Who is like the beat? Who can make war against him?'…All inhabitants of the earth will worship the beast— all whose names have not been written in the book of life belonging to the Lamb that was slain from the creation of the world…Then I saw another beast coming out of the earth. He had two horns like a lamb, but he spoke like a dragon. He exercised all the authority of the 1st beast on his behalf, and made the earth and its inhabitants worship the 1st beast, whose fatal wound had been healed."

So where are we now in the middle of all this? Just how much have people regressed in their spiritual health and well-being over the years that would indicate that the world is dangerously close to being in the same shape it was at the time of Noah? In preparation for this message, this morning, I got on the internet and looked up some current crime statistics for the US. Now, whereas it might have been that, in the distant past, most violently criminal offenders were well into their adult years, as of 1993, the most common ages for "multiple assailant offenders" (the crime in question was perpetrated by a gang), were ages twelve to twenty! Kids, children, are committing crimes in gangs/groups. In 1994, there were 1,271 child abuse/neglect fatalities in the US. That works out to a death of a child once every seven hours: 46% of those almost 1,300 children that died that year—almost half—were under the age of one-year-old, 42% of those kids died from neglect, 54% died from outright abuse, and the remaining 4% from both abuse and neglect. And lastly with these statistics, nationally in 1998, 156 wives killed their spouses, and 275 husbands did the same.

How can people allow themselves to do such things? Do they not have a sense of wrong/right? Do they not have a conscience? Well, I think that Oswald Chambers may have been on to something in addressing that question when he once asked a question we all might want to ask ourselves every once in a while: "Am I becoming more and more in love with G as a Holy G, or with the conception of an amiable being who says,

'Oh, well, sin doesn't matter much'?" And see, when we get to that point where we can easily think/say to ourselves that it doesn't matter what I think or how I behave; that's when we begin to set ourselves up for a huge fall. J pointed out that in Noah's day, not only were people thoroughly corrupt, but in being so, they apparently didn't give much thought to the consequence of their thoughts and behaviors. Combining the passages of Matthew 24:36–39 and Luke 17:26–33, J stated in Scripture, "No one knows about that day or hour, not even the angels in Heaven, but only the Father. As it was in the days of Noah, so it will be at the coming of the Son of Man. For in the days before the flood, people were eating and drinking, marrying and being given up in marriage, and they knew nothing about what would happen until the flood came and took them all away. It was the same in the days of Lot. People were eating and drinking, buying and selling, planting and building. But he day Lot left Sodom, fire and sulfur rained down from heaven and destroyed them all.

"It will be just like this on the day the Son of Man is revealed. On the day, no one who is on the roof of his house, with his goods inside, should go down to get them. Likewise, no one in the field should go back for anything. Remember Lot's wife! Whoever tries to save his life will lose it, and whoever loses his life will preserve it."

I believe that with the passage of time, we come to have more and more the perception that there truly isn't anyone alive who can be called "a good person." Scripture demonstrates that fact twice, once in Psalm 14:2–3: "The Lord looks down from heaven on the sons of men to see if there are any who understand, any who seek G. All have turned aside, they have together become corrupt, there is no one who does good, not even one." Then Romans 3:10–12 states, "As it is written: There is no one righteous, no, not even one; there Is no one who understands, no one who seeks after G. All have turned away, they have together become worthless; there is no one who does good, not even one."

But even though we're all tainted with the spiritual stain of sin, we nevertheless ought to totally against the thought of it in our own lives. Calvin Coolidge once turned home from church one Sunday, and since his wife was unable to attend, she wanted to know what the topic of the sermon was. Coolidge's one-word response to her inquiry was simply "sin." She pressed him for a few details, naturally, and being a man of few words with his wife, Coolidge said, "Well, I think he was against it." (I certainly hope so.)

But even though we know that we ought to do everything to avoid getting involved in sin, admit it: that's easier said than done. An overweight man was in the habit of stopping by the bakery on the way to work for goodies to have during the staff coffee break. But when this man went on a diet, the practice stopped with the okay from the rest of the staff. One day, he had to drive past the bakery on a work-related errand. As he neared the bakery, he said to himself, "Maybe G wants me to stop by the bakery and get some donuts for the staff today." So he told the Lord he would stop, but only if G made a parking space open up right in front of the bakery. And sure enough, there is was, a parking space, right in front—on his eighth trip around the block!

The late Pope John Paul II was once quoted as saying, "Man creates culture, and through culture, creates himself." I think that's true. We create the circumstances that society latches onto as a whole, and in doing so, we become identified with the type of culture in which we live. No wonder, then, that after the Great Flood, Genesis 8:21 states, "The Lord said, 'Never again will I curse the ground because of man, even though every inclination of his heart is evil since childhood.'"

You know, it's interesting. I discovered while researching for this sermon that it was usually after the death (or other removal) of a prophet that the Israelites would significantly digress in the strength of their faith. For instance, Moses warned according to Deuteronomy 31:29, "For I know that after my death, you are sure to become utterly corrupt and turn from the way I have commanded you." Likewise, Judges 2:18–19 says, "Whenever the Lord raised up a judge for them, he was with the judge and saved them out of the hands of their enemies as long as the judge lived; for the Lord had compassion on them as they groaned under those who oppressed and afflicted them; but when the judge died, the people returned to ways even more corrupt than those of their fathers, following other gods and serving and worshipping them." That's the truth from Scripture, folks—scary, isn't it?

Many electronic fire alarms have an internal switch triggered by a beam of light. As long as light is received unbroken by the photosensitive receiver, the detector is quiet. But if smoke, moisture, or even an insect should obstruct the beam for a split second, the alarm sounds. Our conscience resembles such an alarm. When sin obstructs our connection with the light of G's Spirit, the conscience signals us that there's life-threatening danger—or, at least it should.

In his book *Fuzzy Memories*, the author Jack Handey writes, "There used to be this bully who would demand my lunch money every day. Since I was smaller, I would give it to him. Eventually though, I decided to fight back. I started taking karate lessons. But then the karate lesson guy said I had to start paying him $5 a lesson. So, I just went back to paying the bully. The lesson from this story? Too many people would rather pay the bully than learn how to defeat him. Too many people today would rather give in to the moral, ethical and spiritual decay we see all around us rather than to figure out how to beat the devil at his own game."

And that's what I think Scripture says will happen in the last days—indeed, what has already well begun to happen in this day and age—according to 1 Timothy 4:1–2: "The Spirit clearly says that in later times some will abandon the faith and follow deceiving spirits and things taught by demons. Such teaching come through hypocritical liars, who consciences have been seared as with a hot iron."

To show you how much some people act as if their consciences have been seared with a hot iron, the story is told of a little girl who was always in the habit of lying. Once when she was given a St. Bernard dog for her birthday, she went out, telling all the neighbors that she had been given a lion. Her mom scolded her, "I told you not to lie! Go to your room and tell G you're sorry. Promise G you will not lie again." The girl went to her room, said her prayers, then came out.

"Did you tell G you were sorry?" her mom asked.

The girl responded, "Yes, I did, and G said sometimes, he finds it hard to tell my dog from a lion, too."

Some people have had their consciences so ruined by constant "soaking in sin" that they even dare to speak lies in the name of G. What has happened is that many people today spend the first six days of each week sowing wild oats; then they go to church on Sunday and pray for a crop failure!

In Max Dupree's book *Leadership is an Art*, Dupree pointed out that the early church fathers and later church reformers came up with two lists known as the seven deadly sins and the seven virtues. The seven deadly sins include pride, envy, anger, sloth, avarice, gluttony, and lust. The virtue list includes wisdom, justice, courage, temperance, faith, hope, and love. Mahatma Gandhi came up with his own list of the seven deadly sins, updating their applications for today: wealth without work, pleasure without conscience, knowledge without character, commerce without morality, science without humanity, worship without sacrifice and politics without principle. Can't we see how much of that list is prevalent today in our world—just as in the days of Noah.

A Russian parable tells of a hunter who raised his rifle and took careful aim at a large black bear. When he was about to pull the trigger, the bear spoke in a soft, soothing voice, "Isn't it better to talk than to shoot? What do you want? Let's try to negotiate this matter."

Lowering his rifle, the hunter replied, "I want a fur coat."

"Good," began the bear, "That's a negotiable situation. I only want a full stomach, so let us negotiate a compromise."

Well, they sat down to negotiate, and after a while, the bear walked away alone. The negotiations had been "successful": the bear had a full stomach, and the hunter "had his fur coat." Compromise is such a nasty concept to the Christians. We should look at things as either right or wrong.

Compromise is simply a recipe for chicken soup. Someone once stated that "if you put a spoonful of wine into a barrel full of sewage, you'll get sewage. If you put a spoonful of sewage into a barrel of wine, you'll get sewage."

Just a little bit a sin allowed to creep into our lives is enough to cause terrible trouble for us. But unfortunately, that's how a lot of contemporary people operate their spiritual lives—just as in the days of Noah.

It's not easy—in these updated days of Noah—to live our lives fully for Jesus. After all, we know from experience that the trouble with opportunity is that it just/only knocks. Temptation kicks the door in! Are trying to live your life more like Noah instead of like the people all around him at the time?

March 22 Lessons from the Gym
Acts 10:34; Ephesians 6:1-4 and 5:22-23; 1 Peter 1:6-9

Ever since I was in college, I've made it a practice to exercise three times a week, if possible. By exercise, I mean not jog or do aerobics, but go to work out in a gym. I presently exercise in the Gilkerson Community Center on Dogwood Avenue in H-burg, using all the different types of weights and weight lifting equipment, and throughout my time since college, in the different places I've lived, I've made use of the various gyms in the neighborhoods in which I've lived. But even though I've "worked out" in numerous physical exercise facilities, there are certain things in common that they all have had, regardless of the types of equipment they've contained.

For one thing, I have found many different types of people, who care to exercise like I do. Exercising, after all, isn't just for one or two types of people. Everybody needs to exercise (just like the fact that there are many different types of people—everybody, really—who need to be in church on a regular basis). Just as everybody should exercise, in some way regularly in order to stay healthy physically, everybody also needs to regularly exercise spiritually in order to stay healthy spiritually. And by exercising spiritually, I'm talking about things like reading/studying the Bible, spending time in prayer, attending church services and other church activities, to name of few examples.

Now, one way in which this inclusiveness of people needing to exercise their souls as well as their bodies is seen in the example of people of various races. A biblical proof text for that statement, then, can be seen in a statement made by Peter, according to Acts 10:34–35, when the Bible says there, Peter began to speak: "I now realize that it's true that G treats all men on the same basis. Whoever fears him and does what is right is acceptable to him, no matter what race he belongs to."

Yes, on one hand, it's true that all races and cultures of people need to keep themselves physically fit. At the Gilkerson Community Center, we have plain white guys like me, but also African Americans, Mexicans, and if I'm not mistaken, several people who look like to me of being from Middle Eastern ancestry. But the same is true of our spiritual health and well-being. Last time I checked, the Bible seems to indicate that J died for all, including people of all nations and racial backgrounds.

Now, a second point to consider is along the lines of a point once made by a man named Edward Bratcher, when he one time stated, "Ministers can't walk on water; but they can learn to swim." In other words, in the physical sense, I've told you that I exercise regularly, and have for years. Yet you can plainly see for yourself that I do not exactly have an Arnold Schwarzenegger-type of body shape. Nope, I'm no Sly Stallone. But hey, at least I'm fairly physically fit. The same thing goes spiritually. We may be the type to study the Bible and pray for a total of two or more hours a day, and yet, we certainly don't feel as spiritual or as holy as we think Billy Graham might feel. But you know, that's okay. God didn't intend for us all to be like Billy Graham. He intended that we reach the responsible spiritual levels of health that fit the people. If you keep yourselves spiritually healthy by taking part in regular daily devotions, attend church and church activities when you can and are daily seeking, finding and doing G's will for your life, then, by and large, you're probably right where to you ought to be, spiritually speaking for yourself, and that's all right.

But now an unfortunate thing about this topic is that just as there are many people who are just plain lazy when it comes to physical exercise, there are those who are just as lazy when it comes to the spiritual kind. And different people use different sorry excuses as to why they can't exercise either way, to defend the laziness. For example, a lady once said, "When the doctor asked what I did for exercise, I said that pushing eighty was exercise enough!" And it's also been said that the only exercise that some people get in this day and age is jumping to conclusions, running down their friends, sidestepping responsibilities, and pushing their luck! But in all seriousness, it's time to stop making excuses, and start putting forth a little effort by making it a priority to exercise our souls, by studying, praying, being active in church, and fulfilling G's purpose and plan for our lives.

Now, beside people of all races and cultures who need to keep in spiritual shape, people of all ages need to do this as well, as Ephesians 6:1–4 points out, when there, the Bible says, "Children, the right thing for you to do is to obey your parents, because G has placed them over you. This is the first of G's 10 Commandments that ends with a promise, and this is the promise: that if you honor your father and mother, your will be a long life, full of blessing. And now, a word to you parents: Don't keep on scolding and nagging your children, making them angry and resentful. Rather, bring them up with the loving discipline and instruction the Lord himself approves."

I've noticed during my time of exercising at the gym that people from junior high schoolers to senior citizens come in to work out, there. Well, just as people of all age ranges need to stay healthy and strong physically by exercising, people (from the time they're able to understand the gospel message as a growing child) to people in their "golden years" who maybe have been in church even for decades, should never stop growing and learning about G and his plan for them.

But no matter what age-range we might be talking about, people of all ages have used all kinds of excuses for not exercising, and one of those pitifully poor reasons for not working out is that "we might hurt ourselves" (said sarcastically). After all, we wouldn't want to wake up all sore and achy in the morning. But spiritual as well as physical exercise demands that we put forth some effort—even if it hurts to some degree. Hey, you get out of something what you put into it. So if we decide that we simply want to play it safe and not risk getting hurt, then, no, we successfully avoid getting hurt, but we'll also not reap the benefits of that kind of exercise, either. As Ignatius Loyola was once quoted as saying, "Teach us, Lord, to serve you as you deserve, to give and not to count the cost, to fight and not to heed the wounds, to toil and not to seek for rest, to labor and not to ask for any reward except that of knowing that we do your will."

No, many people just don't want the possibility of having to suffer any kind of pain, due to serving Christ. Little kids, apparently, can even pick up on that concept, as a friend of Brenda Goodine's found out. Goodine once explained, "My friend decided it was time to talk to her bright four-year-old son, Benji, about receiving Christ."

"Benji," she began to ask softly, "would you like to have J in your heart?"

Benji rolled his eyes and matter-of-factly answered, "No, I don't think I want the responsibility."

Can you imagine a little kid saying something like that?

Well, that's just one example of the many things people will say/do in order to get out of almost anything—whether you're talking about physical or spiritual exercise. For instance, Ruth Graham tells the story of the early days of missionary work in China. The missionaries knew the importance of relaxation and thus built a tennis court out of dirt, to play for fun. On one occasion, a group of Chinese gentlemen came calling in the middle of a game. They first watched with interest, but then with growing concern. As the game drew to a conclusion and the overheated players joined their Chinese friends, they were greeted with genuine sympathy. Being careful as to not offend their American friends, one of the Chinese men spoke up and said, "We were talking among ourselves. Can you Americans not afford to hire someone to hit that ball back and forth for you?" You know, there are people who wouldn't think twice about hiring someone else to do hard physical work for them, which is bad enough. But we also need to understand that we CAN'T possibly get someone else to "do the spiritual growing part for us." It doesn't work that way. Only each of us, ourselves, can reap the benefits of spiritual exercise.

Now, another aspect of this subject of spiritual exercise is that—just as there are both men and women who work out in most gyms I've frequented—both men and women make up necessary parts of the church. The church is not complete without one of them or the other. As Paul wrote in Ephesians 5:22– 33, "Wives, submit yourselves to your husbands, as to the Lord. For a husband has authority over his wife in the same way Christ has authority over the church; and Christ is himself the Savior of the Church, his body. And so wives must submit themselves completely to their husbands, in the same way that the church submits itself to Christ. Husbands, love your wives in the same way that Christ loved the church and gave his life for it. He did this to dedicate the church to G, by his word, after making it clean by the washing in water, in order to present the church to himself in all its beauty, pure and faultless, without spot or wrinkle, or any other imperfection. Men ought to love their wives just as they love their own bodies. A man who loves his wife loves himself. (No one hates his own body. Instead, he feeds it and takes care of it, just as Christ does the church; for we are members of his body). As the Scripture says, 'For this reason, a man will leave his father and mother, and unite with his wife, and the two will become one.' There is a great truth revealed in this Scripture, and I understand it applies to Christ and the Church. But it also applies to you: every husband must love his wife as himself, and every wife must respect her husband."

Yes, both genders on earth have value and importance in the roles they play in their place in the world. So it's important to include both men and women in various discipleship programs in the church, so they can both contribute to the church's growth.

"What are you planning to do about that excess weight you're carrying around?" the doc asked his patient.

"I just can't seem to lose the weight," the patient began to respond.

"I guess I must have an overactive thyroid."

"The tests show your thyroid is perfectly okay," the doctor stated.

"If anything is overactive, it's your fork!"

Face it; it's possible to get the wrong kind of exercise—one that does us more harm than good. But one the other hand, it's certainly possible that we can grow strong, spiritually, when we apply the right kind of discipleship to our spiritual walk, since it's been said that the church is the only hospital where you can go in as a patient and come out as a doctor.

But just because it's true that we can grow into strong and solid witnesses for J, we need to realize that to do so requires much time and effort, much like it does for building our bodies up in a gym workout. No one becomes an Arnold Schwarzenegger overnight, and they don't become a Billy Graham overnight, either. In the book *First Things First*, Roger Merrill tells of a business consultant who decided to landscape his grounds. He hired a woman with a doctorate in horticulture who was extremely knowledgeable. Because the business consultant was very busy and traveled a lot, he kept emphasizing to her the need to create his garden in a way that would require little or no maintenance on his part. He insisted on automatic sprinklers and other laborsaving devices.

She eventually looked at him and declared, "Look, there's on thing you need to deal with before we go any further. If there's no gardener, there's no garden!" There are no labor-saving devices, folks, for growing a garden of spiritual virtue. Becoming a person of spiritual fruitfulness requires time, attention, and care. In full agreement, then, with this point Roger Merrill made in that book, a man named Doug Rumford was once quoted as saying, "Full grown oaks are not produced in three years; neither are servants of G." And although we Christians understand that we're not saved by our good works, we also know that once we are saved, to finish the race of life as G would want us to requires that we do put forth quite an effort, as Tom Landry explained when he once said, "The job of a football coach is to make men do what they won't want to do, in order to achieve what they've always wanted to be." Just as we might not always want to go to the gym to do our daily workout routine, we might not always want to show up at church so often. But if we want to get something worthwhile out of our spiritual as well as physical health, we need to put forth some extra effort.

Unfortunately, it's possible to be a follower of J without being a disciple; to be a camp follower without being a soldier of the king; to be a hanger-on in some great work without pulling one's weight. In his book The Gospel of Luke, Will Barclay related that someone was once talking with a great scholar about a young man. The first man said to the teacher, "So and so tells me that he was one of your students."

The teacher then retorted, "He may have attended my lectures, but he was not one of my students."

You see, there's a world of diff between attending lectures and being a student. It's one of the supreme handicaps of the Church that in the Church, there are so many distant followers of J and so few real disciples.

Yes, we can spend all kinds of time in the gym, working out, and after just a little while later, wonder whether it's doing us any good at all. But eventually, if we don't quite our exercise routine, we clearly see the benefits of having kept ourselves in shape. The same thing holds true in the spiritual sense, as 1 Peter 1:6–9 explains: "Be glad about this, even though it may now be necessary for you to be sad for a while because of the many kinds of trials you suffer. Their purpose is to prove that your faith is genuine. Even gold, which can be destroyed, is tested by fire; and so your faith, which is much more precious than gold, must also be tested, that it may endure. Then you will receive praise and glory and honor on the Day when JC is revealed. You love him, although you have not seen him. You believe in him, although you do not see him now. And so you rejoice with a great and glorious joy, which words can't express, because you are receiving the purpose of your faith, the salvation of your souls."

Now admittedly, some people need to exercise more than others. When a lady was once signing up for exercise classes, the instructor told her to be sure to wear loose clothing to class. She then responded by saying, "Look, buddy, if I had any loose clothing, I wouldn't need this class." We all have our phases in life where we're a little less spiritually unfit than at other times. So there may be points in our lifetimes where we need to spend more time involved in being discipled than others.

So let's never stop growing in J, thinking that we've reached the top level of spiritual growth and that we don't need to grow anymore. That simply doesn't happen. If you think yourself green, you will grow. But if you think yourself ripe, you will rot. For instance, a lady named Jana Jones once recalled, "During each day, I take a few minutes to read my Bible. After having once witnessed me doing this for several weeks in a row, my four-year-old granddaughter became concerned and asked me, 'Aren't you ever going to get finished reading that book, Granny?'"

October 18 Refuting Some Lies about Our Faith
John 9:24-25; Acts 1:1-9

A university alumnus, shown a list of examinations questions by his old economics professor, exclaimed, "Why, those are the exact same questions you asked when I was in school twenty years ago!"

"Yes," said the professor, "we ask the same questions every year."

The former student asked, "But surely you know that the students pass along those questions from one year to the next."

"Of course," the professor began to reply, "but in economics, we change the answers."

Well, considering the economic climate of today, I'm not surprised that "those in the know" have changed some of the economic answers, and in doing so, have helped lead us to the financial state our country is in at the moment. But as Flannery O'Conner once put it, "The truth doesn't change with our ability to stomach it" (two times). In other words, just because we may not like to hear a certain piece of truth and the message it contains for us, that doesn't mean that we can dismiss it or choose to twist and distort that piece of truth in order to discourage ourselves and others from accepting it. Unfortunately, that's the kind of thing that people do with biblical truth all the time.

So what are we supposed to do when people try to tell us that Christianity is not worth following and trusting in, especially since 2 Corinthians 5:7 reminds us, "We walk by faith, and not by sight?" Well, one thing we can do is to combat that falsehood by exhibiting the truth in us—to share our verbal testimony and life example with others. That's really the best strategy we could use to do battle with lies being spread about our faith. What we should do, then, is to respond to lies about Christianity like the blind man J healed responded, in John 9:13–25, when the Bible says there, "Then, they took the man to the Pharisees. Now, as it happened, this all happened on a Sabbath. Then, the Pharisees asked him all about it. So he told them how J had smoothed the mud over his eyes, and when it was all washed away, he could see!

"Some of them said, 'But how could an ordinary sinner do such miracles?' So there was a deep division of opinion among them.

"Then, the Pharisees turned on the man who had been blind and demanded, 'This man who opened your eyes—who do you say he is?'

"'I think he must be a prophet sent from G,' the man replied.

"The Jewish leaders wouldn't believe he had been blind, until they called in his parents and asked them, 'Is this your son? Was he born blind? If so, how can he see?'

"His parents replied, 'We know this is our son and that he was born blind, but we don't know what happened to make him see or who did it. He's old enough to speak for himself—you ask him.' They said this in fear of the Jewish leaders who had announced that anyone saying J was the Messiah would be excommunicated.

"So for the 2nd time, they called to the man who had been blind and told him, 'Give the Glory to G, not to this man, for we know he is a sinner. 'I don't know whether He's a sinner or not,' the man began to reply, 'But I do know this: I was blind, but now I can see.'"

You see, the first myth about Christianity that we might want to refute, today, is that, supposedly, Christianity is based on blind faith. But we Christians don't believe in something that has no factual basis. What we believe to be true has been proven true. Acts 1:3, for example, explains that J showed himself to numerous people after his death, and gave ample proof that he was alive; over a period of forty days, he appeared to them.

Now, to be fair to some, people sometimes pass on mistruths and lies about Christianity to others simply because they don't know any better. They may not be intentionally trying to distort the faith, but just simply mistaken, based on what they've been told about the faith by others. And admittedly, sometimes mistakes can have comical consequences, and not much more than that. For instance, Evangelist Jack Van Impe was once closing a citywide crusade in Green Bay, Wisconsin, and it was to end on a Sunday afternoon. The very same public arena also featured wrestling, regularly, on Sunday nights. Interestingly, on very next day (Monday evening), Rex Humbard was scheduled to begin a new series of evangelistic meetings. One wonders if the man who set up the marquis in front of the arena didn't have his tongue in his cheek when he arranged the letters on the sign to read, "Jack Van Impe— Wrestling—Rex Humbard."

However, there are those times, where, if we should get our information just a little bit wrong, it can be enough to make a serious difference—and a dangerous one at that. For example, an error in a chemical formula can be lethal. In fact, to remind science students of that fact, there's a little jingle that's sung in some high school chemistry classes, and it goes like this: "Say a prayer for Jimmy Brown, for Jimmy is no more. What he thought was $H2O$, was really $H2O$," Now, $H2O$, of course, is the chemical name for water. But I had no idea what $H2SO4$ was, so I called the chemistry department for JMU and asked…it's a type deadly poison. You see, just a few letters/numbers can make a tremendous difference in science, and the same is no less true in Christian theology.

So after the falsehood that Christianity is based on "blind faith," the next misnomer about Christianity we'll look at today is the infamous one that "people get to Heaven based on how good they are." That may sound like a great thing to believe in, but the Living Bible explains to us that that's not the case, in Romans 3:20, when it says there, "No one can ever be made right in G's sight by doing what the Law commands, for the more we know of G's laws, the clearer it becomes that we aren't obeying them. His laws serve only to make us see that we are sinners." Likewise, the Phillips Modern English Bible relates to us in Ephesians 2: 8–9, "For it is by grace that you have been save, through faith. This does not depend on anything you have achieved, it is the free gift of G, and because it is not earned, no man can boast about it."

Now, stop and think for a moment how many people you've met who are under the impression that we're saved by being good. So many people believe that lie. Well, that is unfortunate, but at least that truth that we're saved by faith through G's grace doesn't change. That will always remain the same as it's ever been. As Will Rogers once noted, "Rumor travels faster, but it don't stay put as long as truth."

Okay, so another big error people make it summing up major parts of the faith is once you're saved, it doesn't matter what you do in life. If you're saved, you can do anything you want and it doesn't matter to G. Well, I think Scripture would beg to differ. Here's what the Bible would have to say on that subject, according to Romans 6:1–2 and 1

Corinthians 10:23–24: "Now what is our response to be? Shall we sin to our heart's content and see how far we can exploit the grace of G? What a terrible thought! We, who have died to sin —how could we live in sin a moment longer?…We are allowed to do anything,' so they say. Yes, but not everything is good. We are allowed to do anything, but not everything is helpful. No one should be looking out for his own interests, but for the interests of others."

The fact that many people get the gospel all mixed up is why it's so important for those of us in the church to "get it right," so that there will be no misunderstanding when we witness to people. As we're discovering here today, the things that go in one ear and out the other don't hurt nearly as much as the things that go in one ear, get all mixed up, and then come out the mouth.

Well, one of the biggest and most prevalent errors about Christianity is that there's more than one way to get to Heaven, and Christianity is simply just one of those many ways. Another way people might phrase that same idea is "It doesn't matter what you believe, as long as you're sincere." Gee, I think Bible would take issue with that, since J plainly said in John 14:6, "I am the Way, the Truth and the Life, and no one comes to the Father except through Me." Add to that verse the passages found in Acts 4:12 ("Salvation is found in no one else, for there's no other name under Heaven, given to us, by which we must be saved") and 1 Timothy 2:5 ("There is one God, and there is one mediator between G and man, the man JC"), and I think you'd agree the Bible is making it clear that faith in Christ is the *only* way to be saved.

Now, some lies and falsehoods are really easy to detect. To illustrate that point, there's the story of a little boy who one day shouted to his mother, "Look, there's a bear in our yard!"

His mother looked out and said, "That's not a bear. It's our neighbor's dog. Now go to your room and ask G to forgive you for telling a lie." The boy went to his room and later came back downstairs. His mother asked, "Did you ask G to forgive you?"

The boy then said, "Yes, and G said it was all right. He said the first time he saw our neighbor's dog, he thought it was a bear, too."

Yes, it would be helpful if all lies about Christianity were as easy to detect as *that* one, but that's just not the case. One such lie that a lot

181

of people fall for is the statement that the Bible has been changed and altered over the years by various groups or individuals with their own agenda. But the Bible itself lets us know that we can be assured that what's contained in the record of Scripture is supposed to be there, and that there's nothing in the Bible that shouldn't be. After all, the Bible states, in Matthew 5:18, John 10:35, 2 Timothy 2:8–9, and Hebrews 4:12, "As long as heaven and earth last, the least point or the smallest detail of the Law will not be done away with—not until the end of all things... We know that what the Scripture says is true forever...But they cannot chain up the word of G...For the word that G speaks is alive and active; it cuts more keenly than any two-edged sword; it strikes through to the place where soul and spirit meet, to the inner most intimacies of a man's being; it examines the very thoughts and motives of a man's heart."

Edward R. Murrow once said of the topic of honesty: "To be persuasive, we must be believable. To be believable, we must be credible. To be credible, we must be truthful." Yes, despite what some people may say, I think the Bible is tough enough to defend itself against being tampered with.

A. W. Tozer once stated, "The untended garden will soon be overrun with weeds; the heart that fails to cultivate truth and root out error will shortly be a theological wilderness." That's why it's important for us, everybody, to take this lies about Christianity seriously. We'll never be able to totally suppress them and keep them from spreading to those who don't know any better, but we can at least do what we can to see as little damage is done as possible.

So as we get to excuses that more and more people use in order to not believe in the Christian faith—excuses which, remember, are based on misunderstandings and lies—we come to the one that states that the G of the Bible is mean, cruel, vicious, and hateful. "Just look at the Bible," they say. "G had the Israelites kill many people without any mercy. Why would I want to follow a god like that?" Sure, there are portions of Scripture where G shows his stern side that demands that justice is to be done. But to those who reject the Faith based on that argument, we ought to remind them of passages from the Bible such as 1 John 4:7–12 and 16 (Phillips Modern English) and Romans 5:8–9 (PME): "To you whom I love I say, let us go on loving one another, for love comes from G. Every man who truly loves is G's son and knows him. But the man who does not love cannot know him at all, for G is love. To us, the greatest demonstration of G's love for us has been his sending his only Son into the world to give us life through him. We see real love, not in the fact that we loved G, but that he loved us and sent his Son to make personal atonement for our sins. If G loved us as much as that, surely we, in our turn, should love each other!"

Now, I ask you—does that seem like a G who is mean, cruel, vicious, and hateful?

Stanford Research Institute was studying the differences in vocation perceptions. They devised a short but succinct test. The first to be tested was an engineer. The researchers asked him, "What does two plus two make?"

The engineer said, "In absolute terms: four."

The researchers made their notes and dismissed him. They called in an architect. They asked him the same question, and he said, "Well, there are several possibilities: two and two make four, but so do three and one, or two and a half and one and a half—they also make four. So it is all a matter of choosing the right option."

The researchers thanked him and made their notes. The last of the three to come in was an attorney. They said to him, "What does two and two make?"

The attorney looked around as if to make sure that nobody else was listening, closed the door for privacy, leaned toward them, and asked, "Well, tell me, what would you like it to be?"

You see, the truth doesn't change just because it doesn't suit our purposes and we'd like it to be adjustable.

Finally, one last lie that many unfortunately believe about Christianity is that our faith is narrow-minded and too exclusive. It's perceived by some that only certain people are let into the "exclusive church club." But you know what? The Christian church is open to everyone. There are no limitations or restrictions on who can become a Christian. Remember, the Bible reassures us in Romans 2:11 that "God does not show favoritism," reiterating that very truth in Acts 10:34–35, when it says, "Peter said, 'I know realize it is true that G treats all men on the same basis. Whoever fears him and does what is right is acceptable to him, no matter what race he belongs to.'" And Titus 2:11 fully agrees with the idea, when it states, "For the free gift of eternal salvation is now being offered to everyone." Now I ask you, after hearing those passages, does it sound like Christianity is some kind of exclusive club to you?

Yes, we Christians really have to be careful to accurately and precisely share the gospel with others so that there are no mistakes. Otherwise, it could mean trouble in a lot of ways. For instance, the *LA Times* recently printed a sampling of signs from around the world that attempted to communicate in English. A Paris hotel elevator: "Please leave your values at the front desk." Russian newspaper announcement: "There will be an exhibition of arts by fifteen thousand Soviet painters and sculptors. These were executed over the past two years." And a Bucharest hotel lobby: "The lift is being fixed for the next day. During that time, we regret that you will be unbearable."

Winston Church once was quoted as saying: "The great thing is to get the true picture, whatever it is." Let's make sure we have the true picture of our faith.

When There's Little to Be Thankful For
Habakkuk 3:17-19; Joel 1:10-12; Amos 5:16

It was Thanksgiving season at the nursing home. The small resident population were gathered about their humble Thanksgiving table, and the director of the facility asked each one in turn to express one thing for which they were thankful. Thanks were then given for typical things— food to eat, a house to live in, loving family, etc. But then, one little old lady took her turn by saying, "I thank the Lord for two perfectly good teeth, one in my upper jaw, and one in my lower jaw, that match so that I can chew my food."

Now, it obviously doesn't sound much like this lady had much to give thanks for—especially when it came to the matter of oral health. But you know what? At least she was thankful for what little she did have, no matter how little it was. Hearing that story, then, reminds me of a couple of passages of Scripture —Joel 1:10–12 and Amos 5:16–17 specifically, when the Bible points out together in those passages, "The fields are ruined, the ground is dried up; the grain is destroyed, the new wine is dried up, the oil fails. Despair, you farmer, wail you vine growers; grieve for the wheat and the barely, because the harvest of the field is destroyed. The vine is dried up and the fig tree is withered; the pomegranate, the palm and the apple tree—all the trees of the field are dried up. Surely, the joy of mankind is withered away...Therefore, this is what the Lord, the Lord G Almighty, says: 'There will be wailing in all the streets and cried of anguish in every public square. The farmers will be summoned to weep and the mourners to wail. There will be wailing in all the vineyards, for I will pass through your midst,' says the Lord."

But then, even though we, today in 2008, can relate personally to a lot of what those verses share with us, since the entire world at this point in history is going through a financial recession and food famine, and our own country is constantly facing job layoffs and cut-backs, listen to what the similar passage in Habakkuk 3:17–19 has to say: "Though the fig tree does not bud and there are no grapes on the vines, though the olive crop fails and the fields produce no food, though there are no sheep in the pen and no cattle in the stalls, yet, I will rejoice in the Lord, I will be joyful in G my Savior. The Sovereign Lord is my strength; he makes my feet like the feet of a deer, he enables me to go on the heights." So, you see, even when things seem their darkest, it's more than possible to have a spirit of thankfulness to G.

One thing, however, is that many people today, who've suffered due to the present worldwide economic crisis, might look at their neighbor, who, unlike themselves, hasn't experienced a job loss or gone through having their home foreclosed on them. We need to understand that even people who seem to have escaped experiencing such tragedy have their own difficulties to deal with and survive. In connection with that, there's the story of a man who looked like he lived life on top of all circumstances. He never seemed to have a down day. He went to work and came home happy. People around him wondered what his secret was.

One, day, however, a friend of his discovered that the man was faking it. The friend confronted the man and exclaimed, "Now I know why you're always so cheery. You've really got it made! Just yesterday afternoon I was riding a taxi when I passed you. You were sitting there listening intently to this beautiful young woman whose back was to the street, and you were enjoying a snack in a lovely sidewalk café."

"Well," the man began to whisper back in response, "let me tell you the truth. That lovely young woman is my wife who was telling me she was leaving me, and that was our furniture on the sidewalk." No, things aren't always what they seem—sometimes, they're a lot worse.

Now, I don't want to suggest that every time someone suffers a significant loss of material blessings and personal finances that it's always "because they deserve it," and that G is punishing them for some specific sins of theirs. But the Bible does indicate, at times, that people often reap what they sow when it comes to dealing less than honorably with material things. For instance, the Bible states in Isaiah 17:10–11, "You have forgotten G your Savior; you have not remembered the Rock, your fortress. Therefore, though you set out the finest plants and plant imported vines, though on the day you set them out, you make them grow, and on the morning when you plant them, you bring them to bud, yet the harvest will be as nothing in the day of disease and uncurable pain."

A farmer once had a cow that gave birth to twin calves. That afternoon at the supper table he was just delighted when he was able to tell his wife, "Ol' bossy had twins today. You know, honey, we're gonna give one of those calves to the Lord and we're gonna keep one for ourselves. That's the way it ought to be." A couple of days later, he was rather quiet and solemn, and she asked what was wrong.

He answered by saying, "Well, honey, I walked into the barn just a few minutes ago, and I found that the Lord's calf had died."

You know, I'm convinced that it's because America, as a whole, has strayed from faith in G so much, that, over time, we've suffered a great loss of the many things He's blessed us with. But for those who seem to think that the US doesn't have anything to worry about, that everything will naturally and automatically be just fine, they need to take a look at verses like Isaiah 16:6–13: "We have heard of Moab's pride—her overwhelming pride and conceit, her pride and insolence—but her boasts are empty. Therefore, the Moabites wail, they wail together for Moab. Lament and grieve for the men of Kir Hareseth; The fields of Heshbon whither, the vines of Sibmah also. The rulers of the nations have trampled down the choicest vines, which once reached Jazer and spread toward the desert. Their shoots spread out and went as far as the sea. So I weep, as Jazer weeps, for the vines if Sibmah. O Heshbon, O Elealeh, I drench you with tears! The shouts of joy over your ripened fruit and over your harvests have been stilled. Joy and gladness are taken away from the orchards; no one sings or shouts in the vineyards; no one treads out wine at the presses, for I have put an end to the shouting. My heart laments for Moab like a harp, my inmost being for Kir Hareseth. When Moab appears at her high place, she only wears herself out; when she goes to her shrine to pray, it is to no avail. This is the word the Lord has already spoken concerning Moab. But now, the Lord says: "Within three years, as a servant bound by contract would count them, Moab's splendor and all her many people will be despised, and her survivors will be very few and feeble."

The thing to do, then, is to be thankful for *whatever* it is that G has given us, no matter how little it might be, or seem. After all, the Bible says in 1 Timothy 6:7–8, "What did we bring into the world when we were born? Nothing! What can we take out of the world when we die? Nothing! So, if we have food and clothes, that will be enough for us."

You know, considering the alternative to a particular situation has a way of helping a person's perspective. An example of that is seen in the instance of a fellow who had a heavy pack of worries, cares and responsibilities of life on his back as he trudged along on his journey. The road seemed rougher and rougher, and the pack seemed to get heavier and heavier. Finally, he just dropped down and said out loud, "I'm ready to die!"

Suddenly, the grim reaper appeared and said, "Did you call for me?"

Rising up quickly from his kneeling position, the man said, "Yeah, can you help lift this pack onto my back so I can continue walking?"

Yes, things could probably be a lot worse. After all, there could be any number of things other than our monetary resources that could pose a concern to us at this point. Rick Majerus, men's basketball coach at the University of Utah, recently captured some common concerns when he said, "Everyone's worried about the economy this year. Hey, my hairline is in recession, my waistline is in inflation, and altogether, I'm in depression."

Now, to continue to reap lessons along these lines from the world of sports, it's been pointed out that no professional football team that plays its home games in a domed stadium with artificial turf has ever won the Superbowl. Yes, while it is true that a climate-controlled stadium protects players and fans from the misery of sleet, snow, mud, heat, and wind, players who brave the elements on a regular basis are disciplined enough to handle hardship wherever it's found. Now, the Green Bay Packers were the 1996 Super Bowl champions, in part, because of the discipline gained from regularly playing in some of the worst weather in the country. That fact, then, reminds us of the truth mentioned in the Bible, specifically in Hebrews 12:7 and 11, "Let G train you, for he is doing what any loving father does for his children. Whoever heard of a son who was never corrected?…Of course, any punishment is most painful at the time, and far from pleasant; but later, in those on whom it has been used, it bears fruit in peace and goodness."

Yes, I will fully agree that sometimes, we find ourselves having to go through a heck of a lot of "messy stuff," in life. Either something happens to us beyond our control that we'd really rather not have to deal with (something very unpleasant) or it's a case where maybe God has called on us to do something for him, something that we're not exactly crazy about and wouldn't have chosen to do on our own, for various reasons. But you know, sometimes, when we allow ourselves to go through those periods, we come to a point where we actually reap a blessing from having to go through "all that stuff." Case in point comes from the March 1995 instance, where the New England Pipe Cleaning Company of Watertown, Connecticut, was digging away, twenty-five feet beneath the streets of Revere, Massachusetts, in order to clean a clogged ten-inch sewer line. Yuck! Well, in addition to the usual materials one might expect to find in a clogged sewer line, the three-man team found sixty-one rings, vintage coins, eyeglasses, and silverware, all of which they were allowed to keep. So whether it's pipes, people, or some other rather difficult experience in life, if we are able to put up with some mess, we just might be able to discover some real treasure for ourselves.

But we also need to realize, this morning, that if we happen to be out of a right relationship with G (and that's maybe at least part of the reason for our suffering) then if we turn back to him, G will bless us and begin to take care of the evils that have been visiting us. Such a promise is made by G himself to the people, according to Haggai 2:15–19: "Now give careful thought to this from this day on—consider how things were before one stone was laid on another in the Lord's temple. When anyone came to a heap of 20 measures, there were only 10. When anyone went to a wine vat to draw 50 measures, there were only 20. I struck all the work of your hands with blight, mildew and hail, yet you did not turn to me,' declares the Lord. For this day on, from this 24th day of the 9th month, give careful thought to the day when the foundation of the Lord's temple was laid. Give careful thought: Is there yet any seed left in the barn? Until now, the vine and the fig tree, the pomegranate and the olive tree have not borne fruit. From this day on, I will bless you."

The following came to me in an e-mail from Lisa Lloyd, and it's entitled "I Am Thankful": "I am thankful for the wife who says, "It's hot dogs, tonight," because she's home with me and not out with someone else; for the husband who is on the sofa being a couch potato, because he's home with me and not out at the bars; for the teenager who is complaining about doing the dishes, because it means he/she is at home and not out on the streets; for the taxes I pay, because it means that I'm employed; for the mess to clean up after the party, because it means that I have been surrounded by friends; for the clothes that fit a little too snug, because it means I have enough to eat; for the lawn that needs mowing, the gutter that needs cleaning and windows that need washing, because it means I have a home; for all the complaining I hear about the government, because it means we have freedom of speech; for the parking spot I find at the far end of the lot, because means that I am capable of walking and have been blessed with transportation; for my huge heating bill, because it means I'm warm; for the lady behind me in church who sings off key, because it means I can hear; for the pile of laundry and ironing I have, because it means I have clothes to wear; for weariness and aching of muscles at the end of the day, because it means I've been capable of hard work; for the alarm that goes off in the early morning hours, because it means that I'm alive; and I am thankful for the CRAZY people I work with, because they make life fun and interesting! The key, then, is to be satisfied with whatever level of material blessings and comforts we have to call our own."

As Philippians 4:11 and 1 Thessalonians 5:18 together say, "I have learned to be content, whatever the circumstances may be…no matter what happens, always be thankful, for this is G's will for you who belong to Christ Jesus."

The story is told of two men, walking through a field one day, who spotted an enraged bull, up ahead of them. Instantly, they darted toward the nearest fence. The storming bull followed in hot pursuit, and it was soon apparent they would not make escape.

Terrified, the one shouted to the other, "Say a prayer for us, John. We're in for it."

John answered, "I can't. I've never made a public prayer in my life."

"But you have to," implored his companion. "It's catching up to us."

"All right," panted John. "I'll say the only prayer I know, the one my father used to repeat at the table: 'O Lord, for what we're about to receive, make us truly thankful!'"

That story reminds us of a valuable truth: no matter how severe the trial, Christians ought to give thanks in everything.

March 15 Me and My Big Mouth
James 3:1-12; Matthew 12:36-37

You know, whenever someone is dealing with the issue of talking and the many types of words that often come falling out of our mouths, they just might want to stop and consider the whale for just a second. After all, it's whenever the whale spouts off that he takes the chance on getting harpooned. Possibly that's why James 3:1–12 says: "My brothers, not many of you should become teachers, for you may be certain that we who teach shall ourselves be judged with greater strictness than others. All of us often go wrong. The man who never says a wrong thing is a perfect character, able to bridle his whole being. If we put bits into horses' mouths to make them obey our will, we can direct their whole body. Or think of ships: no matter who big they are, even if a gale is driving them, the man at the helm can steer them anywhere he likes by controlling a tiny rudder. The human tongue is physically small, but what tremendous effects it can boast of! Think how small a flame can set fire to a huge forest; the tongue is a flame like that. Among all the parts of the body, the tongue is a whole wicked world in itself; it infects the whole body; catching fire itself from hell, it sets fire to the whole wheel of creation.

"Wild animals and birds, reptiles and fish can all be tamed by man, and often are; but nobody can tame the tongue—it is a restless evil, full of deadly poison. With it, we praise our Lord and Father and with it, we curse men, who have been made in G's likeness. Out of the same mouth come praise and cursing. My bros, this should not be. Can both fresh water and salt water flow from the same spring? My bros, can a fig tree bear olives, or a grapevine bear figs? Neither can a salt spring produce fresh water."

So according to this Bible passage, the words we speak can either have a positive or negative effect, and either way, the resulting effect can be powerful. Maybe this is why J is recorded as having said in Matthew 12:36–37, "But I tell you that men will have to give account on the Day of Judgment for every careless word they have spoken. For by your words, you will be acquitted, and by your words, you will be condemned." And when we do talk excessively, the Bible would thus indicate that we're setting ourselves up to sin, maybe more than we originally planned, since Proverbs 10:19 proclaims, "When words are many, sin is not absent, but he who holds his tongue is wise."

Well, speaking of Proverbs 10:14, 12:23, and 18:6–7, the Bible goes on to indicate in the book that when we do talk a bit too much, we not only get ourselves into trouble, but we also many times end up playing the part of a fool, in the process: "Wise men store up knowledge, but the mouth of a fool invites ruin…A prudent man keeps his knowledge to himself, but the heart of fools blurts out folly…a fool's lips bring him strife, and his mouth invites a beating. A fool's mouth is his undoing, and his lips are a snare to his soul."

Now, one way in which our mouths and words get us into so much trouble occurs when we find our anger getting the best of us. I think that's what a man named Lawrence J. Peter might have been getting at when he was once quoted as saying, "Speak when you're angry, and you'll make the best speech you'll ever regret." The fact that excessive anger and too many spoken words don't make for a great combination, then, is also why Francois de la Rochefoucauld once said, "90% of the friction of daily life is caused by the wrong tone of voice."

So what's a good strategy or technique to use to help keep us from saying too much—in anger or in any other mood? Well, one way to look at it is to realize that most of the time, when we are less than careful with the words that come out of our mouths, they come back to bite us—and I am talking about our words, and not our mouths when I say that. Yes, we often pay dearly for having stated our feelings carelessly, as Psalms 140:9 and 64:8, Proverbs 12:13, and Ecclesiastes 10:12 indicate when the Bible says in those passages, "Let the heads of those who surround me be covered with the trouble their lips have caused…He will turn their tongues against them and bring them to ruin…An evil man is trapped by his sinful talk, but a righteous man escapes trouble… Words from a wise man's mouth are gracious, but a fool is consumed by his own lips."

Yeah, it can be kind of embarrassing when we say things we shouldn't and then we reap what we've sown. As Adlai Stevenson once put it, "Man doesn't live by words alone, despite the fact that sometimes, he has to eat them." But remember, everybody, what our passage for today from James indicates: that both good and bad arise from our mouths.

For instance, in his book *The Behavior of Belief*, the author Spiros Zodhiates writes, "The ancient philosopher, Xanthus, once told his servant that the next day, he was going to have some friends for dinner, and that he should get the best thing he could find at the market. The philosopher and his guests sat down the next day at the table, and they ended up having nothing but tongue (4 or 5 courses of it)—tongue cooked one way, then another. The philosopher eventually lost his patience and said to the servant, "Didn't I tell you to get the BEST thing in the market?"

The servant replied, "I did get the best thing in the market. Isn't the tongue the organ of sociability, the organ of eloquence, the organ of kindness, and the organ of worship?"

Well, for whatever reason, after dinner, the philosopher requested of his servant, "Tomorrow, I want you to get me the worst thing in the market." (Maybe he thought they'd wind up getting something pleasantly different, I don't know.) Anyway, the next day, the philosopher and his friends sit down at the table at meal time, and once again, there was nothing but tongue—four or five courses of it, like the previous time— tongue prepared in different ways, in different shapes and styles.

Well, once more, the philosopher lost his patience and yelled at his servant, "Didn't I tell you to get the worst thing in the market?"

The servant then replied, "I did. Isn't the tongue the organ of blasphemy, the organ of defamation, the organ of lying?"

So Proverbs 14:3 then is shown to be extremely accurate in describing the dichotomy of effects the tongue can have when the Bible states there, "The talk of fools is a rod for their backs, but the words of the wise keep them out of trouble."

You see, even when we're talking about verbally sharing the gospel with someone, we really should try to keep our words to a minimum, to help the person we're witnessing to from getting confused or bored with what we're saying. As the famed preacher Charles Spurgeon once pointed out, "If you ask me how you may shorten your sermons, I should say, study them better. Spend more time in the study that you may need less time in the pulpit. We are generally longest when we have the least to say."

Well, not only should we be concise, when we witness to and interact with others, but we also need to be tactful, as well. In his book *How to Win Customers and Keep Them for Life*, Michael LeBoeuf tells of a man who lacked tact. He was the type of person who just couldn't say it graciously. He and his wife owned a poodle. They loved this dog and it was the object of their affection. His wife was, one time, to take a trip abroad, and the first day away, she made it to NYC.

She called home and asked her husband, "How are things?"

He said, "The dog died!"

She was devastated. After collecting her thoughts, she asked, "Why do you do that? Why can't you be more tactful?" He answered, "Well, what do you want me to say? The dog died." She countered, "Well, you can give the news to me in stages. For example, you could say, 'The dog is on the roof.' And then when I travel to London the next day and call you, you could say, 'Honey, the dog fell off of the roof.' And when I call you from Paris, you could add, 'Honey, the dog had to be taken to the vet. In fact, he's in the hospital and not doing well.' And finally, when I call you from Rome, you could say, 'Honey, brace yourself. The dog died.' I could handle that."

Her husband paused and said, "Oh, okay."

Then she inquired, "So, how's my mom doing?"

The husband then replied, "Well, she's on the roof."

Honestly, everybody, nobody we witness to wants to be beaten over the head with the gospel. Although we don't necessarily disguise our message, we may need to go gently with it to the unsaved people around us so they can be receptive to it rather than offended by it.

All this is to say that maybe it's a good idea, then, to take the advice found in Psalms 141:3 and 39:1, when the Bible says, "Take control of what I say, Lord, and keep my lips sealed...I said to myself, 'I will watch what I do and not sin in what I say. I will curb my tongue when ungodly people are around me."

But unfortunately, when it comes to things like gossip, there's a saying that all too many people hold to, which unashamedly says, "Some secrets are worth keeping and others are too good to keep."

But as a man named Elbert Hubbard so wisely once pointed out, "Discretion is leaving a few things unsaid."

And it's also very likely how William Norris came up with the brief but helpful poem that says, "If your lips would keep form slips / Five things observe with care / to whom you speak; of whom you speak; and how, and when, and where."

Still, the Bible continues to be full of advice and wisdom in assorted topics when it comes to the things we say. For example, Proverbs 18:21 lets us know that there's often a price to pay for being loose with our tongue, when the Scripture states there, "Those who love to talk will experience the consequences, for the tongue can kill or nourish life."

James 1:26 speaks to the Christians who might tend to think a little too highly of their spiritual healthiness, when it says, "If you claim to be religious, but don't control your tongue, you are just fooling yourself, and your religion is worthless."

1 Peter 3:10, though, speaks with a tone that's a little more encouraging than convicting, when the Bible reads, "If you want a happy life and good days, keep your tongue from speaking evil, and keep your lips from telling lies."

And a chapter later, 1 Peter 4:11 instructs us to speak for G. Now, that's an awesome thought—to realize that when we open our mouth to talk, we shouldn't do so flippantly but as though G was using us as his mouthpiece. It's there, then, that we read in Scripture, "Are you called to be a speaker? Then, speak as though G himself were speaking through you."

And yet, another lesson we can get out of all this, today, concerns how we verbally witness to people about J. A nine-year-old boy, Danny, came bursting out of SS like a wild stallion. His eyes were darting in every direction as he tried to locate either his mom or dad. Finally, after a quick search, he grabbed his daddy by the leg and yelled, "Man, that story of Moses and all those people crossing the Red Sea was great!" His father looked down, smiled, and asked the boy to tell him all about it.

"Well, the Israelites got out of Egypt, but Pharaoh and his army chased after them. So the Jews ran as fast as they could until they got to the Red Sea. The Egyptian army was getting closer and closer. So Moses got on his walkie-talkie and told the Israeli air force to bomb the Egyptians. While that was happening, the Israeli navy built a pontoon bridge so the people could cross over. And so, they made it across!"

As you can imagine, by now, Dad was shocked. "Is that the way they taught you the story?" he questioned.

"Well, no, not exactly," Danny began to admit, "but if I told it to you the way our SS teacher told us, you'd never believe it, Dad!"

In his book *Living on the Ragged Edge*, Chuck Swindoll explains that a doctor friend of his was treating a woman in her mid-eighties who was in fairly good shape, and who jogged every day. The doctor became concerned about her, though, and he warned her about exerting herself. She heeded his advice and ceased most of her activity. Several months later, he sat in the funeral parlor, attending her memorial service. Later, he commented to Swindoll, "You know, Chuck, I could cut my tongue out for ever having told her to be careful, to stop exerting herself. I doubt that I will ever give that advice again… especially to older people who are enjoying life as much as she was." So you see, even when we believe that we're being helpful, we need to choose what we say to people very carefully since even if we mean well, we can possibly lead them in the wrong direction.

Let's be smart, then, and be led by G's Spirit in knowing what to say, how, when, and where. As John Wanamaker wisely advised, "Whatever you have to say to people, be sure to say it in words that will cause them to smile, and you will be on pretty safe ground. And when you do find it necessary to criticize someone, put your criticism in the form of a question, which the other fellow is practically sure to have to answer in a manner that he becomes his own critic." Fascinating. You know, that can be done—we can get people to admit their faults (if we're truly called to do so) by using appropriate tactfulness."

So maybe today's message can be summed up in a short, sweet sentence that gets to the point effectively enough, and that sentence is, simply, "The trouble with people who talk too fast, is that they often say something they haven't thought of yet." So they next time we're about to say anything, let's think before we speak.

January 20, 2008 Wait Till Momma Finds Out
Psalms 11:4; 40:9; 139:2, 4

When I was a teenager, there used to be a TV show on called *What's Happening?* The show dealt with an African American teen named Raj, his bratty little sister, Dee, and Raj's two hilarious friends, Duane and Rerun. They were a riot. Well, Raj's and Dee's widowed mother was a strict disciplinarian. So since Raj, Duane, and Rerun were forever doing things to get them in hot water, Dee would typically look at her brother once during each episode and proclaim, "Oooh, Raj...you in trouble. Wait till Momma finds out!" And believe me—Momma *always* found out. And that's just it—Momma had to find out, someway. She wasn't omniscient. She didn't just magically/automatically know what her son and his friends were up to. After all, she was only human. She either had to be told by someone (more than likely tattle-tale sister, Dee) or find out on her own through the eventual results of Raj's, Duane's, and Rerun's misadventures.

But you know something? G already knows anything and everything about what we're up to. There's nothing that we can think, say, or do (or plan on saying or doing) that G doesn't already know. Now, it's not just the bad/sinful stuff about us that G already has knowledge of. He knows about everything concerning us. Everything—the good as well as the bad. That's why David penned what he did in Psalm 40:9: "I proclaim righteousness in the great assembly, I do not seal my lips, as you know, O Lord."

J said according to Matthew 6:7–8, "And when you pray, don't keep on babbling like the pagans, for they think that they will be heard for their many words. Don't be like them, for your Father knows what you need before you ask him." Yes, as this verse indicates, G knows our needs ahead of our letting him know about them. That's why Psalm 34:15 points out to us, "The eyes of the Lord are on the righteous, and his ears are attentive to their cry."

Now, of course, it's not just our needs and concerns that G knows very well. He knows the entirety of what's in our hearts. You know, I could have very easily entitled this sermon "He Knows," since that's the main message for this morning. No matter what it is that a person thinks, says, does, or experiences, no one has to tell G to inform him—he already knows. As Psalm 11:4 explains, "The Lord is in His Holy Temple; the Lord is on His heavenly Throne. He observes the sons of men; his eyes examine them."

Along those same lines, Psalm 139:2 points out, "You, G, know when I sit and when I rise; you perceive my thoughts from far off." Psalm 94:10–12 states, "Does He who disciplines the nations not punish? Does he who teaches man lack knowledge? The Lord knows the thoughts of man; he knows that they are futile. Blessed is the man you discipline, O Lord, the man you teach from your law." Look again at the first half of verse 11: "The Lord knows the thoughts of man." That's pretty short, sweet, and simple, and to the point, wouldn't you say? You see, as this verse indicates, human wisdom can't be compared to G's, since he knows all we know, and much more.

So when we go through trying and difficult times, we may think that "G must not know how we feel" or be unaware of what we're going through. But that's not the case at all. Now, I'm not suggesting that "we deserve it, every time we experience suffering," but G's instruction is often closely related to his punishment and discipline. The contented and secure individual learns from life's trying times and difficulties and acknowledges the fact that G's law points to discipline for the disobedient. The greatest human intellectual achievements are puny and insignificant in comparison to G's wisdom.

Well, what if we're trying to hide something from G. Maybe there's a part of our thinking and/or life that we'd rather him not know. Is it possible to keep secrets from him? I kind of doubt it. Especially since King David instructed in 1 Chronicles 28:9, "And you, my son Solomon, acknowledge the God of your father, and serve him with whole-hearted devotion and with a willing mind, for the Lord searches every heart and understands every motive behind the thoughts." Wow. It doesn't sound like anybody's gonna hide anything from G according to that passage. Likewise, Psalm 44:20–21 bring to our attention that "If we had forgotten the name of our G or spread out our hands to a foreign god, would not G have discovered it, since he knows the secrets of the heart?" It's because of verses like this that we can rest assured that "G knows our situation, and because of that, he also knows what we deserve."

But it's not only when we've greatly sinned or spiritually messed up that G is aware. He also knows, thankfully and very fortunately, when we're blameless and innocent. Job was defending his honesty and sincerity to his friends, when he's recorded in Job 31: 5–6, "If I have walked in falsehood or my foot has hurried after deceit, let G weigh me in honest scales, and he will know that I am blameless."

Likewise, David wrote in Psalm 37:18, "The days of the blameless are known to the Lord, and their inheritance will endure forever."

And Psalm 119:168 states, "I obey your precepts and your statutes; for all my ways are known to you."

But obviously, as we've alluded to already this morning, it's not only the good things we think, say and do that G knows all about. Remember, anything that we think we could get away with doing so that no one will know about will be seen and therefore known by God. A large bowl of Red Delicious apples was placed at the front of the cafeteria line at Asbury College. The note attached read, "Take only one, please. G is watching." Well, some joker later attacked a note to a tray of peanut butter cookies at the other end of the line that read, "Take all that you want. G is watching the apples."

Now, part of what all this means is that, G knowing everything, nothing in connection with ourselves is hidden from him. I honestly don't know what many Christians are thinking as they go through their lives, but many people in the church today act as if G is totally unaware of the evil found within them. So when we say that there's nothing in connection with ourselves that is hidden from G, what we're meaning is that the three main areas of human life —the thoughts we think, the words we say, and the actions we commit—all lay bare before him, and the Scripture address that fact in each of those areas.

For instance, when speaking of G knowing our thoughts, the Bible proclaims together in Psalm 94:11 and 139:2, "The Lord knows the thoughts of men...you perceive my thoughts from far away." Now, it would make perfect sense, then, that if G knows our thoughts, then it would follow that he knows not only the words we speak, but he would then obviously know what we would say before we say it. That truth, then, is indicated in Psalm 139:4, when it's there the Bible points out, "Before a word is on my tongue, you know it completely, O Lord." Yes, G is fully aware of the words we let come out of our mouths. How else would J's statement in Matthew 12:36–7 be accurate, when the Bible records him as saying there, "But I tell you that men will have to give account on the day of judgment for every careless word they have spoken. For by your words, you will be acquitted, and by your words, you will be condemned."

And then, of course, it we accept the fact that J is fully aware of both our thoughts and words, we could never deny that He's also completely "onto us" in the things we actually do. The Bible couples the topics of G knowing both our words and actions in 1 Samuel 2:3, when there, it warns, "Do not keep talking so proudly or let your mouth speak such arrogance, for the Lord is a God who knows, and by him deeds are weighed." Likewise, 2 Chronicles 6:30 informs, "Forgive us, G, and deal with each man according to all he does, since you know his heart—for you alone know the hearts of men."

Now, all of us here this morning know that a lot of people don't believe in G, because they cannot perceive him with their five natural senses. Well, once again, there are apparently a lot of Christians who seem to feel as though they can get away with all kinds of sinful thoughts, words and deeds, and G will not hear or see them in action. But that's just not the case. Job pointed out in Job 23:8–10, "But if I go to the east, G is not there; if I go to the west, I do not find him. When he is at work in the north, I do not see him; when he turns to the south, I catch no glimpse of him. But he knows the way I take."

You know, a lot of people in this life are very concerned with how they look, physically. Well, yes, I do believe G wants us to take care of ourselves in every way, and that includes our outward, physical appearance. But our outward attractiveness—or lack thereof—is not what concerns G so much. After all, the Bible states in Galatians 2:6 that "G does not judge by external appearance." Of course, that's all that we humans can truly see of each other—what we see people look like and act like on the outside. But it's a very different thing with G, since he knows what's happening on the inside of us. As 1 Samuel 16:7 puts it, "But the Lord said to Samuel, 'Do not consider Saul's appearance or his height, for I have rejected him. The Lord does not look at the things man looks at. Man looks at the outward appearance, but the Lord looks at the heart.'"

So for those who sit Sunday after Sunday in church, playing the religious game, pretending to be right with G that one day a week (but all through the rest of the week living as if there was no difference between themselves and the people of the world), there's no escaping the fact that G knows where we truly stand with him. If we are sincerely right with Christ, then G will recognize that fact. After all, 2 Timothy 2:29 proclaims, "G's solid foundation stands firm, sealed with this inscription: 'The Lord KNOWS those who are His.'" But we shouldn't try to kid ourselves into thinking and believing that we've somehow managed to fool God, living a sinful life and believing at the same time that "G hasn't found out about it." G doesn't have to be told, like Momma...He already knows! That's why, everybody, Jeremiah 17:10 points out, "I, the Lord, search the heart and examine the mind, to reward a man according to his conduct, according to what his deed deserves."

I'd like to read to you the words to a song by a Christian singer named Steve Taylor, called "Sin for a Season." The song goes like this: "There's a sweaty hand handling his cocktail napkin. 'Come on up and see me' is scribbled with a gold pen, 'but you'd better ring twice.' / Seven months after his little indiscretion, he sits with his wife at a therapy session for a little advice. / 'If the healing happens as the time goes by, tell me why I still can't look her in the eye' / God, I'm only human, got no other reason—sin for a season. / There's a shaky hand shaking with the hand of her hostess; drank a little much, but she'll drive herself home—if she can make it to the car / She never saw the sign or the boy with his daddy driving home late from their very first ballgame, and they don't get far / Now, the years run together as her guilt goes wild—she still see the body of an only child / God, I'm only human, got no other reason—sin for a season. / Wealthy lips say 'Keep us for the evil one,' while praying hands prey with deliberate cunning on the carcass of the cold. / Gonna get the Good Lord to forgive a little sin, get the slate cleaned so he can dirty it again / and no one else will ever know. / But he reaps his harvest as his heart grows hard—no man's gonna make a mockery of God. / I'm only human, got no other reason —sin for a season." To put a well-known scripture to back up Mr. Taylor's song, the Bible flatly states in Galatians 6:7, "Do not be deceived: God cannot be mocked. A man reaps what he sows."

The Bible records a prayer spoken by Solomon, in 1 Kings 8:39: "Forgive and act; deal with each man according to all he does, since you know his heart (for you alone know the hearts of all men)." And for the Scriptural conclusion for the message this morning, we read in Joshua 22:21–22: "Then Reuben, Gad and the half-tribe of Manasseh replied to the heads of the clans of Israel, 'The Mighty One, God, the Lord! The Mighty One, God, the Lord! HE KNOWS!"

He knows. God knows. There's really no way He can't know. He's God, after all.

A father was once telling his son about "the facts of life." As they were nearing the end of the conversation, the boy looked at his dad and asked, "Do you think God knows about this?"

I had a cousin whom I grew up with during my teenage years, who was also a fan of the TV show *What's Happening?* And he, too, loved that infamous line that Dee, the bratty little sister, would pronounce during every episode. Well, my cousin, Jonathan, thought it was just great that my name also happened to be Rog. So anytime I did anything the least bit out of the ordinary that could have sparked some trouble for myself, Jon would look at me and say, "Oooh, Rog…you in trouble! Wait till Momma finds out!" Yeah, I guess my mom always did have to wait to find out, eventually—one way or another. But G doesn't. He already knows! Have you realized that truth for yourself today?

May 17 Not-So-Silly Warnings
Psalms 19:7-11; Ezekiel 3:18-21

You know, I get a kick out of a lot of WARNING LABELS you see attached to various products that you buy at the store. Although they mean to convey a serious message, some of these "warnings" can be downright hilarious. Take, for instance, the following true examples. On the side of the cup of McDonald's coffee: "Caution—hot!" The side of the tube of Chapstick lip moisturizer warns you to keep the Chapstick out of your eyes. The package that holds the Homelite Zip Start Vac Attack leaf blowers cautions you to not point the blower in the direction of people or pets. (Gee, why ever not?) And then, there's the Web Filter Fresh air freshener, which warns the purchaser, "Not for human consumption."

Okay, whatever. There are a lot of absolutely ridiculously silly warnings on a lot of things we purchase, and the Bible itself contains a lot of cautions and warnings, but there all quite serious, to the point, direct, and very accurate in what they say. A couple of those instances, then, come from Psalm 19:7–11 and Ezekiel 3:18–21 and 33:1–9. It's in those passages together, then, that the Bible states, "The law of the Lord is perfect, reviving the soul. The statues of the Lord are trustworthy, making wise the simple. The precepts of the Lord are right, giving joy to the heart. The commands of the Lord are radiant, giving light to the eyes. The fear of the Lord is pure, enduring forever. The ordinances of the Lord are sure and altogether righteous. They are more precious than gold; they are sweeter than honey from the comb. By them is your servant warned; in keeping them there is great reward…When I say to a wicked man, 'You will surely die,' and you do not warn him or speak out to dissuade him from his evil ways in order to save his life, that wicked man will die for his sin, and I will hold you accountable for his blood. But if you DO warn the wicked man, and he does not turn from his wickedness or from his evil ways, he will die for his sin; but you will have saved yourself.

"Again, when a righteous man turns from his righteousness and does evil, and I put a stumbling block before him, he will die. Since you did not warn him, he will die for his sin. The righteous things he did will not be remembered, and I will hold you accountable for his blood. But if you DO warn the righteous man not to sin, and he does not sin, he will surely live because he took warning, and you will have saved yourself."

Now, one problem with receiving fair warning about a potential danger— spiritual and otherwise—is that we often cannot imagine the possible danger sin poses until we actually get close enough to it, where we can at least see for ourselves its devastating effects on somebody else. In connection with that thought, then, Chuck Swindoll once stated that he never had the right perspective on what Daniel must have faced, until he and his family took a trip through Lion Country Safari. Swindoll had been to zoos in several major cities, but he had never been through that tourist safari that was an attraction in Orange Country. For some strange reason, there was a rather sizeable beast that took a liking to their type of car, or something inside the car. Swindoll says he can remember there weren't a lot of animals, but that one king of the jungle seemed to like them and he just sort of walked along with them. They were able to stop and study them, with a very thick car door between them and those creatures. But he said that as he studied that particular regal lion, he got a whole new appreciation for what it must have been like for Daniel to have been in a den filled with several carnivorous beasts like that one. Now, I'm not suggesting that we "push it" by getting only so far away from temptation and sin (determined not to go too far), just so we can see and/ or imagine what the potential consequence might be, but sometimes, if we educate ourselves enough to come to understand what could happen to us if we went in a certain ungodly direction in our life, if might scare us enough to deter us from ever getting involved that far in whatever type of activity or behavior we're talking about.

The July 7, 1993, issue of the *San Francisco Examiner* reported that the California State Automobile Association claims office received a package by FedEx. The unknown contents were bundled in a Fruit Loops cereal box. Workers quickly became suspicious. The FBI had only days before uncovered a terrorist bombing ring in New York, and the media had been crackling with stories of terrorist bombing. Security guards called the police, and about four hundred office workers were evacuated from the building. The bomb squad soon arrived on the scene. The Fruit Loops cereal box was "neutralized," with a small cannon, and its contents were blasted into the air. The bomb squad, however, found no explosives. Inside the suspicious package had been $24,000 in cash. The box contained bundles of $20 bills, $1,000 of which were destroyed in the blast.

"This was a first, finding money," said platoon leader Jim Seim. The package "arrived in such a way that it aroused our suspicions," he said. "We were able to render it neutral. We always err on the side of caution." In our world, then, especially today, it's prudent to use caution, but on the other hand, blanket suspicion can help to destroy things much more valuable than money. Maybe that's why J warned us in Matthew 10:16, to be as wise as snakes but as gentle as doves.

Yeah, some warning can be pretty much what you might call no-brainers," like the one for STP Power Steering Fluid, which simply says, "Do Not Swallow"; the warning label on the package for Gummy Guard, the candy mouth guard, which advises, "Fun candy—not intended to protect you in contact sports"; or the caution notice that comes with the Panasonic industrial oven, which very fortunately warns the potential user, "Caution—hot. Do not touch hot oven."

Well, fortunately, the Bible is full of very helpful warnings, many of which are not too overly obvious. One other lesson-warning, then, the Bible gives us is the truth that we can learn from the grievous errors of others, to keep the same punishments from falling on us. It's in the Living Bible's version of 1 Corinthians 10:1–12, then, that we read, "For we must never forget, dear bros, what happened to our people in the wilderness long ago. G guided them by sending a cloud that moved along ahead of them, and he brought them all safely through the waters of the Red Sea. This might be called their 'baptism,' baptized both in sea and cloud—as followers of Moses—their commitment to him as their leader. And by a miracle, G sent them food to eat and water to drink there in the desert; they drank the water that Christ gave them. He was with them there as a might Rock of spiritual refreshment. Yet, after all this, most of them did not obey G, and in he destroyed them in the wilderness.

"From this lesson, we are warned that we must not desire evil things as they did and not worship idols as they did. [The Scriptures tell us,

'The people sat down to eat and drink and then got up to dance,' in worship of the golden calf.] Another lesson for us is what happened when some of them sinned with other men's wives, and 23,000 fell dead in one day. And don't try the Lord's patience—they did, and died from snake bites. And don't murmur against G and his dealings with you, as some of them did, for that is why G sent his Angel to destroy them. All these things happened to them as examples—as object lessons to us—to warn us against doing the same things; they were written down so that we could read about them and learn from them in these last days, as the world nears its end. So be careful. If you are thinking, 'Oh, I would never act like that!' let this be a warning to you. For you, too, may fall into sin."

On November 20, 1959, a small amount of solvent exploded and blew the door open of a processing cell at the Atomic Energy Commission Oak Ridge Laboratory. About one-fiftieth of an ounce of plutonium was scattered into the air—only one-fiftieth of an ounce! The AEC later reported what it took to clean up this "minor atomic mishap."

(1) Everyone within a 4-acre area turned in their clothing to be decontaminated. (2) Each person was thoroughly examined to ensure that they had not inhaled or ingested any plutonium. (3) The processing plant and nearby research reactor were completely shut down. (4) Buildings were washed with strong detergent—and all the buildings' roofs were resurfaced. (5) The surrounding lawn was dug up and the sod carried to a deep burial place a long distance away. (6) One hundred yards of the surface of a nearby asphalt road was chiseled off. And finally (7), to anchor the slightest speck of plutonium that might have remained, every building was totally repainted with heavyduty paint. The total cost of this renovation and cleaning process was $350,000.

A man named Henri-Frederic Amiel once pointed out that "An error is the more dangerous the more truth it contains." Now, if just one-fiftieth of an ounce of plutonium can have that much of a devastating effect on its surroundings, imagine what just a "little sin" in a person's life can do to their eternal future, if not taken care of by the blood of J.

Still, some people just don't use their head, at all, when going through life, and they need all the warnings they can get to keep them out of trouble— warnings like the one found on the Weber Genesis Silver C Gas Grill: "Caution: Surface will be warm when in use. Do not use matches, lighters, or flame to check for leaks," or the caution label printed on Black Cat Black Snake Fireworks—"Caution flammable. Do not put in mouth." Personally, I always liked the one you typically see on fireworks—the one that says, "Light fuse, and get away." No kidding. I was going to light the silly thing, continue to hold it and let it blow my hand clean off my arm.

Now, specifically, one of the most important warnings we could give people is that of their approaching death. You know this—we all die, and we Christians need to remind the unsaved around us about that fact constantly, since it's so easy to forget and ignore.

"In connection with that practice, Isaiah 40:6–8 reads, 'A voice says, "Cry out.'"

"And I said, 'What shall I cry?'

"'All men are like grass, and all their glory is like the flowers of the field. The grass withers and the flowers fall, because the breath of the Lord blows on them. Surely the people are like grass. The grass withers and the flowers fall, but the word of G stands forever.'"

Likewise, Ecclesiastes 7:2, 2:14–16, and 3:19 together warn, "Death is the destiny of everyone, and the living should take that fact to heart... The wise man has eyes in his head, while the fool walks in darkness, but I came to realize that the same fate overtakes them both...Like the fool, the wise man, too, must die...Man's fate is like that of the animals; the same fate awaits them both. As one dies, so does the other."

So why do we often ignore perfectly good warnings that might come our way and present themselves to us? I mean, when we're given every opportunity to avoid trouble—by having been sufficiently cautioned ahead of time—why do we so often go ahead and get into that very trouble as if "no one had ever told us" not to? Probably because we don't often make good use of the brains G gave us. Yes, along those lines, it's been pointed out that the average human body contains sixty-six pounds of muscle, forty-two pounds of bone, and only three and a half ounces of brain, which probably explains a lot of things.

Yeah, some product warnings just seem so obvious, they hardly seem to be needed. Take, for example, the caution for Vick's Nyquil: "When using this product, drowsiness may occur."

Okay, well, Nyquil *is* a cold remedy that's to be taken at night to help you sleep. Band-Aids have been known to carry the warning, "For medical emergencies, seek professional help." Then, there's the warning included on the back of boxes of Clorox cleaner which states, "If vapors bother you, leave the room," as well as on Coppertone sunblock bottles that advises, "For external use only."

And you know, when we ARE given fair warning about impending danger— spiritual, physical or otherwise—we'd do well, I think, to immediately and fully get moving. To delay or only halfheartedly get moving probably won't do us a whole lot of good. We might as well take no action at all. It's like when a group of senior citizens was lounging on the patio of their retirement community. One man looked up as a large flock of birds flew overhead. He then elbowed his friend sitting next to him who had dozed off. "Frank, you better move around a little bit," he began to advise, "those buzzards look like they're closing in on us."

But maybe the most important thing we can warn people about is that G will, one day, judge us on how we lived our lives. After all, the Bible warns us all together in Job 34:11, Psalm 62:12, Jeremiah 17:10 and 32:19, Matthew 16:27, Romans 2:9–10, and 2 Corinthians 5:10, "G repays a man for what he has done; he bring upon him what his conduct deserves; Surely, Lord, you will reward each person according to what he has done; I, the Lord, search the heart and examine the mind, to reward a man according to his conduct, according to what his deeds deserve; You, G, reward everyone according to his conduct and as his deeds deserve; For the Son of Man is going to come in his Father's glory with his angels, and then he will reward each person according to what he has done; There will be trouble and distress for everyone who does evil: first for the Jew, then for the Gentile; but glory honor and peace for everyone who does good: first for the Jew, then for the Gentile; For we must all appear before the judgment seat of Christ, that each one may receive what is due him for the things done while in the body, whether good or bad."

Yes, there are a *lot* of warnings all around us that just seem like "no one needs to tell us that." A case in point is the caution label on the Amana Stainless Designer Series washing machine, which reads, "For your safety: do not let children play in the washer." Gee, why in the world not? I always wanted to see my kids have the opportunity to go through the wash, rinse, and spin cycles. But the Bible is full of helpful and useful warnings—please determine for yourself not to ignore them.

July 20 Powerful Productiveness Out of Personal Pain
2 Corinthians 1:3-7

I think you're probably very familiar with that TV commercial for the medication known as Lipitor. The ad starts out with a man looking straight at the camera, saying, "When I went to college, I wanted to be an architect. But then, my father had a heart attack, so I decided to study the heart." Then the narrator of the commercial introduces the man, "Inventor of the Jarvik artificial heart, Dr. Robert Jarvik." The ad then goes on to describe Jarvik's role in the development of Lipitor. Now, stop and just think for a moment. Here's a guy who, originally, felt it was his calling in life to build houses, and instead, due to the fact of his heart attack, winds up literally mending hearts. Yes, even after his dad fell victim to one of the most common ailments on the face of the planet, Jarvik could have continued on his original course of architecture. But I guess he decided to take the threat to his father's life and well-being as a call for him to at least attempt to do something about the medical condition.

Well, our focal passage of Scripture, today, reminds us that it's when we ourselves suffer that we're able to relate to—and therefore are better able to— help others in their time of suffering. As the Bible puts it in 2 Corinthians 1:3– 7, "Praise be to the G and Father of our Lord JC, the Father of compassion and the God of all comfort, who comforts us in all our troubles, so that we can comfort those in any trouble with the help we ourselves have received from G. For just as the sufferings of Christ flow over into our lives, so also through Christ our comfort overflows. If we are distressed, it is for your comfort and salvation. If we are comforted, it is for your comfort, which produces in you patient endurance of the same sufferings we suffer. And our hope for you is firm, because we know that just as you share in our sufferings, you also share in our comfort."

In his book *The Pursuit of Excellence*, author Ted Engstrom gave the following incredible examples of the type of thing we're talking about today: "Cripple him, and you have Sir Walter Scott; Lock him in a prison cell, and you have John Bunyon; bury him in the snows of Valley Forge, and you have Geo Washington; raise him in abject poverty, and you have Abe Lincoln; Subject him to bitter religious prejudice, and you have Disraeli; Strike him down with infantile paralysis, and he becomes a Franklin D. Roosevelt. Burn his so severely in a schoolhouse fire that the doctors say that he will never walk again, and you have a Glenn Cunningham, who set the world's record in 1934, for running a mile in 4 minutes and 6.7 seconds. Deafen a genius composer, and you have a Ludwig van Beethoven. Have him or her born black in a society filled with racial prejudice and you have a Booker T. Washington, a Geo Washington Carver or a Martin Luther King, Jr. Make him the 1st child to survive in a poor Italian family of 18 children, and you have an Enrico Curuso. Have him born of parents who survived a Nazi concentration camp, paralyze him from the waist down when he is four, and you have incomparable concert violinist, Itzhak Perlman. Call him a slow learner, 'retarded,' and write him off as uneducable, and you have an Albert Einstein."

You see, as a man named Leith Anderson once pointed out, "Adversity is often the window of opportunity for change. Few people or organizations want to change when there is prosperity and peace. Major changes are often precipitated by necessity."

Yes, it is very possible for good things to come out of bad ones, as is indicated in Paul's letter in Romans 5:3–5: "But we also rejoice in our suffering, because we know that suffering produces perseverance, perseverance character, and character hope. And hope does not disappoint us, because G has poured out his love into our hearts by the Holy Spirit, whom he has given us."

You see, when we follow through with the steps of the process of grief appropriately, according to G's direction, we can end up feeling more blessed than cursed in times of pain and trouble. But, as Plutarch once so eloquently put it, "Those who aim at doing great deeds must also suffer greatly."

Harry Adams tells the story of Jean Dominique Bauby, a French journalist who had been editor in chief of the fashion magazine Elle suffered a stroke in December of 1995. It left him unable to either speak or move, although his mind was left unaffected. The only part of his body still left under voluntary control was his left eyelid.

Bauby learned to communicate with the eyelid. First, he learned a signal for yes and another for no.

Then when a therapist recited or pointed to the letters of the French alphabet, he would blink when she reached the letter he wanted. In that way, he formed words, then sentences. Difficult though it was, he composed an entire book *The Diving Suit and the Butterfly*, prior to his death on March 9, 1997. In its first week of publication, it sold 146,000 copies. Bauby did what he could with what he had. To each of us, G has given some ability and some the opportunity for service.

Now so far, we've been talking about people who have accomplished typically one significant achievement in their life, despite great obstacles. Well, there are some people who, though they might not face incredible opposition, nevertheless employ their G-given talents and abilities in extreme ways. Let me give you a well-known example.

Many of us here today use eyeglasses to see to read printed material. The inventor of eyeglasses? Ben Franklin, at age seventy-nine. Now, the printing press that printed those pages that we read are powered by electricity. Who was one of the first harnessers of electricity? You know, Ben Franklin, at age forty. Some people might even spend a lot of their time reading on the campus of one of the Ivy League universities. The founder of the university was Ben Franklin, age forty-five. Most other people, however, never make it to an Ivy League school. Instead, they might spend their time reading and researching in any one of the thousands of libraries in the US. Who founded the first library in the US? You know what I'm going to say—Ben Franklin, age twenty-five. Who started the first fire department? Ben Franklin, age thirty-one. Who invented the lightning rod? Ben Franklin, age forty-three. Who designed a heating stove still in use today? Ben Franklin, age thirty-six.

Witty, conversationalist, economist, philosopher, diplomat, printer, publisher, and linguist (he spoke five languages), Franklin was also an advocate of paratroopers from balloons, a century before the airplane was invented. All of this, until the age of eighty-four. But maybe the most incredible part of all this is that he had exactly two years of formal schooling. It's a good bet that you already have more sheer knowledge than Franklin ever had when he was your age. Maybe you think there's no use in trying to think of anything new, that everything's been done. Wrong—go do something about it.

But just because someone winds up accomplishing a lot throughout their lifetime, that doesn't necessarily mean they're doing G's will. After all, that's what true success is, doing G's will. Picture the scenario of two friends graduating. One goes to India as a missionary, the other becomes a successful businessman. Both get the announcement of a class reunion, and at the meeting, compare where they've been since graduating. It would be very easy for the missionary to think of himself as a failure. We need to clear the hurdle of comparison. True achievement for each one of us is listening to and obeying the voice that says, "Follow me."

Now, along the same lines, we need to remember that we shouldn't let failure stop us from trying to get done whatever it was we originally set out to accomplish, since it's a truth that, with G, even if our original goal is missed, we can still end up doing a lot of good in the world for Christ. As Thomas J. Watson Jr. once pointed out, "Strangely, the expounders of many of the great new ideas of history were frequently considered on the lunatic fringe for some of all of their lives. If one stands up and is counted, from time to time, one may get knocked down. But remember this: A man flattened by an opponent can get up again. A man flattened by conformity stays down for good. And (I really like this next statement) a man named Les Brown encouraged, "Shoot for the moon. Even if you miss it, you'll land among the stars."

Yes, there is often powerful productiveness that is to be found in personal pain. When a Christian suffers, there is the potential for them to accomplish much for Christ, and in doing so, wind up being a powerful witness for him, as Colossians 1:24 points out in the Jerusalem Bible, when it says, "It makes me happy to suffer for you, as I am suffering now, and in my own body to do what I can to make up all that has till to be undergone by Christ for the sake of his body, the Church."

Even in the face of great peril, there is an opportunity to do great things. For example, there's the story of Marine Corps General Chesty Puller, who made a landing at Inchon. There were Koreans in front of them, there were North Koreans to the flank, there were North Koreans to the other flank, there was the ocean behind them, and Puller commented, "This is great! They'll never get away this time."

As famed golfer Arnold Palmer once put it, "The most rewarding things you do in life are often the ones that look like they can't be done."

But a large part of the problem is that, for whatever reason, many people resist even attempting to do whatever it is that G might be leading them to do, because they look at the obstacles in front of them, and they get scared and frightened and then wimp out. If we should ever be tempted to take that view, then, we need to remind ourselves not to fear that our life will come to an end, but that it might not ever have a beginning.

Bill Plummer and Bonnie Bell wrote in *People* magazine, "The Northwestern University Wildcats shocked the world of college football in 1995 by making it to the Rose Bowl Tournament. The man behind the team's turnaround was coach Gary Barnett. He was determined to prove that kids at the Big Ten's smallest and most academically demanding school could actually play football. He ordered a Tournament of Roses flag for the football building and kept a silk rose on his desk to remind everyone where they were headed. 'At the first meeting,' says kicker Sam Valenzisi, 'he told us we needed belief without evidence. He asked us, "Do you know what that is? That's faith."'"

However, let's not forget the first part of the equation today—that before people may talk about helping others in their need, God can, and does, help us in our own. As the Bible reminds us in Isaiah 49:13 and 66:13, "Shout for joy, O heavens; rejoice, O earth; burst into song, O mountains! For the Lord comforts his people and will have compassion on his afflicted...As a mother comforts her child, so will I comfort you; and you will be comforted over Jerusalem."

Yes, even the least of us, in the midst of pain and suffering, can do great things for G, as Jr. Samples, from the TV show *Hee Haw* once observed when he said, "Size ain't got nothing to do with it. If it did, a cow could outrun a rabbit." So if we have already decided to attempt to do a tremendous work for Christ, we then need to do our best to finish it before we leave this earth. For instance, it's been pointed out that Geo Washington Goethals, the man responsible for the completion of the Panama Canal, had big problems with climate and geography. But his biggest challenge was the growing criticism back home from those who predicted he'd never finish the project.

A colleague once then asked him, "Aren't you going to answer your critics?"

"In time," said Goethals.

"When?" the other man asked.

Goethals responded, "When I'm finished."

Chuck Swindoll wrote in his book *Starting Over*, "Teddy Roosevelt believed, 'Far better it is to dare mighty things, to win glorious triumphs, even though checkered by failure, than to take rank with those poor spirits who neither enjoy much nor suffer much because they live in the gray twilight that knows neither victory nor defeat.'" In other words, everybody, if you don't at least try to do something significant for Christ and the church, you'll never know.

And of course, the last thing we need to worry about is the criticism from outsiders that whatever we're attempting for J can't be done. For example, in 1870, the Methodists in Indiana were having their annual conference.

At one point, the president of the college where they were meeting said, "I think we live in a very exciting age."

The presiding bishop said, "What do you mean?"

The college president responded, "I believe we're coming to a time a great invention. For instance, I think that men will fly through the air like birds." The bishop said, "That's heresy! The Bible says that flight is reserved for the angels. We will have no such talk here." After the conference, the bishop, whose name was Wright, went home to his two sons—Orville and Wilbur. You know what they did to their father's opinion of human flight. As the saying goes, "The one who says 'it can't be done' shouldn't interrupt the one who's doing it.'"

So when we are faced with trouble and difficulty, the thing to do is to rely on G to get us through. Once we have recovered, then, we can go on to be a help and support to others in trouble. As the Good News Bible puts 1 Peter 1:6–9, "Be glad about this, even though it may now be necessary for you to be sad for a while because of the many kinds of trials you suffer. Their purpose is to prove that your faith is genuine. Even gold, which can be destroyed, is tested by fire; and so your faith, which is much more precious than gold, must also be tested, that it may endure. Then, you will receive praise and glory and honor on the Day when JC is revealed. You love him, even though you have not seen him. You believe in him although you do not see him now. And so you rejoice with a great and glorious joy, which words cannot express, because you are receiving the purpose of your faith, the salvation of your souls."

The thing to do, then, when attempting to do something significant for Christ, while in the presence of some formidable obstacle, is to go at the task with full force. As James Hewett recorded in the book *Illustrations Unlimited*, "Zig Ziglar says that he's such an optimist, he'd go after Moby Dick in a rowboat and take a jar of tartar sauce with him." How about you? Can you create powerful productiveness, in the name of J, out of personal pain?

June 14, 2009 I Read Your Obituary Today
Ecclesiastes 7:2; 2:14, 16; 3:19

I read your obituary in the paper, today. It was interesting. It told me a lot of stuff about you that I never knew, it omitted some information that I wish it had included, and it included some things I wish I hadn't known. But seeing your obit in the paper today reminded me the cold, hard fact that someday, each of us has to die. There's no escaping it. Now, I've ready plenty of other people's obits in the paper over the years, but guess what? Someday other people will be reading mine. After all, the book of Ecclesiastes 7:2, 2:14, 2:16, and 3:19–20 (Life Application Bible) lays it on the line about the fact that we will one day "meet our Maker": "It is better to spend your time at funerals than at festivals, because you are going to die, and you should think about it while there is still time...For the wise person sees, while the fool is blind. Yet I saw that wise and foolish people share the same fate: both of them die. Just as the fool will die, so will I...for the wise person and the fool both die, and in the days to come, both will be forgotten...For humans and animals both breathe the same air, and both die. So people have no real advantage over the animals. How meaningless! Both go to the same place—the dust from which they came and to which they must return."

Yes, I took the time to thoroughly ready through the list of all your ten dozen relatives in your obit—all your kids, grandkids, great-grandkids, etc. Yeah, while most everybody else who read your obit was probably gawking at "what a great family man you must have been" by all the family relatives indicated in your obit, you and I both know that it was a much different story. Yeah, you beat your wife, you neglected your kids and you even abused your ailing elderly parents. Yeah, you might have put on a good show in public, but G knows just exactly how you treated your family members. He knows how you ignored the Bible passage found in Ephesians 5:25 and 6:4, which reads, "And further, you will submit to one another out of reverence for Christ. You wives will submit to your husbands as you do to the Lord. For a husband is the head of his wife as Christ is the head of his body, the church; he gave his life to be her Savior. As the church submits to Christ, so you wives must submit to your husbands in everything.

"And you husbands must also love your wives with the same love Christ showed the church. He gave up his life for her to make her holy and clean, washed by baptism and G's word. He did this to present her to himself as a glorious church without a spot or wrinkle or any other blemish. Instead, she will be holy and without fault. In the same way, Husbands ought to love their wives as they love their own bodies; for a man is actually loving himself when he loves his wife. No one hates his own body but lovingly cares for it, just as Christ cares for his body, which is the Church. And we are his body.

"As the Scripture says, 'A man leaves his father and mother and is joined to his wife, and the two are united into one.' This is a great mystery, but it is an illustration of the way Christ and the church are one. So again I say, each man must love his wife as he loves himself, and the wife must respect her husband.

"Children, obey your parents, because you belong to the Lord, for this is the right thing to do. 'Honor your father and mother.' This is the first of the 10 Commandments that ends with a promise: If you honor your father and mother, 'you will live a long life, full of blessing.' And now a word to you fathers. Don't make your children bitter by the way you treat them. Rather, bring them up with the discipline and instruction approved by the Lord."

Now, a lot of people might listen to my next statement, in regards to your obit, and criticizing me for pointing out that you apparently lived a life of business but without any real purpose, but I wonder if you lived your life with a crazy schedule that didn't allow your life to really leave anything constructive behind. I mean, I could see you your obit that you were the president of the local garden club for the past sixty years, that you were instrumental in helping to build the town's mud-wrestling pit, and that your number one favorite hobby that you spent hour after hour participating in was underwater basketweaving. All those things are fine, in and of themselves. There's nothing wrong with any of them, really.

But along with noticing all that, there was absolutely no mention anywhere in your obit about what church you belonged to, or any mention of church activities. And couple that glaring omission with the fact that your funeral will be held at the local funeral home is probably a good indication that you were not presently connected with a church at all. Oh my. That's not good. That aspect of your life reminds me of a young business woman I once knew. She was one day approached by a real estate agent, who wanted to sell her a home. "A home?" she began to respond. "I was born in a hospital, educated in a boarding school, dated my boyfriends in a car, and married in a courthouse. My dates and I would eat in restaurants, spend our weekends playing golf and bridge at the local Country Club. At night, we'd go to the movies, and when I die, I'm going to be buried near the funeral home. I don't need a house. All I need is a garage!" Now, don't get me wrong. It's nice to be busy and we all need some things to do just for the sheer enjoyment. But we also need to get—and stay involved in—activities in the church, during our life on earth, which apparently, you never did.

However, I also realize that there are a lot of people out there who do have a church name listed in their obit, and they have a ton of church-related activities mentioned after the name of their church. I have to admit, somewhat in your defense, that the people who died who had participated in all those activities didn't necessarily make it to heaven, since the Bible makes it plain and clear that we're not saved by the good things we do, in Romans 3:20 and 4:2–4 and Ephesians 2:8–9 when together they say, "For no one can ever be made right in G's sight by doing what his law commands. For the for more we know G's la, the clearer it becomes that we aren't obeying it…Was it because of his good deeds that G accepted Abraham? If so, he would have had something to boast about. But from G's point of view, Abraham had no basis at all for pride. For the Scriptures tell us, 'Abraham believed G, so G declared him to be righteous.' When people work, their wages are not a gift. Workers earn what they receive. But people are declared righteous because of their faith, not because of their work." No, just because somebody has an entire list of activities they took part in throughout their life in the church, that doesn't automatically indicated that they were right with J.

There are so many people who you can see listed in obits, today, who lived incredibly hypocritical lives. They were the type to tell you, if you asked them, that they were indeed a Christian, but then would demonstrate living the opposite of a strong Christian, every opportunity they got. And to make matter worse, other people in and outside the church would see that behavior, and that lifestyle would actually, then, serve as being a type of anti-witness, making people to want to have nothing to do with the church, instead of helping them be drawn to it. I even heard one critic of the church proclaim that a Christian (in *his* opinion) was a person who feels repentance on Sunday for what he did Saturday and is going to do all over again Monday. And yet, an absence of such a list in one's obit might also indicate that they were saved.

The thing that those churchgoers who are still living need to remember and think about every so often is that people are watching their every move, and that while no one has the right to judge anybody else, it surely doesn't help the church one iota when those who are in it give unbelievers reason to reject receiving the church's message over and over again. It actually reminds me of what happened back in the summer of 1805, when a number of Indian chiefs and warriors met in council at Buffalo Creek, New York, to hear a presentation of the gospel by a Mr. Cram, from the Boston Missionary Society. After the sermon, a response was given by Red Jacket, one of the leading chiefs. Among other things, the chief said in his response, "Brother, we are told that you have been preaching to the white people in this area. These people are our neighbors. We're acquainted with them. We will wait a little while and see what effect your preaching has had on them. If we find it does them good, makes them honest and less disposed to cheat Indians, we will then consider once more what you've said."

Yes, I know we just got done saying a few minutes ago that we aren't saved by doing good things—even in and for the church. But for those who claimed, as they lay dying, that they were "headed for heaven" who— at the same time —never bothered to lift a finger to give to—or to serve in—the church, a person like that might want to look at the passage in the Bible found in James 2:14–26, which explains, "Dear bros, what's the use of saying you have faith, if you don't prove it by your actions? That kind of faith can't save anyone. Suppose you see a bro or sis in need of food/clothing, and you say, 'Well, good-by and G bless you; stay warm and eat well,' but then, you don't give that person ay food or clothing. What good does that do?

"So you see, it isn't enough just to have faith. Faith that doesn't show itself by good deeds is no faith at all—it is dead and useless. Now, some may argue, 'Some people have faith, others have good deeds.' I say, 'I can't see you faith if you don't have good deeds, but I will show you my faith through my good deeds.' Do you still think it's enough just to believe that there is one G? Well, even the demons believe this, and they tremble in terror! Fool! When will you ever learn that faith that doesn't result in good deeds is useless?

"Don't you remember that our ancestor Abe was declared right with G because of what he did when he offered his son Isaac on the altar? You see, he was trusting G so much that he was willing to do whatever G told him to do. His faith was made complete by what he did—by his actions. And so it happened just as the Scriptures say, 'Abe believed G, so G declared him to be righteous.'"

He was even called "the friend of G." So you see, we are made right with G by what we do, not by faith alone.

A man once said that when he was 9-y-o, his dad broke the picket line in the machinist's union, which was threatening to go on strike. The man went on to say that his dad's patriotism and love for his family were greater than his loyalty to the union, so his father found himself one day driving the family car back home, with a cracked windshield and broken eggs running down the side of the car, because he was willing to be called a scab for his convictions. It left an impression on the man, as a young boy, and his siblings. They then learned that there are times when it's important enough to stand alone, even when friends don't understand and coworkers disagree.

And who knows? By standing your ground, it's very possible—though it might take a good long while—to help change the hearts and minds of people. For example, after serving Christ for fifteen years in Pakistan, missionary Warren Webster was invited to speak at the Urbana Missionary Conference. Part of his message are these words: "If I had my life to live over again, I would live it to change the lives of people, because you have not changed anything until you've changed the lives of people." Yes, changing the world requires changing people's lives.

Yes, I read your obit today. And as I did, I was reminded of the reality mentioned in Hebrews 9:27, when the Bible says there, "It is destined that a person is to die one time, and then is judged." But I take comfort in the fact that I knew you personally, and therefore, I'm able to know that it's a fact that you had accepted Christ as your Savior years ago. Since then, you did everything you could to further G's kingdom on earth. After all, I remember like it was yesterday, when you and I were in that church service together— way back when—when you took the advice found in Romans 10:9, and confessed with your mouth that 'J is Lord' and believed in your heart that G raised Him from the dead, and so you were saved.

Yes, I read your obituary in the paper, today, and it was quite interesting. I honestly don't know how you keep all those two hundred grandchildren and great-grandchildren's names all straight. I also thought it was interesting to see all about your hobbies and interests. I never knew you so whole-heartedly supported the sport of mud-wrestling to the point that you wanted to start a team for it out of the high school. And I'm still not sure how you got interested in that underwater basket weaving thing. That's definitely not for me. But the most important aspect of my having read your obituary was to know for certain where you ended up for eternity, because of your faith in J. However, it might be a different case for someone reading or listening to this message today. Where do you stand with having a relationship with J at this point in your life?

November 16 The True Sign of the Fish (No Sharks or Crabs)
Galatians 5:15; 1 Corinthians 1:10-17

It's interesting how different areas of life are analogous to parts of the Christian walk and life. For instance, have you ever considered that various kinds of Christians can be compared to diff kinds of fish. I'd like to suggest, to start off with, then, that some people in the church can be likened, strangely enough, to numerous types of ocean animal life.

One example of Christians acting like sharks, then for example, can be seen in the Bible passage mentioned in Galatians 5:15. It's here that the Phillips Modern English version of the Bible warns, "But if freedom means merely that you are free to attack and tear each other to pieces, be careful that it doesn't mean that between you, you both destroy your fellowship together!" Doesn't that sound like what a shark would do to a fresh piece of meat—attack it and tear it to pieces? Well, sad to say, that's how some Christians behave in and out of church.

So how do they demonstrate that kind of behavior? Well, Paul addressed this issue, among other places in the New Testament, in 1 Corinthians 1:10-17: "I appeal to you, Bros, in the name of our LJC, that all of you agree with one another so that there may be no divisions among you, and that you may be perfectly untied in mind and thought. My bros, some from Chloe's household have informed me that there are quarrels among you. What I mean is this: One of you say, 'I follow Paul'; another, 'I follow Apollos'; another, 'I follow Peter'; still another, 'I follow Christ.' Is Christ divided? Was Paul crucified for you? Were you baptized in the name of Paul? I am thankful that I did not baptize any of you except Crispus and Gaius, so no one can say that you were baptized into my name. (Yes, I also baptized the household of Stephanus; beyond that, I don't remember if I baptized anyone else). For Christ did not send me to baptize, but to preach the gospel—not with words of human wisdom, to keep Christ's death on the cross from being robbed of its power."

Now a real-life example of what we're talking about at this point comes from Jim Bakker's book *I Was Wrong*, where he details the before, during and afterward events of his "fall from grace" and his television ministry. On page 157, Bakker details some of the letters he received while he was in prison. "Many of the letters I received were kind and encouraging, but I also received a few vile letters. The hat email jolted me. I could not fathom why anyone would want to send such letter to me now that I was out of the public arena. Perhaps some people felt they could say anything they wanted to a convicted prisoner who was locked away for life.

"More than one person wrote to me: 'I hope you die in prison.' One wrote, 'I hope you get attacked by the biggest man in prison.' Some of the oddest mail I received came from individuals who felt compelled to shred me into tiny pieces, and the sign their letter 'In Christian love.'"

I don't know about you, but that sounds pretty similar to sharklike behavior to me.

Now, part of the reason why some Christians choose to live like sharks in the church (and in other areas of their life) is because they become jealous of each other's work and progress for Christ. So they choose to form "camps" to side against each other, as Paul indicated in a similar passage to what we heard from in 1 Corinthians 1:10–17, just a few minutes ago. Two chapters later, he writes in verses 1–9, "Brothers, I could not address you as spiritual, but as worldly— mere infants in Christ. I've had to feed you with milk, and not with solid food, because you couldn't digest anything strong. And even now, you still have to be fed on milk. For you are still only baby Christians, controlled by your own desires, not G's. When you are jealous of one another and divide up into quarreling groups, doesn't that prove you are still babies, wanting your won way? In fact, you are acting like people who don't belong to the Lord at all. There you are, quarreling about whether I am greater than Apollos, and dividing the church. Doesn't this show how little you have grown in the Lord?

"Who am I, and who is Apollos, that we should be the cause of a quarrel? Why, we're just G's servants, each of us with certain special abilities, and with our help, you believed. My work was to plant the send in your heart and Apollos' work was to water it, but it was God, not we, who made the garden grow in your hearts. The person who does the planting or the watering isn't very important, but God is important, because he is the one who makes things grow. Apollos and I are working as a team with the same aim, though each of us will be rewarded for our own hard work. We are only G's coworkers. You are God's garden, not ours; you are God's building, not ours."

In his book entitled *Great Church Fights*, the author Leslie Flynn wrote, "I read of a father who was in his study reading, and he heard a commotion outside the door. It was his daughter who was playing with her friends. The noise got louder and louder, and their talking got more and more heated and argumentative, until finally, the father couldn't restrain himself any longer. He pushed the door all the way open and said, 'Stop it. Now, honey, what's wrong?' After that brief reprimand, she responded without a second thought, 'But Daddy, we were just playing church.'"

Well, maybe "shark" is not the best term to use to describe numerous people in the church, today. After all, people can be more annoying to churches, than actually destructive to church life. So possibly some in the church act more like the barracuda or a crabby crab than they do as a shark, but even a lower level of negativity in the church is still a problem in the body of Christ that doesn't need to exist and does need to be dealt with properly.

The apostle Paul, then, goes on to admonish Christians for their cantankerous behavior once more in 1 Corinthians 6:1–8: "How is it that when you have something against another Christian, you take him to court and ask the heathen to decide the matter, instead of taking to other Christians to decide which of you is right? Don't you know that some day, we Christians are going to judge and govern the world? So why can't you decide even these little things among yourselves? Don't you realize that we Christians will judge and reward the very angels in Heaven? So you should be able to decide your problems down here on earth easily enough. Why, then, go to outside judges who are not even Christians, I am trying to make you ashamed. Isn't there anyone in all the church who is wise enough to decide these arguments? But, instead, one Christian sues another and accuses his Christian bro in front of unbelievers. To have such lawsuits at all is a real defeat for you as Christians. Why not just accept mistreatment and leave it at that? It would be far more honoring to the Lord to let yourselves be cheated. But, instead, you yourselves are the ones doing the wrong, cheating others, even your own bros."

And don't kid yourself thinking that "people who act like the human equivalent to sharks surely don't exist in the Church." No, maybe not in all, or even most, churches. But they do exist in them from time to time. Such a mindset is demonstrated, for instance in an Irish prayer, which reads, "May those that love us, love us; and those that don't love us, may G turn their hearts; and if He doesn't turn their hearts, may He turn their ankles, so we'll know them by their limping." Not exactly along the lines of "love your enemies and pray for those who persecute you," huh?

So, now we might want to answer the question, "If I know of a shark in my family, at work/school, or even in church, how should I go about relating to them?" Well, J gave us a direct, albeit maybe not simple or easy, guideline in Luke 6:27–31, when he said, "But I tell you who hear me: Love your enemies, do good to those who hate you, bless those who curse you, pray for those who mistreat you. If someone strikes you on one cheek, turn to him the other also. If someone takes your cloak, do not stop him from taking you shirt as well. Give to everyone who asks you, and if anyone takes what belongs to you, do not demand it back. Do to others as you would have them do to you."

Now, we have to realize that J didn't just preach this message, and then not follow through with it himself. Think about it: if there ever existed anyone in "the church" that we could label as "sharks," it would have been the Pharisees that were responsible for having put J to death. They, by and large were cold, cruel and calculating. But instead of J striking back and taking revenge on them, 1 Peter 2:23 tells us, "When they hurled their insults at him, he did not retaliate; when he suffered, he made no threats. Instead, he entrusted himself to him who judges justly."

But it was more than just verbal insults that J put up with coming from the "sharks" of the church of that day. He, of course, endured physical abuse on the cross. But as we also know, he was able to act kindly toward them even in *that* instance, since He's recorded as having prayed to G the Father in Luke 23:34, "Forgive them, Father, because they don't know what they're doing." And obviously, Stephen was able to follow that example of J's, since he's recorded in Acts 7:60, at the point of his being stoned to death, as praying, "Lord, don't hold this sin against them."

Now, once again from Jim Bakker's story, he demonstrates a contemporary example of someone today who was able to follow the same principle after he had once more receiving a lot of "hate mail" while in prison. Bakker began to teach and preach to the other inmates in the prison where he was serving time, and at one point, he details part of the lesson that he communicated to them. He writes, "I told the men about Booker T. Washington, founder of the Tuskegee Institute, a school known primarily for its education of black men and women. In the middle of awful racial prejudice, Washington said, 'I will permit NO man to narrow and degrade my soul by making me hate him.'"

Still, Scripture has yet more to say on the topic of how to properly deal with the sharks of society. As the Bible relates together in Romans 12:14 and 1 Corinthians 4:12, "And as for those who try to make your life a misery, bless them. Don't curse, bless…When we are curse, we bless; when we are persecuted, we endure."

Now, two men named Gary Samlley and John Trent put on a seminar in which they discuss the temperaments in a typical family (or other people groups). The lion temperament is the strong hearted, determined, resilient individual, as well as decisive, opinionated and usually loud. Then, there's the golden retriever—care-giving and compassionate. You can unload on a golden retriever. He lies right there and understands. Next is the otter—fun loving and relaxed. Usually, they're the youngest in the family/group. "Relax, everything's cool" is the attitude they have. Then, there's the hard working and diligent Beaver, responsible and organized. These, then, are the kinds of people that you actually want to have in your church, family and place of work, and you want to have a lot of them.

So when I was planning this sermon a few months ago, I was explaining it to Lisa and the kids, and I asked them for their help. I said, I know what kinds of fish I can use to illustrate the "dark" side of personalities—sharks, barracudas, and crabs—but what kind of fish do I use to support the Christian side of my sermon?

Well, Candace almost immediately responded, "I know Dad, use the angelfish."

And I said, "That's perfect!"

Well, an example of an angel fish in action came once again from Jim Bakker's experience. At times, we can choose to be an angelfish (instead of a shark) in people's lives when we do something as simple as write a short, encouraging note or letter to them, just right when it might mean the most. Bakker details, at one point, about the encouraging letters he received while in prison. He then tells of a letter he received from a fellow pastor, named Owen Carr. Bakker writes Owen seemed to recognize that I was not in prison by accident, without G being aware of my whereabouts and circumstances. It was as though Owen had sense what G was beginning to teach me. "I have confidence in you, Jim," Carr wrote, "that you will walk near to the heart of G, and that you will let him bring peace and quiet to your heart, and keep victory in your soul." Now, everybody, can you see how powerful and yet simple that was? Can you see from Owen Carr's example of ministering to Jim Bakker at that point, how easy, and yet effective, it can be to be an angelfish in somebody else's life, rather than a shark, barracuda, or crab?

Pat Boone and Charles Colson both not only wrote Bakker encouraging letters while he was in jail but also wrote the judge presiding over Bakker's case, as character witnesses. Other well-known Christian ministers who took this way of ministering to him were Kenneth Copeland, Oral Roberts, and Rex Humabard. Yes, it's true, that to behave like a shark toward people around us, to do so can take a lot of work and effort. Sometimes, it takes a lot of hard work to carry off really destructive behavior. But other times, all it takes is a simple sentence or two to tear someone down to their face or ruin their reputation. Likewise, whereas at times there needs to be a lot of preparation in order to bless someone in a mighty and powerful way, at other times, all it takes to be angelfish in someone's life is to say something nice, to them or about them.

Remember, everybody, we're not to be like sharks in the church and other areas of life, separating and dividing people. We're supposed to be about loving and honoring people, keeping the Body together. As Ephesians 3:4–6 says, "Do your best to preserve the unity which the Spirit gives, by the peace that binds you together. There is one body and one Spirit, just as there is one hope to which G has called you. There is one Lord, one Faith, one baptism; there is one God and Father of all men, who is Lord of all, works through all, and is in all."

All right. Take a look at the cartoon I've got included in the bulletin, today. Sherman, the shark, and his crab friend are talking, and the crab starts the conversation: "Doesn't it irk you how sharks get portrayed in the media? According to all those nature documentaries, sharks are just mindless eating machines that think of nothing but food."

It's at that point that Sherman notices a little fish skeleton on the floor of the ocean, so he says to the crab, "You gonna eat that?"

And the crab responds, "Gross, no. Go for it." He then continues: "And crabs don't fare any better. According to them, we're short-tempered, conceited and ego-maniacal. Hmph! Why is it such a well-kept secret that crabs are smooth and sophisticated and warm, and just a little bit sweet and a little bit spicy, with a generous portion of crab on the inside?"

Sherman continues to munch away on that fish skeleton. "That's you?" Sherman asks.

"Yeah!" says the crab.

Sherman then says, "Sounds more like crab ravioli."

"It's me!" the crab says.

If we were to compare ourselves with the various kinds of ocean life, how would we fit in, in connection with how we treat others? A shark? A barracuda? A crab? Or an angelfish?

So You Used to Worship Satan, Eh?
Acts 7:54; 8:3; 9:1-22

All right, let me get this straight. You used to worship the devil, but now you worship J. What's the catch? Is this some sort of publicity stunt? This can't be real! What? You used to be a devil worshipper, but now you're a Christian? Ah man, you're not going to be any fun to hang around with anymore, Mr. Goody Two-Shoes. So you say you used to worship Satan, but now you're following J. Man, I'm gonna be praying for you.

I'm going to talk to you today about two people, besides the apostle Paul, who (as you know) actually persecuted the church before he became a devoted follower of J. Those two other men are Brian Welch and Dave Mustaine, both of whom have had histories of being heavy metal rock band members who used to sing about death, the occult and sinful acts, recently had a total change of heart by accepting Christ as their Savior.

To begin with, though, let's take a look at the tremendous difference that took place in the apostle Paul, when he 1st came to J. Acts 7:54–8:3 tells of what Paul (Saul) was like to start with: "When they heard this, they were furious and gnashed their teeth at him. But Stephen, full of the HS, looked up to heaven and saw the glory of G, and J standing at the right hand of G. 'Look,' he said, 'I see heaven open and the Son of Man standing at the right hand of G.' At this, they covered their ears and yelling at the top of their voices, they all rushed at him, dragged him out of the city and began to stone him. Meanwhile, the witnesses laid their clothes at the feet of a young man named Saul. While they were stoning him, Stephen prayed, 'Lord J, receive my spirit.' Then he fell on his knees and cried out, 'Lord, do not hold this sin against them.' When he had said this, he (fell asleep). And Saul approved of his death. On that day, a great persecution broke out against the church at Jerusalem, and all except the apostles were scattered throughout Judea and Samaria. Godly men buried Stephen and mourned him deeply. But Saul began to destroy the church.

Going from house to house, he dragged off men and women and put them into prison."

Okay. He may not have started out worshipping the devil, but Paul (when he was still known as Saul) was certainly doing the devil's work. But this is what Acts 9:1–22 says, "Meanwhile, Saul was still breathing out murderous threats against the Lord's disciples. He went to the high priest and asked him for letter to the synagogues in Damascus, so that if he found any there who belonged to the Way, he might take them prisoners to Jerusalem. As he neared Damascus, suddenly a light from heaven flashed around him. He fell to the ground and heard a voice say to him, 'Saul, Saul, why do you persecute me?' 'Who are you, Lord?' Saul asked. 'I am J, whom you are persecuting. Now get up and go into the city, and you will be told what you must do.' The men traveling with Saul stood there speechless; they heard the sound but did not see anyone. Saul go up from the ground, but when he opened his eyes, he couldn't see anything. So they led him by the hand into Damascus. For 3 days, he was blind and didn't eat or drink anything."

When G spoke to a disciple in Damascus named Ananias and told him about Saul, Ananias replied that he had heard all about the harm that Saul had done to followers of J in Jerusalem. "But the Lord said to Ananias, 'Go. This man is my chosen instrument to carry my name before the Gentiles and their kings and before the people of Israel. I will show him how much he must suffer for my name.'" After Ananias goes, then, to see Saul and lay hands on him, Saul is healed of his temporary blindness.

Acts 9:20–22 then say this: "At once, Saul began to preach in the synagogues that J is the Son of G. All those who heard him were astonished and asked, 'Isn't he the man who raised havoc in Jerusalem among those who call on this name? And hasn't he come here to take them as prisoners to the chief priests?' Yet, Saul grew more and more powerful and baffled the Jews living in Damascus by proving that J is the Christ."

Well, just as people had a hard time accepting the fact that Saul—this persecutor of the Church—could possibly become a Christian, people today might have a hard time coming to believe that someone like Dave Mustaine, a guitarist and signer for the heavy metal band Megadeath, could become a Christian as well, but it's true. It seems that Mr. Mustaine recently became ill with an affliction that caused great pain in his arm.

He tried to find the cause of the pain, and a cure for it, so that he could continue to play guitar comfortably, but he couldn't find relief in the least. Finally, as a last resort, he turned to G in prayer, asking to be healed, and G saw to it that that is just exactly what happened.

We know by the Scripture we just read that Saul was transformed by his healing, how was Dave Mustaine affected? Well, instead of singing about heathenism and the occult, he seems to have changed considerably. Take for example a sample of the words from a song off of Megadeath's latest album. The song is entitled "Truth Be Told": "This is the 1st tale of death in the world, when Cain struck down Abel, a family broken. Since then mankind's dominated his own kind to insult and injure. There's no such thing as peace, 'til death do us part. Truth be told—Sin lies at the doorway. Truth be told— Hell's open for business now. Truth be told, the soil cries out for revenge. Truth be told, death is upon the ground, all around. Tribulation strikes and we're his hand, still, you just go on your way: head in the sand, ignoring the rain, just like the flood in Noah's day, in his day." Another song on the same album consists of Psalm 23, recited in the King James Version, set to heavy metal in the background. Now, you may not think much of that idea, but regardless of your personal musical taste, you have to admit: it sounds a lot like Dave Mustaine has had a personal experience in Christ.

A number of years ago, a minister of the Church of England attended a meeting at which the people prayed for Israel, while in a London Jewish mission. Coming out on the street, he met a fellow minister, who had attended a special service at St. Paul's Cathedral on the anniversary of the conversion of the apostle Paul. After greeting each other, the second minister asked the other where he had been. He told him he had attended a Jewish mission meeting, but the second minister expressed surprise that the 1st minister would actually believe in the possibility of Jews coming to faith in Christ. The minister who had attended the mission meeting asked the other minister where he had been, and he was told that the other pastor had been to a special service in honor of St. Paul at the cathedral bearing his name.

The clergyman who had attended the Jewish service asked, "Who exactly was Paul?"

The hesitant reply came: "I guess you could call him a 'believing Jew.'"

"What music did they have at the service?"

"Why, Mendelssohn's 'St. Paul,' of course."

"Who was Mendelssohn?"

"Why, a German."

"No, he wasn't—he was a believing Jew."

The minister who didn't believe in the possibility of Jews coming to Christ had been in a church dedicated to the memory of a Jewish believer, attending a service honoring this Jew's conversion to Christianity, had been listening to music composed by a Jewish believer, and was talking to a fellow minister— who was Rev. Aaron Bernstein, a converted Jew! This story, as well as the stories of the apostle Paul and that of Dave Mustaine should remind us that we should never give up on anyone coming to faith in Christ.

Now, it's sad to say, but there will undoubtedly be those who used to like the type of words Dave Mustaine and Megadeath used to sing to, but who now will be bitterly disappointed that Megadeath has changed its tune. Those particular people are likely to think of Mustaine as being an absolute fool for the decision he's made. But as a man named Jim Elliot once pointed out, "He is no fool who gives what he cannot keep to gain what he cannot lose." Dave Mustaine is no longer a fool, no longer a loser.

You know, when many people are converted, they make the mistake of thinking that "their battle has already been fought and won." But after serving Christ for a while, they realized that coming to J is a lot like enlisting in the army: there's not only the battle they're presently in, but there are many more to follow. We need to pray for the Dave Mustaines of the world, those who come to Christ unexpectedly, that they would not eventually throw in the towel and walk away, but that they would hang on tight to Christ throughout the entirety of their life. J's parable of the sower and the seeds demonstrates that not everybody who starts out living a life in Christ is successful in following him to the end. As Alan Redpath wrote in his book *The Making of a Man of God*, "The conversion of a soul is the miracle of the moment, but the making of a saint is the task of a lifetime."

But even though there is a long road ahead for people like Dave Mustaine, we rejoice for people like him who have made the transition of going from an earthly life that WAS headed for eternity in hell to a life aimed toward a heavenly existence once death occurs. Romans 6:4 expresses that idea when, there, the Bible states, "By our baptism, then, we were buried with him and shared his death, in order that, just as Christ was raised from death by the glorious power of the Father, so also we might live a new life."

Now, though we ourselves are responsible for our own spiritual health and well-being, we need to understand that as fellow Christians with one another, we need to always support and uplift others up in prayer and in any other way possible when someone who used to live a life opposed to Christ comes to him in faith. To illustrate that point, there's the story of a young man, aptly named Sinner, who once received from his Heavenly Father a beautiful bright-red convertible. He named his new car Salvation, for it was new, clean, modern, and powerful. The car delighted the young man, especially since it was a free gift. He never could have afforded it himself. He was so excited, in fact, that he changed his name from Sinner to Saved.

Well, he washed his car every week, took pictures of it and sent them to friends. He'd look it over—top, bottom, front, back, inside, and out. He never tired of telling his friends about this gift he'd received: "My Father gave it to me...it was free!" A few days later, Saved was out on the highway, pushing Salvation. An individual named Helper walked up and introduced himself and asked if he could assist Saved. "Oh, no thanks," came the reply, "I'm just out enjoying my new car," as he wiped the sweat off his face. "I just had a little trouble because my bumper kept cutting my hands, especially on these hills. But then a nice man helped me by showing me how to mount rubber cushions right here, under the bumper, and now I can push this thing for hours without a blister.

Helper asked, "Have you pushed the car very far?"

"About two hundred miles. It's been hard, but since it was a gift from my Father, it's the least I can do in return to thank him." Helper opened the door on the right side and told Saved to get in. Saved decided to go along, slid into the front passenger side, and rested for the first time since receiving the car. Helper then went around the other side and got in behind the wheel, starting the car.

"What's that noise?" Saved questioned.

Before long, the two of them were driving down the road at sixty miles per hour. You see, for those just starting out in the faith, they just may need a "little extra push," a little help and encouragement from someone else who's had a fair amount of experience in walking the Christian walk. Then, spiritual victory can come.

Someone once wrote that the evangelical church reproduced and improved the old Latin hymns and tunes and produced a larger number of original ones. It introduced congregational singing. The German reformation introduced a hymnal by which the people could sing their faith. The hymn then became, next to the German Bible and the German sermon, the most powerful missionary of the doctrines of sin and redemption. Now, I know that nobody else other than me in the room here today would dare listen to the type of music that Dave Mustaine would put out. But since he has become a Christian and begun to share the Christian message through his type of music, we need to pray that (1) he will stay true to the faith and only grow stronger in his walk with Christ and (2) the people who listen to that group's music from now on will eventually themselves "get the message."

It really does sound as though Mr. Mustaine has made a tremendous change in his life, for the better. It really shouldn't be a concern where he was before now, in his spiritual life, or even "how he got where he is." The important thing is—he's changed. Along those lines, I like what Galatians 6:15 says in the Living Bible: "It doesn't make any difference whether you've been circumcised or not; what counts is whether we really have been changed into new and different people."

May 31, 2009 I Smell Something Funny—
the Story of the People's Temple
Jeremiah 23:9-40

Sometime in 1977, Rev. Jim Jones, who had been influenced in his theology by Unitarian Humanism as well as Marxism, founded his church, which he named, The People's Temple, near San Francisco. Over time, Jones began to make the outrageous claims that he, himself, was God, Buddha and strangely enough Lenin. In the end on November 18, 1978 in Jonestown, Guyana, 914 people, including Jones, lost their lives.

It all got started when Jones promised his congregation to build a utopia where people of all races and classes could work together for the common good. Jones had been well-connected with San Francisco political leaders, and he had been appointed to the San Francisco Housing Authority, so things had been going well, there, for a while. But during the 1970s, the People's Temple was accused of being abusive toward a portion of its church's membership, so the idea to build their own little utopia came into Jones's mind, and they left for Guyana.

In '78, then, due to concerns that relatives of the church's members had that Jones was holding their loved ones against their will, Rep. Leo Ryan traveled to Guyana in order to see for himself what was going on, and to take back home with him any interested People's Temple church members. Sadly, though, Ryan was at the point of getting ready to board planes with his group and a few dozen People's Temple members, when gunmen who had been sent by Jones, killed him and three cameramen, and wounded eleven others. Back at the compound, then, Jones warned the rest of the group of the impending response this action would undoubtedly bring about, with the US government certain to send some kind of physical retribution against them. He then led them all in a mass suicide, which they had actually rehearsed for, many times over.

Cyanide-laced grape Kool-Aid was squirted in the mouths of the babies on the compound and also given to the children. As bodies piled up, the adults drank the poisoned mixture, or were shot to death by gunmen who were charged with enforcing the mass suicide.

Unfortunately, the story of the People's Temple is not the only example of such a tragedy, although I believe it holds the record for the largest number of collective deaths. The real tragedy of all this, however, is that it could have been prevented if those people, who apparently were "religious" people of some kind, had only protected themselves from such a false prophet as Jim Jones by paying attention to passages of Scripture, like the one found in Jeremiah 23:9– 40. Reading selected verses from that passage, here's what G's word has to say:

"The prophets follow an evil course and use their power unjustly. Both prophet and priest are godless; even in my temple, I find their wickedness... Do not listen to what the prophets are prophesying to you; they fill you with false hopes. They speak visions from their own minds, not from the mouth of the Lord...Which of them has stood in the council of the Lord to see or to hear his word? I did not send these prophets, yet they have run with their message; I did not speak to them, yet they have prophesied. But if they had stood in my council, they would have proclaimed my words to my people, and I would have turned them from their evil ways and from their evil deeds.

"I have heard what the prophets say who prophesy lies in my name. They say, 'I had a dream! I had a dream!' How long will this continue in the hearts of these lying prophets, who prophesy the delusions of their own minds? Let the prophet who has a dream tell his dream, but let the one who has my word speak it faithfully. Therefore," declares the Lord, "I am against the prophets who steal from one another words supposedly from Me. Yes, I am against the prophets who wag their own tongues and yet say, 'The Lord declares.' Indeed, I am against those who prophesy false dreams. They tell them and lead my people astray with their reckless lies, yet I did not send them or appoint them. They do not benefit these people in the least," declares the Lord.

"If a prophet or priest or anyone else claims, 'This is the oracle of the Lord,' I will punish that man and his household. You must not mention the oracle of the Lord again, because every man's own word becomes his oracle, and so you distort the words of the living God, the Lord Almighty, our God...Although you claim, 'This is the oracle of the Lord,' THIS is what the Lord says: You used the words, 'This is the oracle of the Lord,' even though I told you that you must not claim, 'This is the oracle of the Lord. Therefore, I will surely forget you and cast you out of my presence.'"

Now, what I'd like to do with the remainder of our time here together today, is to go through this passage from Jeremiah 23, and the examples of Jonestown and other instances, to see what kinds of lessons we ourselves can extract from them, to help make certain that we ourselves never end up like the 914 People's Temple members did on November 18, 1978.

You see, Jim Jones had started off leading his People's Temple church focusing and centering on real Bible doctrine, but over time, he began to preach less and less biblical content and instead focused on social activism. Now, there's absolutely nothing wrong with getting directly involved in helping to make this a better world for those who are oppressed in some way, but when the pastor/preacher of the church you attend at the time starts to ignore Bible content in his messages for anything else, you'll know that something smells funny, theologically speaking.

Well, soon after moving his church community to Jonestown, Guyana, Jones would have the hundreds of his followers practice and rehearse for a ritual of mass suicide, and for them to do so as a test of loyalty to—and faith in—Jones. Rep. Ryan's delegation, then, went to Jonestown to make certain that the people's freedom weren't being restricted. The question that was being asked at that point by many surrounding this group was, "Could Jones's followers leave Jonestown, if they ever wanted to?"

Now, ironic as it might sound, Jones's own wife and son were some of the ones who desperately wanted out. But as it turned out, Jones's wife stayed behind, yet she was able to get their son out of harm's way by arranging for him to go with a group of the Jonestown community who were planning to go to another city in Guyana (Georgetown, in fact), to play in an arranged soccer match. You see, Jones would use fear to control his followers, making them afraid of him so that they would obey his orders. He therefore was able to get most of them to sign a petition to attempt to keep Congressman Ryan and company out of coming to visit Jonestown. But one of his flock is able to talk him into allowing Ryan and his assistants to come visit.

Well, some of the People's Temple members saw an opportunity to sneak out of the community, with Ryan coming to make this visit, so one of them secretly slipped the Congressman a handwritten note, pleading for him to let as many who wanted to come go with him. But when Ryan's group began to get ready to leave to come back to the US, most of them had a nagging feeling that Jones wasn't about to let them be able to leave to go back to the US and tell others what they'd witnessed and experienced. The hopeful deserters of the Jonestown experience, then, knew that Jones would make it tough—if not altogether impossible—for them to leave. Ryan and his group had come to realize just how scary it was that so many people were basically under Jones' total control.

Unfortunately, the "help us escape" note didn't get passed to Ryan himself or another responsible person in his entourage. Although people in the congressman's group had strong unsettled feelings and suspicions about Jones and the whole idea of Jonestown, Ryan himself seemed to be rather impressed and perfectly okay with it all. But he eventually got a hold of the note that had not reached him at first, and he offers the one person who wrote it the opportunity to come back to the US with him. Yet he still didn't realize just how much danger he and his party were in. Within hours of the note having been passed to him, it became clear that actually many people wanted to leave Jonestown. Again, some in Ryan's part knew that there was going to be serious trouble of some kind, before they'd have a chance to leave. Some, however, thought that there was absolutely nothing to worry about.

So why do I remind you of this piece of tragic religious history? That all happened in the 1970s, so why bring it up now? Because the lessons we get from the story of Jim Jones and the People's Temple are as applicable today as they were then. Therefore, the first point about all this I'd like to mention is that spoken of in Ezekiel 44:23, when G is speaking to Ezekiel about the duties and responsibilities of the priests, and he says of them, "They are to teach my people the difference between the Holy and the common, and show them how to distinguish between the clean and the unclean." You see, it's great to be able to simply know the difference between what's true and of God and what's not. A lot of people in the church aren't even certain of that kind of thing. But what's just as important is that we teach ourselves and other Christians around us how to distinguish/tell the difference between the truth and a lie, so that when either of them presents themselves to us, we'd be prepared to figure out just exactly which one it is we're facing. So if you're taking notes on this sermon, this morning, go ahead and write down Ezekiel 44:23. It's the first in a line of Scriptures we'll use this morning that I think will help us keep from following the path of the people in the People's Temple.

And before you say to yourself, "But I would never fall for a false prophet like Jim Jones. I could smell something funny, theologically speaking, about someone like that a mile away," just remember that J warned five times in Matthew 24:4–5, 11, and 23–24 (say twice) that in the last days, there would be false prophets and messiahs who would appear and perform great signs and miracles to deceive even the elect—if that were possible.

So understanding that truth, we then need to take the verse found in 1 John 4:1 to heart and follow it's advice, when the Bible says there, "Dear friends, do not believe every spirit, but test the spirits to see if they are from G, because many false prophets have gone out into the world." I dare say that if more of the members of the People's Temple had "tested" the supposed prophet they had originally thought they'd found in Jim Jones, there probably would have been many less than 914 people who wound up dead on November 18, 1978.

Well, there are numerous other passages in Scripture that pretty much describe numerous aspects of the horrible scenario we've been looking at, today. For instance, Acts. 17:11 points out that "the Berean people were of more noble character than the Thessalonians, for they received the message with great eagerness and examined the Scriptures every to see if what Paul said was true." I can't help but wonder if each of the people who came to be part of the People's Temple had sincerely studied the Bible like they should have during the early years of their Christian growth, if more have them couldn't have seen more clearly just where Jones was beginning to lead them before it was too late. How much did they check what the Bible said, as Jones preached to them, to see if what he was saying was accurate? I guess we'll never know.

Yes, if they had done just that, then they would have seen for themselves— early on in their connection to Jones—what J described in Matthew 7:15 when he warned, "Watch out for false prophets. They come to you in sheep's clothing, but inwardly, they are ferocious wolves." Likewise, the apostle Paul warned the elders at the church in Ephesus, according to Acts 20:29–31, "I know that after I leave, savage wolves will come in among you and will not spare the flock. Even from your own number, men will arise and distort the Truth in order to draw away disciples after them. So be on guard! Remember that for three years I never stopped warning each of you night and day with tears."

But in addition, the Scripture goes on elsewhere within itself to continue to warn against people like this, who are to come with the passage of time. 2 Peter 2:1–3, for instance, cautions, "But there were also false prophets among the people, just as there will be false teachers among you. They will secretly introduce destructive heresies, even denying the sovereign Lord who bought them—bringing swift destruction on themselves. Many will follow their shameful ways and will bring the way of truth into disrepute. In their greed, these teachers will exploit you with stories they have made up. Their condemnation has long been hanging over them, and their destruction has not been sleeping." Did you happen to catch the phrase "Many will follow their shameful ways and will bring the way to truth into disrepute"? Many people, as in 913, who followed Rev. Jim Jones.

And maybe most pointedly and most accurately prophesied about Jones comes the verse found in Ezekiel 13:19, in which G said to the people, "You have profaned me among my people for a few handfuls of barley and a few scraps of bread. By lying to my people, who listen to lies, you have killed those who should not have died."

Remember, J said three times in Matthew 24 that false prophets would arrive on the scene and mislead many. Never allow yourself to be one of those kinds of church goers. Embrace the Truth and nothing else, know who it is that you believe in and why you believe that. Then, don't let anyone mislead you. If you should ever attend a revival or Bible study or other church, and the charismatic, well-like preacher starts making statements about the Faith that you know aren't true, listen to that little voice inside your head. Then get up and run, don't walk, but run to the nearest exit before it's too late.

The Compassionate Greaseman
Proverbs 1:1-7

I listen to a rock radio station in H-burg, WBOP. During the morning show on WBOP, the disc jockey is a guy who calls himself the Greaseman. Don't ask me why—that's just the man's nickname. Anyway, like most morning radio DJs, the Greaseman acts like a real clown on the air. He's forever making wisecracks about politicians and celebrities who figure prominently in the news, often talking in cartoon-character-like voices, and whenever anyone calls into the station to talk to the Greaseman on the air in the morning, he clowns around with them as well. People call with their minor problems and complain: "Hey, Grease, my boss is a jerk! Do you think I ought to quit my job?"

The Greaseman then replies something like, "Yeah, it does sound like your boss is a real loser. It sounds like he's got peas for brains. On Monday, I suggest you tell him to take a hike and quit."

"Thanks, Greaseman," comes the reply. "I knew you'd tell me the right thing to do."

You know that in a case like this, it'd be real easy to look at such a person who calls the Greaseman to give him some true direction and help and point them in the direction of the Bible in order for them to get the help/advice they need. After all, the Bible says Proverbs 1:1–7, "The proverbs of Solomon son of David, king of Israel: for attaining wisdom and discipline; for understanding words of insight; for acquiring a disciplined and prudent life, doing what is right and just and fair; for giving prudence to the simple, knowledge and discretion to the young— let the wise listen and add to their learning, and let the discerning get guidance—for understanding proverbs and parables, the sayings and riddles of the wise. The fear of the Lord is the beginning of knowledge, but fools despise wisdom and discipline."

"To Scripture and to Christians who know the Bible is where people like fellow who called the Greaseman need to go," we might say.

Well, one day not too long ago, a guy calls into the Greaseman, literally in tears. Once Greaseman answered the phone, the guy starts to sob, explaining that he caught the woman that he was planning to marry soon in a less-thanappropriate situation with another man. I'm thinking, "Great. This guy's got a real problem, and he's expecting the Greaseman of all people to help him out. This ought to be good; I wonder what 'the Grease' will tell him."

Well, I simply could not believe the compassion, sensitivity, and sympathy that came out of the Greaseman's mouth! He immediately took this fellow very seriously and began to ask the poor guy a few questions about his relationship with his supposedly future fiancé. After getting all the necessary details from the grieving caller, the Greaseman went on to comfort him, doing a pretty good job: "You know, you sound like an intelligent and decent kind of guy. I know it hurts to have something like this happen, but you know what they say: 'There are plenty of fish in the sea.' With your sincerity, obvious intelligence and friendliness, you have to know that it won't be long before you find 'the right one.'"

Sometime after the guy admitted that the Greaseman had actually helped comfort him and hung up, I thought about the conversation that had taken place. I thought to myself, why didn't the caller go to a preacher for help/counsel? Even if he hadn't been a churchgoing Christian, many non- Christians go to a pastor for help in times of need. Why didn't he go to a professional counselor? No, he didn't do any of those things. Instead, he calls the Greaseman on the live morning radio show. Why? Unfortunately, I think I know not one, but two, good reasons why that guy called the Greaseman, rather than to rely on the church, for help in his time of need.

For one thing, maybe the man's impression of Christians is that—for all the talk to love and compassion that they supposedly exhibit—Christians just really don't care about reaching out to those who are hurting who are also outsiders to the Church. "Christians? Not caring? Who in the church would act like that to set such an example for that young man?" Well, if that young man would say that he'd seen more than one example of someone who called themselves a Christian who avoided showing compassion to those who needed it, it wouldn't be the 1st time such a thing has happened. Many times, the "religious people" are the last ones to show an interest in coming to the rescue when someone is hurting.

Remember J's parable of the good Samaritan? Christ mentioned that the first two of three men to pass by the man who had been beaten and robbed and left for dead were a priest and a Levite. A priest was the first one to come along and notice that this man obviously needed help, but instead of helping, chose to simply go on his merry little way, effectively leaving the man for dead.

Oh, sure. We all have our reasons as to why it would be better "not to get involved" with someone else's problems: "They got themselves into this mess. They can get themselves out. I don't have the time to fool with them because I've got problems of my own (don't we all?). I'd like to help them out, but let's face it—this guy's just too weird!" Who knows? I can't say for certain, of course, but for all we know, the fellow who called the Greaseman on that morning may have tried solicit some sympathy from folks who attend a church near him, but because they felt that he needed to reap what he had sown, because they may have felt that they didn't have the time to devote to helping him out, or because they may have thought he was just a little too weird for them to mess with, they may have told him what the priest in the story of the Good Samaritan basically said as he silently walked by the injured man —"Sorry, I'm not going to help you."

When J spoke the parable of the Good Samaritan, it wasn't the 1st time recorded in the Bible that we see this idea of helping someone out who is in need. In fact, if we should even come across someone who is an enemy of ours who is in need of help, it's written in Exodus 23:4–5, "If you come across your enemy's ox or donkey wandering off, be sure to take it back to him. If you see the donkey of someone who hates you fallen down under its load, do not leave it there; be sure to help him with it." Now let's figure this out right, folks. If Scripture is plainly adamant, here, that we are to help our enemy if they should need rescuing, certainly it would follow that G would naturally direct us to come to the assistance of someone who is just a total stranger to us, someone whom we've never met before but who has called us up or come to see us with the intention of not hanging up or leaving until they get a positive response. Otherwise, they just might figure on going on their own way, continuing their search to find someone who really cares. At that point, they too might figure that the Greaseman is their last hope.

Now, another reason why people might turn to the Greaseman in time of trouble instead of the church is because of their fear of people in the church giving them more words of condemnation rather than words of comfort. I think there's more than one reason why J is recorded as having said in Matthew 7:1–5, "Do not judge, or you too will be judged. For in the same way you judge others, you will be judged, and with the measure you use, it will be measured to you. Why do you look at the speck in your brother's eye and pay no attention to the plank in your own eye? How can you say to your brother, 'Let me take the speck out of you eye,' when all the time there's a plank in your own eye? You hypocrite, 1st take the plank out of your own eye, and then you will be able to see clearly to remove the speck from your brother's eye."

Of course, in this passage, J was warning us to guard against the attitude of excessive spiritual pride, in comparison to others. While that should be the main message of those verses, another lesson we get from that passage is this: When people find themselves in hot water—desperately needing the help of someone else—even if they did something to put themselves in that very situation, the last thing that they need to hear at first from someone in the church is something like, "Boy, did you ever mess up! What were you thinking? How could you be so stupid as to do something like that?"

I'm sure you've heard the saying that "G's army is the only army that shoots its wounded." Unfortunately, that's all too true. Sometimes, when a member of a church gets themselves into trouble, the surrounding church members would rather "sacrifice that person on the altar of their own self-righteousness" rather than to actually think about helping the person first, then after everything has been pretty much resolved, working with them by lovingly confronting them by saying, "You know, that really wasn't the type of activity that Christians need to get themselves involved in—you should have known better. Let's make sure you never do anything like that ever again."

And then, it would be our responsibility, as a church, to support that person as they try to reform themselves—to encourage and do what we could to work with them to see that they never got in that kind of situation ever again. Such an attitude in the church demonstrates to the surrounding outside, unsaved community that here's a church that won't simply condemn me for what I've done, but one that I can go to if I need help. And who knows? After that kind of love is expressed to that person, we just might end up leading them to J. I think the fellow that I heard call into the Greaseman show that morning just might have already solicited help from the Christian community, but having received a less than warm, loving response, he probably felt like, "Well, I'll call the Greaseman—he won't judge me."

After it appears to people outside the church that either (1) Christians in the church just don't give a flip or (2) Christians in the church will just simply condemn them and not help them, (3) probably a final reason why many people choose to call the type of someone like the Greaseman rather than the church for help is because the people in the church, many times, have put themselves in just as much trouble (and often the same kinds of trouble) that the person in need is in. If we ourselves are struggling with the issues of drug/alcohol abuse, the last thing we're going to think about is going to a fellow drug addict for help. Instead, we go to a drug counselor—one who has the solution to our problem. If we're having a problem maintain fidelity in our marriage, then the thing we shouldn't do is to go to a fellow adulterer to ask, "So how should I go about putting an end to my/my spouse's unfaithfulness?" Instead, we go to a marriage counselor.

But when we, who are in the church, play the part of a hypocrite (saying that we live by the standards set forth in the Bible, but then do many things contrary to the teaching of Scripture), why would anyone come to us for advice on how to straighten out their life?

While detailing the story of his act of adultery that got him in so much spiritual and even legal trouble, Jim Bakker writes of his frustration at himself after feeling the effects of his sin, in his book I Was Wrong. On page 455, Bakker writes, "I had already apologized to the Christian community as best I could; I didn't know what else I should do. I continued to grieve deeply over the negative fallout my sin caused to the entire Body of Christ. No amount of apologizing could even make up for the worldwide denigration of the role of evangelists and TV ministries that resulted from my moral failure. Most of all, I had besmirched the name of the Lord JC, my blessed Savior and lover of my soul. What could I possibly do to ever make up for that?"

Now, to be fair to Rev. Bakker, he has learned his lesson, turned his life around, and now uses his past experience to help keep others out of the same trap he fell into. But you can see how the world takes those instances and uses them to say, "Why would I go to someone for help—someone who's life is just as messed up as mine?" That's yet another reason why people often call the Greaseman, rather than the church, when they need help. It's because of that kind of scenario that we need to set the standard of behavior for people to follow so that they might have more of a reason to look up to respect us, rather than laugh at us and thus might be inclined to come to us for help when they need it.

The Difference between Dog and Cat People
Romans 3:10-12; John 10:1-5

How many of you in here, this morning, have either a cat, dog, or both for pets? Dogs and cats are great, aren't they? We happen to have one of each—a cat named Tabby and a dog named Princess. Well, it occurred to me, recently, about just how different dogs and cats are besides the obvious physical differences. And then I thought about how those distinct differences can easily translate to lessons for us, this morning, on our relationship to G. Yes, I'm going to base a sermon on cats and dogs, today. Let me begin to explain by discussing cats, first.

Well, even those of us who don't own cats understand the simple truth that cats do their own thing. They aren't exactly trainable when it comes to most actions and behaviors. So cats—in that respect—remind me of the spiritually lost person, who is described in Romans 3:10–12: "There is no one righteous, no, not one. There is no one who understands, no one who seeks after G. They have all gone out of the way; together, they have gone wrong. There is no one who does what is right, no, not one." You know this—you can call for your cat until you're blue in the face, but if your cat doesn't want to come, they won't come. Why? Because a cat's gonna do what a cat's gonna do. Well, once again from Scripture, we see plainly that we humans are often just like that, according to Isaiah 53:6 and 56:11. It's here in the Bible that, together, these verses say, "We all, like sheep, have gone astray, each of us has turned to his own way...They are (wolves) with mighty appetites; they never have enough. They are shepherds who lack understanding; they all turn to their own way, each seeks his own gain."

But we also are like cats, not only in that we often like to "do our own thing" in the spiritual sense, often ignoring G's will and direction for our life just like a cat often ignores its owner, but cats also have a way of showing up begging for attention when they want it. If a cat is interested in your petting or feeding it, it's right there, where you are. But if a cat wants to play with a cat toy or simply wants to be left alone to sleep, it couldn't care less about you.

Unfortunately, we, too, can get like that in our relationship to G. Simon, the sorcerer, is recorded in Acts 8:14–24 as having an attitude like that. It's there that the Bible says, "When the apostles in Jerusalem heard that Samaria had accepted the Word of G, they sent Peter and John to them. When they arrived, they prayed for them that they might receive the HS, because the HS had not yet come upon any of them; they had simply been baptized into the name of the Lord Jesus. Then, Peter and John placed their hands on them, and they received the HS.

"When Simon saw that the Spirit was given at the laying on of the apostles' hands, he offered them money and said, 'Give me this ability, too, that everyone on whom I lay my hands may receive the HS.'

"Peter answered, 'May your money perish with you, because you thought you could buy the gift of God with money! You have no part or share in this ministry, because your heart is not right before G. Repent of this wickedness and pray to the Lord. Perhaps he will forgive you for having such a thought in your heart. For I see that you are full of bitterness and captive to sin.' "Then Simon answered, 'Pray to the Lord for me, so that nothing you have said may happen to me.'"

You see, Simon wasn't interested in loving Jesus simply for who he is and what he stands for, but Simon was only interested in receiving some of the benefits of having the HS within him, and he wanted those benefits for his own glory, at that. Maybe instead of being known as Simon the Sorcerer, he should have been known as Simon the Catman.

But a dog, on the other hand, is a totally different creature. Whereas you can't exactly train a cat to do anything on command, dogs—as you know—are practically all about being able to be trained. If a dog is adequately trained, they will obey when you tell them to do something. In other words, they act according to your will for them at that time. In connecting that characteristic of dogs, then, to our obeying G, David wrote in Psalm 119:33–34, "Teach me, O Lord, to follow your decrees; then I will keep them to the end. Give me understanding, and I will keep your law and obey it with all my heart." And not only are we who are Christians at the moment to obey G, but we are to teach others to obey G as we go about and witness to people about Christ. As J said when he was giving the Great Commission to his disciples, according to Matthew 28:18–20, "All authority in heaven and on earth has been given to me. Therefore, go and make disciples of all nations, baptizing them in the name of the Father and of the Son and of the Holy Spirit, and teaching them to obey everything I have commanded you."

And we will, in a way, behave like dogs in our relationship to J in that we are to obey him because we love him. I suppose there are people out there who have dogs that "love" them and obey them when given a commanded, but those dogs might do so because they only fear what their Master might do to them if they did not obey. And yes, we know that G will certainly punish us for not doing as he commands. But again, while we ought to have a healthy fear of G, we also ought to desire to serve J because he loves us and we love him. Together in John 14:23 and in 1 John 5:3, the Bible proves this point when the Scripture says in those two passages, "If anyone loves me, he will obey my teaching…This is love for G—to obey his commands." Once more, if you prefer to think if it this way, we are "dogs" for God in that we are to obey his direction in our life, since Deuteronomy 13:4 plainly states, "It is the Lord your G you must follow, and him you must revere. Keep his commands and obey him; serve him and hold fast to him."

Now, another interesting characteristic that separates cats from dogs— and "spiritual men from spiritual boys"—is how dogs and cats relate to a stranger, whenever one enters their living space. You're familiar with what great guardians of the home dogs are. If anyone comes into the house that they're not familiar with, even if it's a friend of the family or another relative who doesn't happen to live in that house, the dog knows something's up. "Something's not right, here," it thinks to itself. "I'm not acquainted with this person—therefore, they don't belong here!" And so, the dog begins to bark loudly and won't shut up until the person leaves the house. And just sticking the dog in a room separate from "the stranger" doesn't help. As long as that person is in the house, the dog knows this and won't be quiet again until that person's left. Cats, once again on the other hand, don't give two flips if you're a total stranger or not. They just want a nice, soft lap to sit and curl up on. I've been to some of your houses, I know. I'll often come away from visiting some folks who have cats, brushing the fur off my pants as I leave. (It's okay; I don't mind.)

Well, yes, it's nice to be friendly and sociable, like cats generally are. Christians ought to be friendly and sociable with whoever they meet. But we Christians also ought to be very careful about who we choose to attach ourselves to. While dogs might go a little overboard, barking wildly at every stranger who comes into their home, you have to admit that they're on guard and nothing is going to get past them that shouldn't. For us humans along those lines, J states in John 10:1–5, "I tell you the truth, the man who does not enter the sheep pen by the gate, but climbs in by some other way, is a thief and a robber. The man who enters by the gate is the shepherd of his sheep. The watchman opens the gate for him, and the sheep listen to his voice. He calls his own sheep by name and leads them out. When he has brought out all his own, he goes on ahead of them, and his sheep follow him because they know his voice. but they will never follow a stranger; in fact, they will run away from him because they do not recognize a stranger's voice."

You know, if cats were people, their tendency to overly trust people could get them in a whole lot of trouble, especially in the spiritual sense. Too many people today are way too accepting when a stranger knocks on their door and begins to talk to them about J. The person in the home just assumes, then, that because the person at the door is invoking J's name while not swearing, they must be okay to associate with and befriend. But when it comes to a scenario like that, we really need to be much more like a dog, who's always on the lookout for something "funny," something that's just not quite right.

But a final way that people are often like either cats or dogs, when it comes to "coming to J," different people are motivated by different methods to do the same thing. Let me explain this by using the example of attempting to get a cat or a dog out of a room or out from underneath a piece of furniture. You know, sometimes, we'd like to do some work in a certain room in the house, and before we get started, we discover that either Tabby or Princess has parked themselves under the couch or is simply playing around in the room where we need to have that space for ourselves, and we want them out of there.

You know what gets a dog moving? Usually, just call his name, and he comes running. Because, as we've just noted, a dog knows his master's voice, when he hears his own named called, that means his master is searching for him, for some reason. So nine times out of ten, when a dog hears his named being called, he comes bounding out from wherever he was at the time, to come greet his master. However, sometimes, simply calling a dog by his given name is not enough. Sometimes, a dog has to be enticed to come out from wherever he is, in order to do his master's bidding. I'll tell you what we do with Princess whenever we want her to come out of a room or out from under a piece of furniture. We go to the storage closet and get the bag of dog treats. We then shake the bag, close to where Princess is hiding so that she hears that familiar sound of those delicious morsels—and then, she comes running.

That's what I think heaven is partly for—to help people understand that G isn't just wanting us to "be good people and follow him blindly" just because he said so. G wants to reward us with a treat—an eternal treat. Certainly, Heaven, as it's described in the Bible, serves in part as a reward for us for living the life G called us to live, as it's described in Revelation 21:2–4: "I saw the Holy City, the New Jerusalem, coming down out of heaven from God, prepared as a bride beautifully dressed for her husband. And I heard a loud voice from the throne saying, 'Now the dwelling of God is with men, and he will live with them. They will be his people, and G himself will be with them and be their G. He will wipe every tear from their eyes. There will be no more death or mourning or crying or pain, for the old order of things has passed away.'"

You know this. The only enticement that some unsaved people need in order for them to agree to accept J as their Savior is for someone to explain to the them promise and glory of heaven, and that's good enough for them. Just the promise of that glorious reward is enough to say, "I'd like to have life after I die on earth, a life without grief, crying or pain."

But some people are like cats—a little less agreeable. For instance, when we want to get Tabby out of a room or out from under a piece of furniture, she won't come on out just because we call her. And she's also not likely to come out of where she is just because we shake the plastic container of cat food. Unlike Princess, the promise of a reward for Tabby doesn't really work. Well, I have a secret for any of you who find yourselves in a situation where you want to get a cat out from somewhere, and she just continues to "dig herself into wherever she is," refusing to come out.

Take a plastic grocery bag like this (show one), walk over to her as close as you can get, and shake the bag. I guarantee it will scare the tar out of her and she'll come running out from under the furniture and out the door of the room as fast as she can go. ("Hey, what was that!" "I think it was a flying ball of fur.") You see, where a reward won't work with enticing Tabby to do something we want her to, a threat will. You know, if there was only a heaven and no hell—if it was such that a person who was saved in J lived for eternity in heaven after they died, but unsaved people just went into a state of nonexistence (like they were before they were born), what would the big deal be? I've talked to people who believe that way. They say, "Wouldn't it be awful just to die and go back into the dust, not being able to have any kind of life anymore? Why would someone need to be tortured in Hell forever for their sin that they never repented for? Just going back into dust in the ground would be punishment enough." No, it wouldn't.

So what? You go back to being what you were before you were born. You didn't know that you weren't living a human life at the time, so where would the punishment be if you went back to being in that same condition? Hell is real, folks, and sometimes, G has to use that extra incentive to get people to see that they truly need to be saved from the penalty of their sins through J. Hell is real. That's why the Bible says in Revelation 20:10, 14–15, "And the devil, who deceived them, was thrown into the lake of burning sulfur, where the beast and the false prophet had been thrown. They will be tormented day and night for ever and ever…Then death and Hades were thrown into the lake of fire. The lake of fire is the 2nd death. If anyone's name was not found in the book of life, he was thrown into the lake of fire."

So not to knock cats. I like cats; I really do. But taking into consideration what we've talked about here today, which do you identify yourself with more in your relationship to Christ—a cat or a dog?

The Ultimate Reality Show
Matthew 25:32-46

I think one of the funniest moments in Hollywood movie history took place in the movie Crocodile Dundee. The movie was about a man from Australia who found himself living in the US for a time, while still holding on to the ways he was used to in the Outback. One of the parts I liked was where Mr. Dundee is walking down the street in metropolitan NYC. A couple of teenagers come up to him and attempt to mug him, by threatening him with a small pen knife. After the teens verbally threatened him and then brandished their "weapon," Dundee looks at them and asks (in an Australian accent, of course) "What's THAT?"

"It's a knife, you idiot!" one of the would-be muggers replies.

"A knife?" Dundee begins to respond. "That's not a knife." He then proceeds to reach into his vest and pulls out a huge, honking machete. He holds the machete up with one hand, points to it with the first finger of his other hand, and says, "Now this, this is a knife!"

The boys' eyes immediately fly wide open, their jaws drop, and they run off like scared rabbits.

You know, there are a lot of so-called reality shows on TV today: *Who Wants to Marry My Dad?*, *The Apprentice*, and *Survivor*. Reality shows? Realityshmeality! those aren't reality shows—there's nothing real about them, for more than one reason. Now, the judgment, the final judgment, the time when J will judge everyone who has ever lived, based on their actions and behavior throughout their lives, will be a reality show if there ever will be one. What will be so real about the final judgment? Well, let's take a look at our Scripture passage for this morning, Matthew 24:32–46, to find out:

"When the Son of Man comes in his glory and all the angels with him, he will sit on his throne in heavenly glory. All the nations will be gathered before him, and he will separate the people one from another, as a shepherd separates the sheep from the goats. He will put the sheep on is right and the goats on his left. Then the King will say to those on his right, 'Come, you who are blessed by my Father; take your inheritance, the kingdom prepared for you since the creation of the world. For I was hungry and you gave me something to eat; I was thirsty, and you gave me something to drink. I was a stranger and you invited me in; I needed clothes and you clothed me; I was sick and you looked after me, and I was in prison, and you came to visit me."

"Then the righteous will answer him, 'Lord, when did we see you hungry and feed you or thirsty and give you something to drink? When did we see you a stranger and invite you in, or needing clothes and clothe you? When did we see you sick or in prison and go to visit you?' The King will reply, 'I tell you the truth, whatever you did for one of the least of these brothers of mine, you did it for me.'

"Then, he will say to those on his left, 'Depart from me, you who are cursed, into the eternal fire prepared for the devil and his angels. For I was hungry and you gave me nothing to eat; I was thirsty, and you gave me nothing to drink; I was a stranger and you did not invite me in; I needed clothes, and you did not clothe me; I was sick and in prison, and you did not look after me.'

"They will also answer, 'Lord, when did we see you hungry or thirsty or a stranger or needing clothes or sick or in prison, and did not help you?' He will reply 'I tell you the truth: whatever you did not do for one of the least of these, you did not do for me.' Then, they will go away to eternal punishment, but the righteous to eternal life."

Christianity Today once printed an article by a man named Gary Thomas, and Thomas wrote there: "Thinking about eternity helps us retrieve perspective. I'm reminded of this every year when I figure my taxes. During the year; I rejoice at the paychecks and extra income, and sometimes, I flinch when I write out my tithe and offering. I do my best to be a joyful giver, but I confess that it's not always easy, especially when there are other perceived needs and wants. At the end of the year, however, all that changes. As I'm figuring my tax liability, I wince at every source of income and rejoice with every tithe and offering check—more income means more tax, but every offering and tithe means less tax. Everything is turned upside down, or perhaps, more appropriately, right-side-up. I suspect," Thomas concluded, "that the judgment Day will be like that." I agree with him. I think there will be a lot of people on that day who will approach the throne of grace will too much confidence in themselves. Then, they will come to see the absolute reality of just exactly how they lived their lives and receive their due.

Yes, the Bible has lots to say on the reality of G passing judgment on us due to how we conducted our lives. Scripture says in Jeremiah 17:10, "I the Lord search the heart and examine the mind, to reward a man according to his conduct, according to what his deeds deserve." And it won't just be the big things (good and bad) that we did throughout our lives that we'll be judged on. Even the little things that we did in connection with, or contrary to, biblical teaching will have an effect on the type of eternal reward that we'll receive. As J plainly stated in Matthew 10:42, "If anyone gives even a cup of cold water to one of these little ones because he is my disciple, I tell you the truth, he will certainly not lose his reward."

And just when will all this passing of judgment take place? Well, different people have differing ideas on the topic, but I think the Bible makes it pretty clear that it'll all take place when J comes back. In speaking about that point in future history, J stated in Matthew 16:27, "For the Son of Man is going to come in his Father's glory with his angels, and then he will reward each person according to what he has done." To reiterate the reality of judgment from Scripture before ending this portion of the message today, we should look at what Revelation 20:11–15 as to say on the matter: "Then I saw a great white throne and him who was seated on it. Earth and sky fled from his presence, and there was no place for them. And I saw the dead, great and small, standing before the throne, and books were opened. Another book was opened which is the book of life. The dead were judged according to what they had done, as recorded in the books. The sea gave up the dead that were in it, and death and Hades gave up the dead that were in them, and each person was judged according to what he had done. Then, death and Hades were thrown into the lake of fire. The lake of fire is the 2nd death. If anyone's name was not found written in the book of life, he was thrown into the lake of fire."

Well, in relation to talking about the final judgment, we might want to touch on this morning this issue of ourselves judging others. You see, people in general, but Christians in particular, tend to divide sins into two categories: their sins and our sins. The Bible, of course, knows of no such distinction. Sin is sin, without partiality shown to the sins of G's people—*our* sins.

But even after all the warnings that the Bible gives us against judging others, many of us still don't get that message. It seems that a court judge was horseback riding with a young lawyer when they came across an open stretch of country. They noticed a noose hanging from a tree they were passing by. The judge raised his voice to the lawyer as they rode and jokingly asked, "If that gallows had its due, where do you suppose you would be right now?"

The young lawyer spurred his horse a few feet forward, then turned back to the judge and called out, "Riding alone."

Now, one thing our topic for today stresses to us is that we will be judged partly on the good things that we should have done but didn't. In stressing that point, the Bible says in James 2:14–26, "What good is it if a man claims to have faith, but has no deeds? Can such faith save him? Suppose a brother or sister is without clothes and daily food. If one of you says to him, 'Go, I wish you well; keep warm and well fed,' but does nothing about his physical needs, what good is it? In the same way, faith by itself, if it is not accompanied by action, is dead. But someone will say, 'You have faith; I have deeds.' Show me your faith without deeds, and I will show you my faith by what I do. You believe that there is one God. Good! Even the demons believe that—and shudder.

"You foolish man, do you want evidence that faith without deeds is useless? Was not our ancestor Abraham considered righteous for what he did when he offered his son Isaac on the altar? You see that his faith and his actions were working together, and his faith was made complete by what he did. And the scripture was fulfilled that says, 'Abraham believed G and it was credited to him as righteousness,' and he was called G's friend. You see that a person is justified by what he does, and NOT by faith alone. In the same way, was not even Rahab, the prostitute considered righteous for what she did when she gave lodging to the spies and sent hem off in a different direction? As the body without the spirit is dead, so faith without deeds is dead."

That's why the goats in the parable of the sheep and the goats were in so much trouble—they knew the good things that they should have done in J's name, and yet they didn't do them.

Yes, indeed, our rewards will match the level of the importance of our earthly behavior. Linus and Lucy were talking one day, and Linus says to Lucy, "You know, Charlie Brown has really been a dedicated baseball manager. He's devoted his whole life to the team. We should give him a testimonial dinner."

Lucy replied, "How about a testimonial snack?"

So other than our actions, is there anything else that we'll be judged on? You better believe it! How about our words that we spoke throughout our lifetime? J strongly indicated that what we say will be judged in Matthew 12:34–37: "You brood of vipers, how can you who are evil say anything good? For out of the overflow of the heart the mouth speaks. The good man brings good things out of the good stored up in him, and the evil man brings evil things out of the evil stored up in him. But I tell you that men will have to give an account on the day of judgment for every careless word they have spoken. For by your words, you will be acquitted and by your words you will be condemned."

Believe it or not, our words will come back to haunt us. A mother was driving with her pre-school aged son in the car. The boy eventually spoke up and asked, "Mommy, why do the idiots only come out on the road when Daddy's driving?"

Yes, the tongue winds up getting us in a lot of trouble that we will be reminded of at the judgment. James 3:3–10 says, "When we put bits into the mouths of horses to make them obey us, we can turn the whole animal. Or take ships as an example. Although they are so large and are driven by strong winds, they are steered by a very small rudder wherever the pilot wants to go. Likewise, the tongue is a small part of the body, but it makes great boasts. Consider what a great forest is set on fire by a small spark. The tongue also is a fire, a world of evil among the parts of the body. It corrupts the whole person, set the whole course of his life on fire, and is itself set on fire by hell.

"All kinds of animals, birds, reptiles and creatures of the sea are being tamed and have been tamed by man, but no man can tame the tongue. It is a restless evil, full of deadly poison. With the tongue, we praise our Lord and Father, and with it, we curse men, who have been made in G's likeness. Out of the same mouth come praise and cursing, my brothers, this should not be." A woman bought a parrot whose previous owner had taught him profanity and decided that she would reform him. He began to learn a number of Christian words/phrases. The new owner caught him cursing one day, and grabbed him, saying, "I'll teach you to never talk that way again."

She put him in the deep freeze and shut the door. A few minutes later, she took him out and asked, "Have you learned your lesson?"

The bird shivered, replying, "Yes, ma'am."

After a couple of months, the lesson got forgotten. She returned the parrot to the freezer but forgot him for some time, almost freezing him to death. After she put him back in his cage to thaw out, he began to move and talk a little. She asked, "Did you learn your lesson?"

"Yes, ma'am," the bird replied.

After a moment of silence, the bird spoke up and said, "I thought I knew all the bad words that there were, but just what in the world did that turkey in there say?"

Make no mistake about it: we will be judged and punished for the things we said that we shouldn't have said.

Lastly, not only will G judge our actions and words, but our thoughts, as well. The Scripture makes this truth plain and clear. Psalm 94:11 says, "The Lord knows the thoughts of man." Hebrews 4:12–13 says, "For the word of G is living and active. Sharper than any double-edged sword, it penetrates even to dividing soul and spirit, joints and marrow; it judges the thoughts and attitudes of the heart. Nothing in all creation is hidden from G's sight. Everything is uncovered and laid bare before the eyes of him to whom we must give account." Matthew 10:26 says, "There is nothing concealed that will not be disclosed, or hidden that will not be made known." 2 Corinthians 5:10 says, "For we must all appear before the judgment seat of Christ, that each one may receive what is due him for the things done while in the body, whether good or bad."

October 26, 2008 The Living Years
Genesis 4:1-10; 33:1-12

(Begin by playing a recording of the song "The Living Years," by Mike and the Mechanics: "The words are as follows: Every generation blames the one before / And all of their frustrations come beating your door / I know that I'm a prisoner to all my Father held so dear. I know that I'm a hostage to all his hopes and fears. I just wish I could have told him in the living years / Crumpled bits of paper, filled with imperfect thought / Stilted conversation— I'm afraid that's all we've got. You say that you don't see it / He says it's perfect sense; we just can't get agreement in this perfect tense. We all talk a different language, talking in defense. / Chorus: Say it loud, say it clear—you can listen as well as you hear. It's too late when we die to admit we don't see eye to eye. / So we pen up a quarrel between the present and the past. We only sacrifice the future—it's the bitterness that lasts. So don't yield to the fortunes you sometimes see as fate. It may have a new perspective on a different day, and if you don't give up and don't give in, you may just be okay. [Repeat chorus.] I wasn't there that morning when my Father passed away. I didn't get to tell him all the things I had to say. I think I caught his spirit later that same year. I'm sure I heard his echo in my baby's new born tears. I just wish I could have told him in the living years. [Repeat chorus.]")

Begin spoken message: Yes, as someone once said, "Home is where we go when we're tired of being nice." Ouch! That wasn't very nice. But you know, in a lot of cases, it's very true. You know, family tension and conflict is nothing new; it's been around ever since biblical times, as demonstrated by the first of our passages for today, Genesis 4:1–10: "Adam lay with his wife, Eve, and she became pregnant and gave birth to Cain. She said, 'With the help of the Lord, I have brought forth a man.' Later, she gave birth to his bro, Abel. Now, Abel kept flocks, and Cain worked the soil. In the course of time, Cain brought some of the fruits of the soil as an offering to the Lord. But Abel brought fat portions from some of the firstborn of his flock. The Lord looked with favor on Abel and his offering, but on Cain and his offering, he did not look with favor. So Cain was very angry, and his face was downcast.

"The Lord said to Cain, 'Why are you angry? Why is your face downcast? If you do what is right, will you not be accepted? But if you do not do what is right, sin is crouching at your door; it desires to have you, but you must master it.'

"Now, Cain said to his bro Abel, 'Let's go out to the field.' And while they were in the field, Cain attacked Abel and killed him.

"Then the Lord said to Cain, 'Where is your bro, Abel?'

"'I don't know,' he replied. 'Am I my brother's keeper?'

"The Lord said, 'What have you done? Listen! Your bro's blood cries out to me from the ground.'"

But fortunately, family conflict doesn't have to end in out and out bloodshed with the taking of a life. Instead, with Christ to guide us in tension-filled situations with family members, there is the distinct possibility that the situation can be resolved peacefully and lovingly, as seen in the instance of bros Jacob and Esau. Remember, it was after Jacob had fled the area after having stolen his brother Esau's birthright and father's blessing that Genesis 27:41 records Esau saying to their mother Rebekah, "The days of mourning for my father are near; then I will kill my bro Jacob."

As we know, Jacob found out about how furious Esau was, and was terrified at the prospect of having to meet up with him again, as described six chapters later. Now, unfortunately, the Bible doesn't say anything about what Esau did —or what happened to him—during the time that lapsed between the point where he discovered Jacob had cheated him and the point where the two of them came face to face again. But Esau took the high road when they met. As Esau and his entourage approached Jacob and his group, Jacob was practically "sweating bullets." But Genesis 33:4–12 tells us what happened: "But Esau ran to meet Jacob and embraced him; he threw his arms around his neck and kissed him. And they wept. Then Esau looked up and saw the women and children. 'Who are these with you?' he asked.

"'They are the children G has graciously given your servant.' Then the maidservants and their children approached and bowed down. Next,

Leah and her children came and bowed down. Last of came Joseph and Rachel, and they too bowed down.

"Esau asked, 'What is the meaning of all this?'

"'To find favor in your eyes,' Jacob replied.

"But Esau said, 'I already have plenty, my bro. Keep what you have for yourself.'

"'No, please!' said Jacob.

"'If I have found favor in your eyes, accept this gift from me. For to see your face is like seeing the face of G, now that you have received me favorably. Please accept the present that was brought to you, for G has been gracious to me and I have all I need.' And because Jacob insisted, Esau accepted." You see, as this portion of the Bible so well points out, even at the point of one sibling wishing to kill the other at one point, it's entirely possible for complete restoration of the relationship as it should be in Christ.

Unfortunately, however, the attitude of un-forgiveness is extremely prevalent in today's world. People hold grudges against one another all over—in the workplace, in the neighborhood, and across international borders. But you know something? When J said, according to Matthew 5:44, to love your enemies and pray for those who persecute you, I don't think he was just/only meaning those people who we don't get along with at work, in town or in other nations. Believe it or not, I think even those obnoxious family members that we just can't seem to get along with are included in that command as well.

I was once made aware of a case of a middle-aged adult pair of brothers and sisters, who were in business together with other family members. Throughout the years they worked together, a lot of pain and anger was exchanged between them, but mostly, the bro was the one who instigated and initiated the situations that helped to create the overall problem. At one point, the entire family hired some professional family-business mediators to help them sort out their problems and to see if the family couldn't learn to live and work in peace with each other. At one point, the sister was asked by one of the mediators to look at her brother and simply tell him that she loved him. You know what her reaction to that instruction was? She just grinned, chuckled slightly, and told the peacemaker that she honestly couldn't do it. Okay, that's pretty bad. When you have two people who grew up in the same house together during tough times like the G. Depression worked like crazy to build a life for themselves and their own families, but then who become so nasty to each other that they don't even care to truly put forth the effort to restore peace between them; that's just outrageous. But stuff like that, sad to say, isn't all that uncommon.

Heck, I even knew of a minister, once, who had had a falling out with his own mother. I don't know what it was that caused the rift between them, but this pastor never did what he could to see that things were made right between them. Well, his mother's health eventually began to deteriorate, and I believe that he could see that the end of her life wasn't far off, but he didn't make any attempt to work things out with her. You guessed it—she eventually died, and the pastor just about went nuts. For months afterward, he was extremely moody in his dealing with others, he constantly forgot about keeping important appointments and exhibited other signs of severe stress. Folks, it doesn't have to be that way. We can make things right with disassociated family members, and as hard as it might be to do such a thing, it's much harder to deal with the effects of not having done so, once that other family member is gone for good. Maintaining a right relationship with our family members is so important, in fact, that football coach Vince Lombardi was once quoted as saying, "Think of three things—your God, your family, and the Green Bay Packers—in that order."

Now, maybe one of the best gospel illustrations that demonstrate the powers of unforgiveness vs. forgiveness is the parable of the unforgiving servant, found in Matthew 18:21–35. Reading from the New English Bible, it's here the Scripture reads, "Peter then came up and asked him, 'Lord, how often am I to forgive my brother if he goes on wronging me? As many as 7 times?'

"J replied, 'I do not say 7 times, I say 70 TIMES 7.'

"The kingdom of Heaven, therefore, should be thought of in this way: There was once a king who decided to settle accounts with the men who served him. At the outset, there appeared before him a man whose debt ran into the millions. Since he had no means of paying, his master ordered him to be sold to meet the debt, with his wife, his children, and everything he had.

"The man fell prostrate at his master's feet. 'Be patient with me,' he said, 'and I will pay in full'; and the master was so moved with pity that he let the man go and remitted the debt.

"But no sooner had the man gone out than he met a fellow servant who owed him a few dollars; and catching hold of him, he gripped him by the throat and said, 'Pay me what you owe.'

"The man fell at his fellow-servant's feet and begged him, 'Be patient with me, and I will pay you'; but he refused, and had him jailed until he could pay the debt.

"The other servants were deeply distressed when they saw what had happened, and they went to their master and told him the whole story. He accordingly sent for the man. 'You scoundrel!' he said to him. 'I forgave the entire amount of your debt when you appealed to me. Were you not bound to show your fellow servant the same pity as I showed you?' And the master was so angry that he condemned the man to torture until he could pay the debt in full. And that is how my Heavenly Father will deal with you, unless you each forgive your brother from your hearts."

Now, we can claim all we want that this parable has to do with needing to forgive anybody but our family members, but that just isn't the way it is. After all, a man named James Strachan explained that for us to have any positive influence in the world at large, we have to start by being a positive force in our families. Strachan once noted, "Abraham was chosen to be a blessing to the whole earth, but his vocation was to begin to take effect in the simplest way. He was called to teach his own household, who again, would hand down the truth to their households. His being a blessing to the world depended on his being a blessing to his own household."

Yes, we all have conflicts with family from time to time, but what we need to realize is that most likely, when that happens, things could be a lot worse. There was once a man who lived with his wife, two small kids, and his elderly parents in a small hut. He tried to be patient and gracious, but the noise and crowded conditions wore him down over time. In desperation, one day, he decided to consult the village wise man.

"Do you have a rooster?" the wise man questioned.

"Yes," the man replied. "Keep the rooster in the hut with your family, and come see me again next week."

The next week, the man returned to the wise man and told him the living conditions were worse than ever, with the rooster crowing and making a mess of the hut.

"Do you have a cow?" asked the sage. The man nodded fearfully.

"Take your cow into the hut as well, and come see me in a week." Over the next couple of weeks, the man, on the advice of the wise elder, made room for a goat, two dogs, and his bro's family.

Finally, he couldn't take it anymore, and in a fit of anger, he kicked out all the animals and guests, leaving only his wife, kids and parents. The home suddenly became spacious and quiet, and everybody lived happily ever after. You see, no matter what kind of conflict we might find ourselves in with family member, we just might be able to find a way to peacefully coexist with them if we begin to put things in the right perspective.

However, J himself, as well as the apostle Paul and other biblical writers, had even more to say on the topic of forgiving others who hurt us. Remember, J said according to Matthew 6:14–15 and in Mark 11:25–26, "For if you forgive men when they sin against you, your Heavenly Father will also forgive you. But if you do not forgive men their sins, your Father will not forgive your sins...And when you stand praying, if you hold anything against anyone, forgive him, so that your Father in heaven may forgive you your sins, but if you do not forgive, neither will your Father who is in heaven forgive your sins." In addition, James 2:13, Ephesians 4:32, and Colossians 3:13 explain, "Judgment without mercy will be shown to anyone who has not been merciful...Be kind and compassionate to one another, forgiving each other, just as Christ G forgave you...Bear with each other and forgive whatever grievances you may have against one another. Forgive as the Lord forgave you."

Schopenhauer, the German philosopher, once compared the human race to a bunch of porcupines huddling together on a cold winter's night. He said, "The colder it gets outside, the more we huddle together for warmth; but the closer we get to one another, the more we hurt each other with our sharp quills. Then, in the lonely night of earth's winter, we eventually begin to drift apart and wander out on our own and freeze to death in our loneliness." Christ has given us an alternative to forgive each other for the pokes we receive. That allows us to stay together and stay warm. And it truly is a work of G when forgiveness between people takes place, since theologian Helmut Thielicke once stated, "It can be the death of our faith if we forget that forgiveness is literally a miracle."

A lady named Jane Schmidt once wrote, "One Saturday morning, I awoke to the delightful smell of waffles and the sound of our two small boys in the kitchen with my husband. Settling down to eat, I sat down on my husband's lap and gave him a big hug for his thoughtfulness. Later that day, we were having a heated discussion in our bedroom when our four-year-old Jacob stopped us in midsentence. Standing in the doorway, he said, 'Mommy, try to remember how you felt when you were on Daddy's lap.'"

Everybody, life is too short to hold a grudge against anybody, especially family member with whom we're supposed to be closer to than anybody else on earth. You know, it'll soon be the holiday season, where family member will be getting together to have dinner and celebrate that time of year. And yet, in many of those same families, fights, arguments, and memories of long-ago offenses will raise their ugly heads. Let's commit ourselves to not fall into giving into that temptation this year.

This I *Do* Know
John 9:1-34 (v. 25)

Shortly after the communist revolution, a spokesman for the party visited one of the peasant villages and began to promote communism. He said, "Thanks to the party, we have increased wheat production by 100%."

One little man stood up in the back and said, "My name is Menski, and I'd like to know where all the wheat is."

The next year, the same official returned to the same village and began the same litany of propaganda, except in this case, he said, "I want you to know by now we have increased the wheat production 200%."

The same little man in the back of the room stood up and said, "My name is Menski, and I have one question. Where is all that wheat?"

Eventually, another year passed. Same official approached these people and began his same talk. And he said, "The communist party has increased the wheat production 300%."

Well, a little fellow stood up in the back. The official started by saying, "I know, I know…you're Menski, and you."

The fellow in the back of the room cut him off, then by saying, "No, my name is Polaski, and I have a question. What I want to know is, where in the world is Menski?"

Sounds like something fishy happened with Menski, doesn't it? I think the story implies that Menski because of his courage to question the state of things as they were being presented by the local authorities may have caused those authorities to finally see that he'd never be around again to be able to continue to question their methods. This also sounds like, to me, like the situation found in the New English Bible's version of John 9:13–34:

"The man who had been blind was brought before the Pharisees. As it was a Sabbath day when J made the paste and opened his eyes, the Pharisees now asked him by what means he had gained his sight. The man told them, 'He spread a paste on my eyes; then I washed, and now I can see.'

"Some of the Pharisees said, 'This fellow who did this is no man of God; he does not keep the Sabbath.'

"Others said, 'How could such signs come from a sinful man?' So they took different sides.

"Then they continued to question the man: 'What have you to say about him? It was your eyes he opened.'

"The man answered, 'He is a prophet.'

"The Jews would not believe that the man had been blind and had gained his sight, until they had summoned his parents and questioned them: 'Is this man your son? Do you say that he was born blind? How is it that he can see, now?'

"The parents replied, 'We know that he is our son, and that he was born blind. But how it is that he can now see, or who opened his eyes, we do not know. Ask him, he's of age; he will speak for himself.'

"His parents gave this answer because they were afraid of the Jews; for the Jewish authorities had already agreed that anyone who acknowledged J as Messiah should be banned from the synagogue.

"That is why the parents said, 'He is of age; ask him.'

"So for the 2nd time, they summoned the man who had been blind, and said, 'Speak the truth before G. We know that this fellow is a sinner.'

"'Whether or not he is a sinner, I do not know,' the man began to reply. 'All I know is this: once I was blind, now I can see.'

"'What did he do to you,' they asked. 'How did he open your eyes?'

"'I have already told you,' he retorted, 'but you took no notice. Why do you want to hear it again? Do you also want to become his disciples?'

"Then, they became abusive. 'You are that man's disciple,' they said, 'but we are disciples of Moses. We know that G spoke to Moses, but as for this fellow, we do not know where he comes from.'

"The man replied, 'What an extraordinary thing! Here's a man who has opened my eyes, yet you do not know where he comes from! It's common knowledge that G does not listen to sinners; he listens to anyone who is devout and obeys his will. To open the eyes of a man born blind—it's unheard of since time began. If that man had not come from G, he could have done nothing.'

"'Who are you to give us lessons?' they retorted, 'born and bred in sin as you are?' Then, they expelled him from the synagogue."

You see, the man who J healed in this biblical account wasn't sure about whether J was a sinner, as the Jews in this story were accusing him of being. And if the man had been asked about the theological likelihood of J being God incarnate or questioned about just exactly how J was able to pull off the miracle of enabling the formerly blind man to see, he probably would have responded with a resounding, "I have no idea." But I believe he would have continued, "All I know is—and I know this for certain—I had been blind, but now I see." That's all he needed to know, for him to know that J was the Son of G. His assurance in his understanding of J, then, is reflected in a well-known statement of Job's, according to Job 19:25, where Job is recorded as saying, "I know that my Redeemer lives, and in the end, He will stand on the earth."

These, then, are good examples of why we need to read the Bible for ourselves. We learn from the experiences others had in Scripture as to who J is and what he's all about so we can have assurance in our own faith. As the great preacher Charles Hadden Spurgeon once pointed out, "The man who never reads will never be read; he who never quotes will never be quoted. He who will not use thoughts of other men's brains proves he has no brain of his own. Brothers, what is true of ministers is true of all people. You need to read the Bible."

Paul Tournier once commented, "The beautiful, good and true can't be weighed and measured. True knowledge is spiritual knowledge, which is beyond the reach of the world of quantity and thus is disregarded by our civilization." What I think Mr. Tournier was saying was that though we Christians have more than adequate reasons for believing in J, the world doesn't necessarily agree. But you know what? I learned a long time ago that we Christians can't pay attention to—or worry about—what the world thinks about what we know is true. Forget them. Don't be embarrassed in front of unbelievers about what you believe as a Christian. As Tertullian once put it, "Truth does not blush."

Now, another thing to consider is that we need to be honest with others when we present ourselves as witnesses to them. We don't need to try to present ourselves as something other than what we really are. King Charles told Oliver Cromwell once to pose for a portrait. He didn't believe in that kind of vain stuff, but he did it because the king said so. Cromwell sat down before an artist who began to put his thoughts together as Cromwell was posing. Now the artist noticed that Cromwell had a rather large wart on the side of his nose, near his cheek. He carefully suggested to Cromwell that he turn his face to the other side so that there might be a better pose.

Cromwell then responded, "Sir, I desire you would use all your skill to paint my picture truly like me, and not flatter me at all; but remark all these roughnesses, pimples, warts, and everything you see, otherwise, I won't pay a cent for it." For us to convince people that we truly believe what we say we do in Christ, they need to see us as we really are—warts and all.

Yes, because of what the Bible says, if we believe what the Bible says, the Living Bible says in Ephesians 3:12, "Now, we can come fearlessly right into G's presence, assured of his glad welcome when we come with Christ and trust in him." Also because of J being who we say he is, we can have confidence in order to hold onto the faith we have and not let go. We have this pointed out to us, then, in Hebrews 4:14, when there the Bible says, "Therefore, since we have a great high priest who has gone into heaven, J the Son of G, let us hold firmly to the faith we profess." And as the Living Bible instructs us in Hebrews 10:35, "Do not let this happy trust in the Lord die away, no matter what happens. Remember your reward!"

Hans Kung once stated that "Understanding someone properly involves learning from them, and learning from someone properly involves changing one's self." You see, as the man in our scripture passage for today found out, the more he learned and understood about J, the more he realized that he needed to change; he needed to complete his faith/belief. Yes, it all goes back to learning about what we believe as Christians before we can go out and witness for Jesus Christ S. Lewis pointed out, "A man can't be always defending the truth; there must be a time to feed on it." Sure, we'd all like to go out into the world and witness effectively to everyone we meet, but we need to make time for ourselves to study the word regularly before we go about telling people, "This I do know." And the thought of learning about what to say to people about our faith shouldn't frighten us, since—when you think about it —our faith is based on a fairly simple premise: G came to earth to live among us and show us ultimate truth; in the form of this person, he died a horrible death that we ourselves deserved; and if we place our faith in that person, J, we will receive the gift of eternal life. It's really not all that complicated.

Now, because it's not a real complex message we have to share with people, there's absolutely no reason for us to lie or be deceptive with people to whom we witness. We've been talking about the truth, this morning, and that's exactly what we need to share with others, and nothing else. For instance, it makes people uncomfortable to think that Christianity says that we're all sinners, destined for hell, unless we humble ourselves and accept J as our Savior. But that's the truth. Some Christians, however, who refuse to take on that air of humility might feel like they still need to claim a certain amount of "goodness" about themselves. A related story tells of the famous actress Sara Adler, who was never willing to accurately admit her age. On one such occasion, a newspaper reporter asked her to tell her age, and without hesitation, she replied that she was sixty-eight.

The reporter objected, "But, Mrs. Adler, how can you be sixty-eight? I happen to know that your son is sixty years old himself."

She replied, "My son lives his life, and I live mine."

Still, another lesson in all of this is that we're not only to tell the truth regarding J with assurance but also with honesty. The story is told of two rich brothers, who were also very wicked. Both lived a wild, unprofitable existence, using their wealth to cover up the dark side of their lives. On the surface, however, few would have guessed it, for these expert con artists attended the same church almost every Sunday and contributed large sums to various church-related projects. Then the church called a new pastor, a young man who preached the truth with zeal and courage. Before long, attendance had grown so much that the church needed a larger worship center. Being a man of keen insight and strong integrity, this young pastor had also seen through the hypocritical lifestyles of the two brothers.

Suddenly, one of the brothers died, and the young pastor was asked to preach his funeral. The day before the funeral, the surviving brother pulled the minister aside and handed him an envelope. "There's a check in here that is large enough to pay the entire amount you'll need for the new sanctuary," he whispered. "All I ask is one favor: tell the people at my brother's funeral that he was a saint." The pastor gave the brother his word; he would do precisely what was asked. That afternoon, he deposited the check into the church's account.

The next day, the young pastor stood before the casket at the funeral service and said with firm conviction, "This man was an ungodly sinner, wicked to the core. He was unfaithful to his wife, hot tempered with his children, ruthless in business, and a hypocrite in the church—but compared to his brother, he was a saint!" Folks, people don't need a dishonest gospel presented to them. They don't need us to give them a plan of salvation that make it any easier or harder than it really is. Yes, we do need to share with others "what we do know" about J, but we need to do so accurately and honestly.

So what else do we know, for certain, about J this morning? Well, according to 1 John 4:21–24, "If our heart does not condemn us, we have courage in G's presence. We receive from him whatever we ask, because we obey his commands and do what pleases him. This is what he commands: that we believe in the name of his Son JC and love one another, just as Christ commanded us. Whoever obeys G's commands lives in G and G lives in him. And this is how we know G lives in us: We know it because of the Spirit he has given us."

We also know for a fact that if we live a solid life in Christ, we can rest assured that we'll have nothing to fear on that great day of judgment that is still yet to come. As 1 John 2:28 and 1 John 4:17 together say, "And now, my little children, stay in happy fellowship with the Lord so that when he comes, you will be sure that all is well, and will not have to be ashamed and shrink back from meeting him...And as we live with Christ, our love grows more perfect and complete; so we will not be ashamed at the day of judgment, but can face him with confidence and joy, because he loves us and we love him too."

When Aleksandr Solzhenitsyn was awarded the Nobel Prize in Literature, the concluded his speech by quoting a Russian proverb: "One word of truth outweighs the whole world." If we could change a couple of words in that proverb for today, it might read, "One person of truth impacts the whole world." I don't have any doubt that the man we've been focusing on this morning, the man who had been born blind whom J healed, had a definite impact on *his* part of the world when he flatly stated, "This I do know...I was blind, but now I see." Can you say the same type of thing with just as much assurance this morning for yourself?

What Keeps You Outta Church
Matthew 13:3-23; Luke 14:15-24

A man was selling "unbreakable combs" in front of a department store. To convince his skeptical audience, he bent two ends of a comb together until they touched. There was a loud crack, and the salesman was left with two pieces of plastic in his hand. Undaunted, he held them up and said, "And this, ladies and gentlemen, is what the comb does when you want to comb." Now, this salesman's claims were obviously proven wrong, right in front of him, and yet, he kept on denying the Truth that was staring him in the face. Likewise, there are many people who are constantly faced with the fact that they need J in their lives, yet they keep on denying that fact, turning around and running away from that truth, for one or more of several reasons, as our first Bible passage—from Matthew 13:3–23—indicates.

"A farmer was sowing grain in his fields. As he scattered the seed across the ground, some fell beside a path, and the birds came and ate it. And some fell on the rocky soil, where there was little depth of earth; the plants sprang up quickly enough in the shallow soil, but the hot sun soon scorched them and they withered and died, for they had so little root. Other seeds fell among the thorns, and the thorns choked out the tender blades. But some fell on good soil, and produced a crop that was 30, 60 and even 100 times as much as he had planned. If you have ears, listen!

"His disciples came and asked him 'Why do you always use these hard-tounderstand illustrations?' Then he explained to them that only they were permitted to understand about the Kingdom of Heaven, and others were not.

"'For to him who has will more be given,' he told them, 'and he will have great plenty; but from him who has not, even the little he has will be taken away. That is why I use these illustrations, so people will hear and see, but not understand.'

"This fulfills the prophecy of Isaiah: 'They hear, but don't understand; they look, but don't see! For their hearts are fat and heavy, and their ears are dull, and they have closed their eyes in sleep, so they won't see and hear and understand and turn to G again, and let me heal them.'

"But blessed are your eyes, for they see, and your ears, for they hear. Many a prophet and godly man has longed to see what you have seen, and hear what you have heard, but couldn't.

"'Now here is the explanation of the story I told about the farmer planting grain: The hard path where some of the seeds fell represents the heart of a person who hears the Good News about the Kingdom and doesn't understand it, then Satan comes and snatches away the seed from his heart. The shallow, rocky soil represents the heart of a man who hears the message and receives it with real joy, but he doesn't have much depth in his life, and the seeds don't root very deeply. After a while, when trouble comes or when persecution begins because of his beliefs, his enthusiasm fades, and he drops out. The ground covered with thistles represents a man who hears the message, but the cares of life and his longing for money choke out G's word, and he does less and less for G.'"

Yes, many people will tell you why they choose not to participate in the life of the Christian church, but what they say are more poor excuses than good reasons. And as far as those excuses go, Michael Green once explained, "An excuse has been defined as the skin of reason stuffed with a lie." You know how it goes—you invite people to accept Christ for themselves and/or to come to church, and they'll often respond by telling you they can't, for whatever reason. They'd like to take you up on your invitation to come to church, but they can't. Well, as Chuck Swindoll pointed out in his book *Come Before Winter*, "Can't and Won't—Christians need to be very careful which one they choose. It seems that we prefer to use 'can't'—'I just *can't* get along with my wife'; 'My husband and I just *can't* communicate'; 'I *can't* discipline my kids like I should'; 'I just can't *give* up the affair I'm in the middle of having'; 'I simply *can't* stop overeating'; 'I *can't* find the time to pray and read my Bible each day'; 'I can't stop gossiping.'"

"No, any Christian who takes the Scriptures seriously will have to confess the word really should be "won't." Why? Because we have been given the power, the ability to overcome. Literally! One of the best books you can read on overcoming depression," Swindoll went on to say, "is a splendid work by two psychiatrists, Frank Minirth and Paul Meier. The volume is appropriately entitled, 'Happiness is a choice.' As psychiatrists, we cringe whenever Christian patients use the word "can't." Any good psychiatrist knows that 'I can't' and 'I've tried' are merely lame excuses. We insist that our patients be honest with themselves and use language that expresses the reality of the situation. So we have our patients change their 'can'ts' to 'won'ts.' If an individual changes all his can'ts to won'ts, he stops avoiding the truth, quits deceiving himself, and start living in reality."

"I just *won't* get along with my wife." "My husband and I won't communicate." "I *won't* discipline my kids." "I just *won't* give up the affair I'm having." "I *won't* stop overeating." "I won't find time to pray and read my Bible each day." "I *won't* quit gossiping." Non-Christians have every right and reason to use "can't," because they *really can't*. They're victims, trapped and bound like slaves in a fierce and endless struggle. Without Christ and his power, they lack what it takes to change permanently. They *don't* because they *can't*. It's a fact— a valid excuse.

But people like us? Hey, let's face it, we don't because we won't. We disobey because we want to, not because we have to—because we choose to, not because we're forced to. The sooner we are willing to own up realistically to our responsibility and stop playing the blame game at pity parties for ourselves, the more we'll learn and change and the less we're burn and blame.

A father was one day reading the Ten Commandments to his son. As he read, he was explaining what each one of them meant. "Thou shall not… Thou shall not…" When they came to commandment 5, "Honor your father and mother," the boy looked at his dad and proclaimed, "Daddy, I'm not thou!" You see, as this story so wonderfully illustrates, one of the things that keeps us out of church (and thus keeps us from coming to J like we should) is that we're often convicted by what G says to us, and we decide at that point that we want no more of it. It's at that point, then, that we come up with some of those lousy excuses for not getting close to J. But the thing to remember whenever that becomes our plan of action is that G sees through the supposed reasons we have for not coming closer to him. It's kind of like the little kid who had obviously been trying, early in the morning, to get out of going to school. But much to his dismay, he found himself on the school bus, talking to his friend, saying, "My stomach hurt at breakfast, I was dizzy and my throat was sore, but my mom didn't buy it." Just like moms of little kids who seem to know everything, G knows what's going on in our minds as well, no matter how much of an act we put on.

Now, I think one of the best illustrations from the Bible as to the types of excuses people give for not coming to Christ is the passage found in Luke 14:16–24: "A man was preparing a great feast and sent out many invitations. At the time for the banquet to begin, he sent his servant to tell those who he had invited, 'Come, for everything is now ready.' But they all alike began to make excuses.

"The first said, 'I have just bought a field, and I must go and inspect it. Please excuse me.'

"The second said, 'I've just bought a yoke of oxen, and I'm on my way to try them out. Please accept my apologies.'

"Still, another said, 'I just got married, so I'm sure you will understand that I cannot come.'

"The servant came back and reported this to his master. Then the master of the house said, in a rage, to his servant, 'Go out quickly into the streets and alleys of the town and bring in the poor, the crippled, the blind and the lame.'

"'Sire,' the servant began to say, 'what you have ordered has been done, but there is still room.'

"Then the master said to his servant, 'Go to the open roads and the hedgerows and force people to come in to make sure my house is full; because I tell you, not one of those who were invited shall have a taste of my banquet.'"

You see, as this story so well illustrates, people have different (and what would seem to be good) reasons for not committing themselves to Christ. It might be their devotion to their family. It might that they feel they have responsibilities on the job that they can't get out of that would conflict with their devotion to J. Maybe they feel that there are just too many things going on in their life at that point that they just don't have any room/time to devote to Christ at that point.

Now, consider this: true sports fans have an amazing ability to remember details, statistics, a little technicality of a rule—you know, stuff nobody really cares to hear about except another sports fan. Another characteristic of a fan is an indomitable sense of commitment sense of commitment or determination. Against incredible odds, sound logic, and even medical advice, sports fans will persevere to the dying end!

Well, I've often wondered what would happen if people were as intense and committed and determined about church as they were about sports—or a number of other pastimes. This was reinforced some years back in a *Moody Monthly* piece which illustrated twelve excuses a person might use for "quitting sports." The analogy, here, isn't hard to figure out:

"Every time I went, they asked me for money / The people with whom I had to sit didn't seem very friendly / The seats were too hard and uncomfortable / The coach never came to see me / the referee made a decision with which I could not agree. / I was sitting with some hypocrites—they only came to see what others were wearing. / Some games went into overtime, and I was late getting home / The band played numbers I had never heard before. The games are scheduled when I want to do other things. May parents took me to too many games when I was a kid. Since I read a book on sports, I feel that I know more than the coaches anyhow." And finally, "I don't want to take my children, because I want them to choose for themselves what sport they like best."

A man one day pulled into a gas station in the deep south, walked to a coke machine, and stared at the sign, which said "$2.00"

"Two dollars for a Coke," he said. "That's incredible."

A friendly serviceman replied, "It ain't really $2.00—the machine's broken, so I put up an out-of-order sign, but people kept putting their money in anyway, and I had to get it out again, so I put that sign up, and I haven't had any trouble since." Isn't that just like us? We keep putting our money, time and efforts into worldly things, instead of investing in G's love, and so we find that we portions of these things, especially money.

And this leads us to another reason of "what keeps people out of church"— the issue of money. The Phillips Modern English Translation of the Bible's portion found in 1 Timothy 6:6–10, then puts it like this: "There are many men who have lost their real hold on the truth and hope to make some profit out of the Christian religion. There is a real profit, of course. It is peace of heart for those who live as G would have them live. We brought nothing with us when we entered this world, and we can be sure we shall take nothing with us when we leave it. Surely, then, as far as physical things are concerned, it is sufficient for us to keep our bodies fed and clothed. For men who set their hearts on being wealthy expose themselves to temptation. They fall into a trap and lay themselves open to all sorts of silly and wicked desires, which are quite capable of utterly ruining and destroying their souls. For loving money leads to all kinds of evil, and some men in the struggle to be rich have lost their faith and cause themselves untold agonies of mind."

There's the story of a doctor who once asked his patient, "What are you planning to do about that excess weight you're carrying around?"

"I just can't seem to lose the weight, Doc," the patient replied.

"It must be an overactive thyroid."

"The tests show your thyroid is perfectly normal," the doctor said.

"If anything is overactive, it's your fork and spoon."

You see, the patient's own response in this story pretty much revealed just exactly what the problem was. Kind of like the rich young man told about in Matthew 19:16–23: "Now a man came up to J and asked, 'Teacher, what good thing must I do to get eternal life?'

"'Why to you ask me about what is good?' J replied. 'There is only One who is good. If you want to enter life, obey the commandments'

"'Which ones?' the man asked.

"And J replied, 'Don't kill, don't commit adultery, don't steal, don't lie, honor your father and mother, and love your neighbor as yourself.'

"'I've always obeyed every one of them,' the youth replied.

"'What else must I do?' J told him, 'If you want to be perfect, go and sell everything you have and give the money to the poor, and you will have treasure in heaven; and come, follow me.' But when the young man heard this, he went away sadly, for he was very rich. Then J said to his disciples, 'It is almost impossible for a rich man to get into the Kingdom of Heaven.'"

This isn't always the case, but many times, when people talk openly and honestly about how they feel, they will admit just exactly what it is that keeps them out of church.

Dani Tyler, third base star for the US Women's Softball Team, thought she'd hit a home run. In her excitement rounding the bases, she accidentally stepped *over* home plate. The umpire disallowed the run. Because of that, the US team experienced only their second loss in international play in ten years. The next evening, Tyler played well. When later asked why her previous error didn't become a mental ball and chain, causing further disappointing performance, she said, "I'm not the best athlete, but I try to have the best attitude and work the hardest. What happened the other night was a freak thing. If I whine about it, or make excuses, what happens? I look like a jerk."

Well, I might suggest that our making excuses as to why we won't follow J doesn't put us in a very good light, either. A man left a bar, got in his car, and drove away. He was soon stopped by a police officer. The officer explained he was testing drivers to determine whether they were driving drunk. "Would you please blow into this machine," he requested.

The driver responded, "Oh, I'm afraid I can't do that—I have asthma. If I blow into that machine, I'll have an asthma attack."

The officer then said, "Then please come with me to the station so that I can give you a blood test."

Protesting further, the man said, "I can't do that. I'm a hemophiliac. If you stick me with a needle, I'll bleed to death."

The officer came back with a third alternative: "Then just get out of the car and walk five yards along this white line."

The man answered, "I'm afraid I can't do that either."

"Why not?" asked the officer.

"Because I'm too drunk!" The man replied.

You see, folks, when we make excuses as to why we can't do something—including why we can't follow J—then eventually, the truth comes out and we pay the price.

When the Rooster Crows
Mark 14:27-31, 66-72

How many of you have ever spent a night on a farm, and thus had the experience of having been woken up not by an alarm clock or by the sunlight light streaming in through your window but by a rooster. That obnoxious little bird. You're all cozy and warm in bed, still very much able to sleep another hour or two, and that stupid bird is outside your window—cock-a-doodle-do! Makes you wish you could, without having to get out of bed, stretch your arm out the window and slap the thing silly until it stopped crowing. Stupid rooster! Yes, roosters are just naturally really good at waking people up, in the physical sense. But think about this: there is at least one recorded instance where a rooster played a big part in waking someone up spiritually, as seen in our Scripture for this morning, Mark 14:27–31 and 66–72: "J told them, 'You will all fall away, for it is written: "I will strike the shepherd, and the sheep will be scattered." But after I have risen, I will go ahead of you into Galilee.'

"Peter declared, 'Even if all fall away, I will not.'

"'I tell you the truth,' J answered, 'today—yes, tonight—before the rooster crows twice, you yourself will disown me three times.'

"But Peter insisted emphatically, 'Even if I have to die with you, I will never disown you.' And all the others said the same...

"Meanwhile, Peter was below in the courtyard. One of the maids who worked for the High Priest noticed Peter warming himself at the fire. She looked at him closely and then announced, 'You were with J, the Nazarene.'

"Peter denied it. 'I don't know what you're talking about!' he said, and walked over to the edge of the courtyard. Just then, a rooster crowed.

"The maid saw him stand there, and she began telling the others, 'There he is! There's that disciple of J!'

"But Peter denied it again. A little later, others standing around the fire began saying to Peter, 'You are so one of them, for you are from Galilee!'

"He began to curse and swear. I don't even know this fellow you are talking about,' he said. And immediately, the rooster crowed the second time. Suddenly, J's words flashed through Peter's mind: 'Before the cock crows twice, you will deny me three times.' And he began to cry."

You see, we can hope and pray that spiritually lost people around us will one day soon get the message for themselves. But oftentimes, it's not until something like a combination of powerful words that are spoken to them and/or events that occur in their life that cause them to realize just how far off the mark they are and how much they need to make a change. It's the kind of feeling people should have when a Christian points out to them that they can name all the characters on their favorite soap opera but couldn't begin to name the twelve disciples; that they can anticipate, in advance, the outcome of an episode of their favorite TV drama, but they can't remember how the New Testament ends; that this churchgoing person's TV cable bill is more each month that their tithe to their church.

The ironic thing, though, is that until that instance of conviction comes— whether it's a matter of the spoken word, an event of some sort, or a combination of both the guilty person involved often has no clue as to the seriousness of the spiritual trouble they have already gotten themselves in to, or are about to get in to. Jim Bakker, former televangelist and leader of PTL ministries relates how he and his wife, Tammy Faye, at one point began to drift apart from each other in their marriage. He explains in his book I Was Wrong that besides the toll of his workaholic schedule on him and his family, he became suspicious of Tammy, strongly suspecting that she was carry on an affair with a ministry associate of Bakker's, named Gary Paxton. One day, during a casual conversation with one of Bakker's other ministry associates, a man named John Fletcher, Bakker told Fletcher flippantly that he ought to have an affair to his own to make Tammy jealous.

"I've tried everything else to win Tammy back. Just think, I could say to Tammy, 'I had an affair, too, baby.' I'd be fighting fire with fire."

"Really," Fletcher asked, "Do you think that would help?"

"Well, you know how jealous Tammy is. She would go nuts if she thought that I was even attracted to another woman."

"Hmmm," Fletcher answered thoughtfully.

Over the next few weeks, Fletcher and Bakker joked occasionally about his having an affair to make Tammy jealous. Bakker then continues to explain: "I didn't really want to have an affair. As a highly visible television personality, and as president of Heritage USA, had I desired to have a relationship with another woman, it would have been relatively easy to do so. Nevertheless, my foolish, male-ego-driven statement soon took on a life of its own, fueled by the hurt in my heart."

I can't say that I was surprised when John showed up in Florida with a woman in tow. I followed him inside the hotel, up the elevator, and down the hallway to room 558. I knew it was wrong; my conscience screamed at me every step of the way. But I stupidly determined to make my wife jealous and get back at her and that was the truth. It was an adulterous act of the first degree. I stifled the screaming voice in my head and heart and stepped inside the room. As I said, I knew I was wrong the moment I entered the hotel room. I should have run out of the place. Nobody was forcing me to stay there. I willfully crossed the line and went through with it. When it was over, I quickly left the room, and in a daze, hurried to the elevator and pressed the button. I was horrified. Oh G! What have I done? I hadn't considered the consequences of my absurd attempt to make Tammy jealous. I hadn't even paused to think of the potential ramifications of my actions while I was giving in to temptation. I had opened the door to attack on the ministry I headed, my family and me personally. Worse yet, the devil had not made me do any of it; I had done it of my own stubborn will. I jumped in the shower, turning the water on as hot as I could stand it. I never felt so dirty in all my life. "Maybe if I make the water hotter, it will wash it all away," he thought.

You see, the problem is that people like Jim Bakker—and the apostle Peter— start out their walk in Christ being quite confident of their ability to fend off temptation, but then find out that it's actually quite easy to run headlong into sin, full force. That's why, in part, I think Sydney J. Harris was once quoted as saying, "Once we soothe our conscience by calling something a 'necessary evil,' it begins to look more and more necessary, and less and less evil." In other words, when people get convicted of their sin—when the rooster crows for them—they often turn and try to run in the other direction in order to escape having to listen to the crowing. An example is seen in a Mrs. Reed, who had been a member of the Little Brown Church for more than fifty years, and loved to hear a fiery sermon. She would rock back and forth in the front pew in time to the minister's cadences, take a dip of snuff, and shout, "A-a-a-amen!" at every ministerial denunciation. When the minister spoke harshly of sex, drinking, smoking, drug abuse, movie-going and dancing, she approved heartedly, taking snuff at each admonition and shouting her enthusiastic "Amen."

One Sunday, the minister began, "And now, let me talk about another vicious habit that, fortunately, is going increasingly out of fashion. I refer to the deplorable practice of snuff-dipping." Whereupon Mrs. Reed sat bolt upright and muttered under her breath, "Wouldn't you know it? He's stopped preaching and has started meddling."

But if we should ever decide to go back on our promise to follow J to the end, and then forsake him out of shame—like Peter did, before he repented in that case—maybe we should call to mind what J said in Matthew 10:32: "Whoever acknowledges me before men, I will also acknowledge before My Father in Heaven. But whoever disowns me before men, I will disown him before my Father in heaven."

But you see, our conscience shouldn't only stop us from doing what we shouldn't—it should also help spur us on to do what we should. In his book *Honesty, Morality and Conscience*, author Jerry White explains, "My dad used to read the cartoon series *Moon Mullins* to the two of us. That was sort of our Sunday ti-me together, when my mother would leave me home with my dad to sort of shame him for not going to church.

"One of the main characters in the comic strip was a guy named Willie. In one strip, he's slumped in front of the television set with a coffee cup resting on his pot belly as he flicks his cigar ashes into his cup. He says to his wife, 'You're awful quiet this morning, Mamie.'

"And she says in reply, 'Willie, I've decided to let your conscience be your guide on your day off.' In the next cartoon panel, then, Willie is surrounded by a lawnmower, an edge-trimmer, a hoe and a shovel, and he's frantically washing the windows and muttering to himself, 'Every time I listen to my dumb conscience, I end up ruining my relaxing.'"

Now, that story isn't meant to encourage staying home from church in order to get house work done, but once again the point is that our conscience does fulfill the purpose in helping us accomplish the tasks G would want us to do.

But the problem with a lot of people in the church today is that their particular brand of faith far too often soothes their conscience, instead of awakening it, and it, therefore, produces a sense of self-satisfaction and eternal safety rather than a sense of our unworthiness. In other words, a warped faith dumbs down our conscience. Former presidential aide, Jeb Stuart Magruder, once commented on his part in the Watergate Scandal, saying, "We had conned ourselves into thinking that we weren't doing anything really wrong, and by the time we were doing things that were illegal, we had lost control. We had gone from poor ethical behavior into illegal activities without even realizing it." It can be seen from Magruder's admission, then, that our conscience will quickly be dulled if we must constantly try to justify our actions.

Remember, as J warned in the Living Bible's Version of J's words found in Mark 8:38, "Anyone who is ashamed of me and my message in these days of unbelief and sin, I, the Messiah, will be ashamed of him when I return in the glory of my Father, with the holy angels."

I think you'll agree that verses like that can be truly convicting. Now, no one likes to be convicted of a wrong attitude or behavior they might have, but some people really don't like it when this kind of thing happens. It's kind of like the lady who, as she was leaving church, shook hands with the pastor and remarked, "Thank you for the sermon, pastor. It was like water to a drowning man."

It sounds like to me that that lady found out the hard way that "the truth might set you free, but first, it'll make you miserable."

A. T. Robertson, a Baptist scholar of years ago, taught for many years at the Southern Baptist Theological Seminary in Louisville. When he began to write on the books of the Bible, he chose on one occasion 3 John, which talks about Diotrephes. Diotrephes was a man who became a self-appointed boss of a church. Over a period of time, he was the one who excommunicated certain people, and he screened whatever was done in the church. As the selfappointed leader, he wouldn't even let John come to speak as a representative of Christ. So John wrote a letter to reprove him. In writing about Diotrephes, then, A. T. Robertson said this: "Some 40 years ago, I wrote an article on Diotrephes for a denominational paper.

The editor told me that 25 deacons stopped the paper to show their resentment against being personally attacked in the paper." Sounds like we've got some Diotrephes in the church today, doesn't it?

Remember Edgar Allen Poe's story, "The Telltale Heart"? The murderer, after retiring that evening, couldn't sleep, because he kept hearing the heart of his victim as it pounded in his chest. He really didn't hear the victim's heart, of course. In all actuality, he was hearing his own heart, and it kept him awake. The guilt of his condition finally led to his revealing that he was a murderer. That's the power of a guilty conscience.

Yes, it's sad, but many times, we'd rather sin than have to face possible retribution for doing the right thing. It's like the example from Peter's life that we're looking at today. He was more willing to lie, denying J for himself, than to have to own up to the fact to others that, yes, he had been a close associate of J's. But face it—many times, it's just easier to do the wrong thing, rather than the right. Yes, it's much easier to lie than to tell the truth for example. One time, a woman drove her friend to see some people who lived about fifty miles away. They had a nice visit, but when it was time to leave, the two of them discovered that the keys had been inadvertently locked in the car. The woman called her husband, who had a spare key. Understandably, he was quite annoyed. A few minutes later, the passenger-friend decided to try to open one of the back doors of the car. Sure enough, one was unlocked. The lady who had been the driver rushed back into the house of the people they'd been visiting, hoping to call and reach her husband, before he left to come bring the spare key, but it was too late.

The passenger friend looked at her and noted, "Just wait till he gets here. He'll be even more upset. What are you going to do?"

"What anyone else would do," she said.

Just then, she walked back over to the car, opened the back door, pushed down the lock button, and slammed the door shut!

Yes, our stubbornness and insistence to do things our way can get us in a lot of trouble with Christ, as seen in 2 Timothy 2:12, when there, the Bible admonishes, "If we deny him, he will deny us."

And as Martin Luther once said, "My conscience has been taken captive by G's Word, and to go against conscience or Scripture is neither right nor safe."

There was once a small Kentucky town that had two churches and one whiskey distillery. Members of the churches complained that the distillery gave the town a bad image. In addition, the distillery's owner was an atheist. They tried to have the place shut down but were unsuccessful. They eventually decided to have a lengthy prayer meeting on a Saturday night. As they got together that night, a might thunderstorm occurred, and lightning struck the distillery, burning it to the ground. The next morning, the sermons in both churches were on "The Power of Prayer." Fire insurance adjusters promptly notified the distillery owner they would not pay for his damages since the fire had been caused by an act of G, and coverage for acts of G was excluded in the policy.

Well, when that decision was made and passed on to the distillery owner, he decided to sue all the church members, claiming that they had conspired with G to destroy his building and business. The church member defendants absolutely denied having anything to do with causing the fire. The trial judge then made an interesting observation: "I find one thing about this case that is truly perplexing. We have a situation where the plaintiff—an atheist—is professing his belief in the power of pray, and the defendants—church members—are denying the power of prayer."

The point, everybody, then is this: when we ever find ourselves having failed our Lord miserably—like Peter did in our passage for this morning and like Jim Bakker did at his moment of spiritual weakness, all hope is not lost. We can get back in a right relationship with G, but we need to do so as soon as possible. None of us knows how long we might have before it will one day be too late to make things right with Christ.

Who Needs a Hot Dog? (I Remember You)
1 Corinthians 1:4-6; Philippians 1:3-6

I remember the time when my brothers, sister and I went to the circus. Now, as you might imagine, it was a memorable experience. There were the usual death-defying stunts of the high wire acts, the exotic animals and humorous clowns that we've all seen whenever we might have gone to the circus ourselves. But do you know what the most memorable part of that trip was for us? It wasn't the death-defying acrobatics, it was the incredible things the animal trainer had the lions, tigers, and elephants do, and it wasn't the clowns as funny as they were. No, the most memorable thing about that trip was the silly guy who sold the stupid hot dogs in the stands. Most circus hot dog vendors have the usual line of "Hot dogs... Get your hot dogs, here. Hot dogs...Get you hot dogs, here!" Not *this* guy—he was a little more over the top than that. This is what he would say (stress loudly): "Hot dogs, I got hot dogs...Who needs a hot dog? You need a hot dog! I got plain hot dogs! I got hot dogs with ketchup, hot dogs with mustard, hot dogs with relish! I got hot dogs with ketchup and/ or mustard and/or relish! I got chili dogs...I got cheese dogs...I got chili cheese dogs! What kind of hot dog you want, sir? I got dogs. Who needs a dog? You need a dog!" The guy was nuts; he was insane. But you know what? He sold a lot of hot dogs. We bought some off him. We'll never forget that guy.

You know, it's interesting how there are people we've all encountered throughout our lives, who will forever remain a part of our memory, especially if either they had a hand in our spiritual growth/development or if we were the one who, at some point, helped them in their spiritual walk. Paul referred to such people in his past, in 1 Corinthians 1:4–6 and Philippians 1:3–6: "I always thank G for you because of his grace given you in Christ Jesus For in him you have been enriched in every way—in all your speaking and in all your knowledge—because our testimony about Christ was confirmed in you...I thank my G every time I remember you.

In all my prayers for all of you, I always pray with joy because of your partnership in the gospel form the first day until now, being confident of this, that he who began a good work in you will carry it on to completion until the day of Christ Jesus."

Yes, having solid Christian friends is not only a natural part of the lives of every other Christian, but being surrounded by friends of a like mindedness in Christ is absolutely necessary for all Christians' spiritual development. While pointing his gun toward his frightened victim, the robber tossed him a large sack and yelled, "Gimme all your valuables!" It's said that the one being robbed then immediately started to stuff all of his friends into the sack. That may not have been a very friendly thing to do, but I think you get the idea of what's being said there.

You see, the word "Philadelphia" means "human affection, brotherly love." It means being an affectionate friend. Sam Coleridge's poem "Youth and Age" contains the line "Friendship is a sheltering tree." That is a wonderful wordpicture. Friends are those whose lives are like branches. They provide shade and refuge from the demanding, irritating and searing rays of the hot sun in life. You can find comfort by them. You can find strength near them. They are treelike in that they bear fruit that provides nourishment and encouragement. Isn't it interesting when some disaster occurs in your life and you happen to be alone at the time, you often pick up the phone and call a friend? You want to connect with someone else. Few things are lonelier than going through a sudden test or joy and having no friend to call.

In their book *Edge of Adventure*, Keith Miller and Bruce Larson point out that the neighborhood bar is possibly the best counterfeit there is to the fellowship Christ wants to give his church. It's an imitation, dispensing liquor instead of grace, escape rather than reality, but it's an accepting, inclusive fellowship. It's unshakeable; it's democratic. You can tell people secrets in a bar, and they usually don't tell others or even wish to do so. The bar flourishes, not because most people are alcoholics, but because G has put into the human heart the desire to known and be known, to love and be loved, and so many seek a counterfeit at the price of a few beers. We should understand that J wants his church to be unshakeable and democratic—a fellowship where people can come in and say, "I'm sunk!"

"I'm beat!" "I've had it!" Alcoholics Anonymous has this quality, but our churches too often miss it.

Paul encouraged us in Galatians 6:10 to "do good to all people, especially to those who belong to the family of believers, whenever we have the opportunity." In doing so, we come to form godly relationships that last a lifetime, relationships where Christians can affect each other and other non- Christians powerfully. For example, there's the story of a number of Indian chiefs and warriors, who lived during the summer of 1805, in which they held their tribal council in Buffalo Creek, New York, in order to hear a Christian message presented by a Mr. Cram from the Boston Missionary Society. After the sermon, a response was given by Red Jacket, one of the leading chiefs. Among other things, the chief said, "Brother, we're told that you have been preaching to the white people in this place. These people are our neighbors. We are acquainted with them. We will wait a little while and see what effect your preaching has on them. If we find that it does them good, makes them honest and less disposed to cheat Indians, we will then consider again what you have said."

But someone doesn't have to be an adult with an important worldly position in order to make a significant impression on people what will positively influence them for a lifetime. A simple child can do that kind of thing as well, as seen in the story of little Teddy Stallard. You see, Teddy certainly qualified as "one of the least." Disinterested in school, musty, wrinkled clothes, with hair never combed. He was one of those kids in school with a deadpan face, expressionless—sort of a glassy, unfocused stare. When Miss Thompson spoke to Teddy, he always answered in monosyllables. Unattractive, unmotivated, and distant, he was just plain hard to like. Even though his teacher said she loved *all* in her class the same, down inside, she wasn't being completely truthful.

Whenever she graded Teddy's papers, she got a certain perverse pleasure in putting Xs next to the wrong answers, and when she put the Fs at the top of his papers, she always did it with a flair. She should have known better; she had Teddy's records, and she knew more about him than she wanted to admit. The records read like this:

First grade: Teddy shows promise with his work and attitude, but poor home situation.

Second grade: Teddy could do better. Mother is seriously ill. He receives little help at home.

Third grade: Teddy is a good boy but too serious. He is a slow learner. His mother died this year.

Fourth grade: Teddy is very slow, but well behaved. His father shows no interest.

Christmas came, and the boys and girls in Miss Thompson's class brought her Christmas presents. They piled their presents on her desk and crowded around to watcher her open them. Among the presents was one from Teddy. When she opened his gift, out fell a gaudy rhinestone bracelet, with half the stones missing, and a bottle of cheap perfume. The other kids giggled at the gift, but she immediately silenced them by putting on the bracelet and putting some of the perfume on her wrist.

"Doesn't it smell lovely?" she asked the kids as she held her wrist up for the kids to sniff. Taking their cue from the teacher, they agreed.

When school was over that day, Teddy came over to Ms. Thompson at her desk and said, "Ms. Thompson, you smell just like my mother, and her bracelet looks real pretty on you, too. I'm glad you like my presents."

When Teddy left, Ms. Thompson got down on her knees and asked G to forgive her. The next day when the kids came to school, they were welcomed by a new teacher. Miss Thompson had become a different person. She was no longer just a teacher; she had become an agent of G. She was now a person committed to loving her children and doing things for them that would live on after her. She helped all the children but especially the slow ones and especially Teddy Stallard. By the end of the year, Teddy showed dramatic improvement. He had caught up with most of the students and was even ahead of some.

After that year, she didn't hear from Teddy for a long time. Then, one day, she received a note that read: "Dear Ms. T., I wanted you to be the 1st to know. I will be graduating 2nd in my class. Love, Teddy Stallard." Four years later, another note came: "Dear Ms. T., They just told me I will be graduating 1st in my class. I wanted you to be the 1st to know. The university has not been easy, but I liked it. Love, Teddy Stallard." And four years later, "Dear Ms. T., As of today, I am Theodore Stallard, MD. How about that? I wanted you to be the 1st to know. I am getting married next month, on the 27th to be exact. I want you to come and sit where my mother would sit if she were alive. You are the only family I have now; Dad died last year. Love, Teddy Stallard."

Ms. T went to that wedding and sat where Teddy's mother would have sat. She deserved to sit there; she had done something for Teddy that he could never forget.

Again, scripture points out to us an instance where Paul very much appreciated the faith of people he once had close contact with, people he'd never forget. It's in 2 Timothy 1:3–6 he writes, "I thank G, whom I serve, as my forefather did, with a clear conscience, as night and day I constantly remember you in my prayer. Recalling your tears, I long to see you, so that I may be filled with joy. I have been reminded of your sincere faith, which 1st lived in your g-mother Lois and in your mother Eunice and, I am persuaded, now lives in you also. For this reason, I remind you to fan into flame the gift of G, which is in you through the laying on of my hands."

Yes, it's often the case that the Christians whom we've come to know personally have a lasting, positive effect on ourselves and most other people around them. After all, isn't that really the point in living the Christian life? And once we begin to live that kind of life faithfully, it can't be helped but that most everybody around us who knows us personally will hear— one way or another—of how we've been living effectively in the name of J. Paul wrote in Romans 1:8, "First, I thank my G through JC for all of you, because your faith is being reported all over the world." Isn't it great to know that because of our positive witness in the world around us, even people whom we haven't even come in direct contact with often come to catch wind of our testimony?

And another great thing about all this is, even when a strong Christian dies, the positive example that they set throughout their lifetime often continues to be a mighty witness. In his book *The Divine Conquest*, A. W. Tozer put it this way: "We can't think properly of G until we start to think of Him as always being there, and there first. Joshua had this to learn. He had been so long the servant of G's servant Moses, and had with such assurance received G's word at his mouth, that Moses and the God of Moses had become blended in his thinking, so blended that he could hardly separate the two thoughts; by association, they always appeared together in Joshua's mind. Now Moses is dead, and because G knew that

Joshua might have then been struck down with despair, G spoke to him with assurance: 'As I was with Moses, so I will be with you.' Moses was dead, but the G of Moses still lived. Nothing had changed; nothing had been lost. Nothing of G dies when a man of G dies."

You know, in regards as to how we ought to go about living our daily lives as a potential witness—who will have an immense impact on other people for Christ—we need to be very careful how we choose to go through our time on earth. The Bible puts it in Ephesians 5:15–6 this way: "Be very careful, then, how you live—not as unwise, but as wise, making the most of every opportunity, because the days are evil." Likewise, Colossians 4:5 instructs us, "Be wise in the way you act toward outsiders; make the most of every opportunity."

Just how important are each of us Christians when it comes to making an impact for J on the lives of others? Well, we might be more important than what you think. A rooster minus a hen equals no baby chicks. Kellogg minus a farmer equals no corn flakes. If the nail factory closes, what good is the hammer factory? The genius of the great classical pianist Paderewski would have amounted to a whole lot if the piano tuner never showed up. A cracker maker will do better if there's a cheese maker nearby. The most skillful surgeon needs the adequate ambulance driver who delivers the patient. Just as Rogers needed Hammerstein, you need someone and someone needs you.

October 14 Why Didn't Anyone Tell Me?
2 Timothy 1:8, 12; Hebrews 5:11-14; Romans 3:23

I listen to a rock music radio station that calls itself 98 Rock. Sometimes, the people at the station find a funny, old movie/TV clip, and then put it in the middle of their name, during the station ID. For instance, in their sound bit archives, once, they discovered this clip of a guy shouting the phrase "Why didn't anyone tell me?" and they put it in the middle of their name that was to be announced. So one day when I was listening to the station, the DJ came on and said, "You're listening to: 98—why didn't anyone tell me?—Rock." Well, I have to ask you today, "Why didn't anyone tell me?" Why didn't anyone tell me *what*, you're probably thinking. Well, over the past couple of years, I had really gained some weight; I had packed on the pounds; I had become slightly fat. I honestly hadn't realized that fact, until I started to lose some, through the men's Body and Soul class here at the church on Thursday nights. But nobody said anything to me about it. Why not? Why didn't anyone point my condition out to me?

Oh, I can hear the excuses, now: (1) Well, I didn't want to be the one to tell Roger he needed to lose weight. I didn't want to offend my preacher. Oh, that would have been great—he never would have come to visit me in the hospital or anywhere else, for that matter. I don't want to get my preacher mad at me. (2) Oh, sure, I could have pointed out the obvious to him—that he needed to lose some weight—but I would have needed to do something more than that, like tell him how to lose the weight, but I'm not a nutritionist. I'm not a dietician by any means. I don't have the knowledge to pass on to him to help with his weight problem. And finally, (3) oh, of course, I recognized that Roger was outgrowing some of his suits and other clothes. But who am I to tell him that he needs to lose weight, when I've got weight issues of my own. How hypocritical it would be for me to try to instruct him on what he needs to do with his life when basically, I've got the exact same problem.

If you listened carefully to the 3 excuses I just gave as to why many people tend not to say anything to their friends about a significant gain in weight, you then heard the basic outline for today's message; that is, three big reasons as to why we Christians in the church today tend not to be the witness for J that we need to—and should—be.

So the first big reason why Christians most often choose not to say anything to spiritually lost friends and loved ones is because of fear— fear of offending the other person, fear of being rejected for ever having brought up such an offensive and controversial topic. Well, yes, it's true that some people—even some of those who we presently know and love—could become highly offended and upset with us if we were to bring up the issue of being in a right relationship with J. But if that possibility is what's stopping us from witness for Christ, could it be that we're basically ashamed to admit that we're a Christian to the people in the world around us? Well, if we're presently ashamed of the gospel message to the point that this shame actually prevents us from sharing the Good News to those who need it, we need to remind ourselves, then, of J's stern warning in the Living Bible's version of Luke 9:26, in which he said, "When I, the Messiah, come in my glory and in the glory of the Father and of the holy angels, I will be ashamed, then, of all who are ashamed of me and of my words now."

If that's anyone's problem here, today, if there's anyone here this morning who's afraid of ticking off their spiritually lost family, friends, neighbors, or coworkers by witnessing the gospel to them, I have news for them. You're going to offend somebody sooner or later in your life, anyway. Eventually in life (and you all know this) we all say and do things to get other people miffed at us. Well, the way I figure it, if we are bound to get other people upset with us from time to time, it might as well be something important and constructive. What better of an issue could we possibly raise with people that would possibly get them angry, miffed, and ticked off with us than the Gospel of Jesus Christ? Do you know what I'm saying? And don't kid yourself, thinking that maybe you can somehow be a strong witness for Christ, and at the same time, avoid being the target of ridicule and rejection. After all, 2 Timothy 3:12 bluntly states, "Everyone who wants to live a godly life in Christ Jesus will be persecuted." But the Bible not only warns us in regards to the issue of being persecuted, but also encourages and consoles us on the same topic, when, together, 2 Timothy 1:8, 12 say, "If you will stir up this inner power, you will never be afraid to tell others about our Lord, or to let them know that I am your friend, even though I am here in jail for Christ's sake. You will be ready to suffer with me for the Lord, for he will give your strength in suffering...That is why I am suffering here in jail and I am certainly not ashamed of it, for I know the one in whom I trust, and I am sure that he is able to safely guard all that I have given him until the day of his return."

Now, a second reason why many Christians choose not to tell anyone about the Good News is that they'd honestly love to be able to do just that, but they can't—because they don't know how. There are too many people in the church today who just don't have the foggiest idea what they should say or do whenever the opportunity to share the gospel presents itself to them. But do you know what? There's absolutely no excuse in today's day and age—and in the area of the world in which we live—for not knowing how to properly share the gospel with others. But before I give you some concrete examples of why that statement is so true, let me remind us all of a couple of Bible passages that are relevant to this concern.

First off, I like how the Philip's Modern English Translation of the Bible convicts the reader of possibly not being educated enough in Christian teaching, when it states in Hebrews 5:11–14, "There is a great deal that we should like to say about this, but it is not easy to explain to you since you seem so slow to grasp spiritual truth. At a time when you should be teaching others, you need teachers yourselves to repeat to you the ABCs of G's revelation to men. You have become people who need a milk diet and cannot handle solid food. For anyone who continues to live on milk is unable to digest what is right—he simply has not grown up. Solid food is only for the adult, that is, for the man who has developed, by experience, his power to discriminate between what is good and what is evil." Hebrews 5 ends at that point, and the same topic is continued to be spoken of in Hebrews 6:1–3 according to the Living Bible. It's there the Bible says, "Let us stop going over the same old ground again and again, always teaching those first lessons about Christ. Let us go on instead to other things and become mature in our understanding, as strong Christian ought to be. Surely, we don't need to speak further about the foolishness of trying to be saved by being good, or about the necessity of faith in G; you don't need further instruction about baptism and spiritual gifts and the resurrection of the dead and eternal judgment. The Lord willing, we will go on now to other things."

So what are we supposed to do about this? If the church is suffering—if not nearly as many people are being won to Christ as there should be, due to people in the church not knowing enough about what to say to them in order to lead them to Christ, what's the answer? The answer is simple enough—get involved in Bible study—one our own (on a daily basis) and in a small group of other people (probably once a week). That kind of practice would go a long way in helping to cure the disease of biblical ignorance that seems to be so rampant in our churches today. After all, that's exactly the strategy that the people of the early church used, in order to grow themselves in Christ.

Acts 2:42 reports, "They devoted themselves to the apostles' teaching, and to the fellowship to the breaking of bread, and to prayer." But just simply attending the first New Testament Bible studies in existence wasn't all that the early disciples of J did to train themselves properly in learning proper Christian doctrine. They didn't just show up at a passive scenario, only listening to what was being said by the teacher—they got involved in what was being presented to them, as Acts 17:11 explains, when the Living Bible says there, "But the people of Berea wee more open minded than those in Thessalonica, and they gladly listened to the message. They searched the scriptures day by day to check up on Paul and Silas' statements to see if they were really so."

Now, a third excuse that people give for not being the witness for Christ like they should come from the thoughts they have of their own particular circumstances in the area of life that's being addressed. On the issue of weight management, for instance, a person who recognizes that they have a loved one that really needs to lose some weight might say something, for example, like, "Hey, I'm the last person who ought to be approaching other people, trying to point out to them that they have a weight problem. After all, I've got weight issues myself I need to get straightened out and take care of. The same kind of statement, then, can be said by people of others, regarding the spiritual health and well-being of them both. "Who am I to tell them how to get right with G?" they might say.

Well, at first, that might sound pretty reasonable. Well, on one side of the coin, that might sound like a valid argument. After all, none of us is perfect, spiritually speaking, according to passages like Romans 3:23 and 5:15, Galatians 3:22, Psalm 106:6, the two identical verses found in 1 Kings 8:46 and 2 Chronicles 6:36 and Revelation 5:1–4. All together, these verses from the Bible state, "There is no difference, for all have sinned and fall short of the glory of God…many died by the trespasses of one man…But the Scripture declares that the whole world is a prisoner of sin…We have sinned, even as our fathers did; we have done wrong and acted wickedly…there is no one who does not sin…Then I saw in the right hand of him who sat on the throne a scroll with writing on both sides and sealed with 7 seals. And I saw a mighty angel proclaiming in a loud voice, 'Who is worthy to break the seals and open the scroll?' But no one in heaven or on earth or under the earth could open the scroll or even look inside it. I wept and wept because no one was found who was worthy to open the scroll or look inside."

So we can see by these verses and passages from Scripture that none of us, technically, are "worthy" to preach the gospel and to share this good news with others. But that's just it—telling others about J isn't based on worthiness or unworthiness…it's a matter of being called by God to go and do just that. Consider for a moment, the apostle Paul. He was very upfront—about the sins from his own past—with the people to whom he was preaching in Jerusalem, according to the Acts 22:2–5: "Then Paul said, 'I am a Jew, born in Tarsus of Cilicia, but brought up in this city. Under Gamaliel, I was thoroughly trained in the law of our fathers and was just as zealous for G as you are today. I persecuted the followers of this way to their death, arresting both men and women and throwing them into prison, as also the high priest of all the Council can testify. I even obtained letter from them to their brothers in Damascus, and went there to bring these people as prisoners to Jerusalem to be punished.'"

And in addition, most if not all of us are very familiar with Paul's statement found in 1 Timothy 1:15, where he writes, "Here is a trustworthy saying that deserves full acceptance: Christ Jesus came into the world to save sinners—of whom I am the worst."

All right, Paul calls himself the chief of sinners in that passage. So if Paul couldn't consider himself "worthy enough" to preach the gospel, then there'd be no way we could ever obtain that kind of goodness within ourselves. Sharing the gospel, then, must not be a matter of "Am I worthy enough?" but more like "Sharing the gospel is what G wants me to do, so I must do it. End of story."

Without Love, We're Zilch
1 Corinthians 13:1-13

(Start by playing a recording of the song "Forgiveness," by Collective Soul; lyrics are printed in the bulletin.)

You know, I really like that song for its beauty, and not just for the musical beauty of it. I love the words. Especially striking to me is the chorus, "It used to be all I'd want was wisdom, trust and truth, but now, all I really want is forgiveness for you." In hearing that, I heard echoes of this morning's focus passage from 1 Corinthians 13:1–13: "I may be able to speak the languages of men and even of angels, but if I have not love, my speech is no more than a noisy gong or a clanging bell. If I have the gift of prophecy, and can fathom all mysteries and all knowledge, and if I have a faith that can move mountains, but have not love, I am nothing. If I give all I possess to the poor and surrender my body to the flames, but have not love, I gain nothing. Love is patient and kind; it does not envy or boast, and love is not proud. It is not rude, it is not self-seeking, it is not easily angered, it keeps no record of wrongs. Love does not delight in evil but rejoices in the truth. Love bears all things, believes all things, hopes all things, endures all things.

"Love never ends; as for prophecies, they are temporary; there are gifts of speaking in strange tongues, but they will cease; there is knowledge, but it will pass away. Now we know so little, even with our special gifts, and the preaching of those most gifted is still so poor. But when we have been made perfect and complete, then the need for those inadequate special gifts will come to an end, and they will disappear.

"It's like this: when I was a child, I spoke, thought and reasoned like a child does. But when I became a man, my thoughts grew far beyond those of my childhood, and now I have put away those childish things. In the same way, we can see and understand only a little about God now, as if we were looking at the reflection in a poor mirror; but someday, we are going to see him in his completeness, face to face. Now all that I know is hazy and blurred, but then I will see everything clearly, just as clearly as G sees into my heart right now. There are 3 things that remain—faith, hope and love, and the greatest of these is love."

You know, there are many questions that have plagued humankind and problems that have confronted people for centuries—problems and questions of all kinds—and most of these problems and questions have to do with how to solve assorted medical diseases/illnesses and how to put a stop to things like crime and war. But I'll tell you what really stumps me, this morning. I've always wondered how people who call themselves Christians—people who claim to faithfully follow the one and only savior of the earth, Jesus Christ— can still find it within their heart (somehow, someway) to allow themselves to feel hatred toward any number of people for assorted reasons, and still believe that they can remain in a right relationship with G. To try to live life as a Christian and, at the same time, hold contempt and disdain for someone unapologetically on pretty much a constant basis is really impossible. As we begin the month of February, the month of Valentines and a celebration of love, I'd like to focus on some "reasons" as to why some people find it very hard and difficult to love others, see what the Bible says on those "reasons" and even maybe what we can do for ourselves to maybe have a better attitude toward those around us.

To begin with, some issues that seem too often divide people from each other is those of envy, greed, and jealousy. Now, most of us would automatically point a finger at those who are presently rich and wealthy, in the material sense in this life, as having a problem of despising people who equally rich and well off, as well as those who are much poorer than themselves. Indeed, that is often the case. That's part of the reason why 1 Timothy 6:9–10 in the Living Bible says, "But people who long to be rich soon begin to do all kinds of wrong things to get money, things that hurt them and make them evil-minded and finally send them to hell itself. For the love of money is the first step toward all kinds of sin. Some people have even turned away from G, because of their love for it, and as a result have pierced themselves with many sorrows."

But the issue of the spiritual dangers of the love for money is not exclusive to those who are rich and materially well-off, as many people might assume. The poor can have a problem in this area as well, since it's many times those who are without material "stuff" in life who envy those who do possess such things. No, I don't believe that G was talking exclusively to the immensely rich, in the last of the Ten Commandments, as listed in Exodus 20. You're familiar with verse 17 of that chapter: "You shall not covet your neighbor's house. You shall not covet your neighbor's wife, or his manservant or maidservant, his ox or donkey, or anything else that belongs to your neighbor." What people who are set against each other over the issue of money, whether they themselves are considered to be rich or poor, need to realize is that human relationships are much more important than material possessions in this life, that people are always to be considered vitally more important than things. As Jesus pointed out, according to the Living Bible's translation of Luke 12:15, "For real life and real living are not related to how rich we are."

There was a man who once spent a 3-week visit to Africa, and during one day of the trip, he went to a game park near Nairobi. It was there that he learned how African monkey are often captured in order to be placed in zoos in the US.

A shining metal object of any type is placed in a long-necked jar, tied to a tree. As monkeys swing through the trees, their eyes catch the reflection of the sun on the shining object (much like the "power" of money catches the attention of many people in the world today). Reaching into the jar poses no problem for the monkeys, but when they try to bring their closed fists through the narrow jar openings, they can't make it. To gain freedom, all the stupid monkeys would need to do is to let go of the worthless object, thus flattening their hands out and sliding their hand easily out of the jar. But instead, the monkeys stay sitting by the jar, possibly continuing to look at their hand stuck in the jar, until the people contracted by the zoo come to pick the monkey up and take him away. I bet if we learned to let go of a lot of the things in the world we find ourselves greatly attached to that our human relationships would improve immensely.

Sad to say, though, there are many people who wouldn't think twice about hurting someone if it meant that there would be a financial reward for it. A pastor was speaking to a Sunday school class of eight-year-olds about things money can't buy. "It can't buy joy," he told them. "That comes from the heart. And money can't buy love."

Driving the point home, he asked, "What would you do if I offered you $1,000 not to love your mom and dad?"

After a few seconds of dead silence, one of the kids raised his hands and asked, "How much would you give me not to love my big sister?"

Now, a second type of animosity that exists between people that shouldn't—especially in the Christian community—is that which is based on the attitudes of racism and racial prejudice. We're all familiar with probably the most common form of racism in our twenty-first century US society—that of racism directed from the Caucasian Americans to African Americans. But that's not the only type of racism that exists in our country today and indeed around the world. In this country, Asians are often targeted for discrimination, harassment, and even for murder, as well. Even certain Europeans would be in danger to simply mind their own business while walking down a US street. But it also works in the opposite way, in that with the unfortunate bad light that the US has been seen in many countries over the past few years since 9/11, we would most likely been in danger of suffering many of these same things ourselves if we were to visit their homelands.

But you know something, folks. G doesn't care what skin color we have. He couldn't care less about the shade of the pigment in our skin as far as how much he's determined to love us. Just as G stated about himself as he was speaking to Samuel, according to 1 Samuel 16:7, "The Lord does not look at the things man looks at. Man looks at the outward appearance, but the Lord looks at the heart."

Some people in our country might respond to some statement like that and say, "Well, it's not people of other races whom I don't get along with—it's simply people of other countries, countries other than the good old US. You know them foreigners. I'll take a fellow American over one of them any day."

Please don't get me wrong. I love America just as much as anybody else. The summer between my junior and senior year in college, I attended that year's session of West Virginia Boys' State, the weeklong event held in every state of the US every summer, in which boys and girls learn all about things like what's it's like to run for public office, to help in the campaign of a certain candidate, to simply what it's like to participate in the voting process. That experience, together with the event of September 11, twenty-one years later, helped instill in me a pride in our country that many people around the world do not have in their own homeland. However, I don't like to discount verses from the Bible, such as Acts 10:34–35 in which Peter is seen speaking to a crowd of people in Cornelius's house. It's here that Peter is recorded as having said, "The truth I have now come to realize is that God does not have favorites, but that anybody of any nationality who fears G and does what is right is acceptable to him."

Now, a third type of animosity that exists between people that shouldn't— especially in the Christian community—is that of a mentality of selfrighteousness toward others. You know, for all the talk in secular realms in which you often hear people halfway quote the Bible by admonishing someone else, "Now, don't judge anybody else" or "Hey, I think you need to take the log out of your own eye before you start to look at the small faults of other people around you," for all the many times that this idea is traded back and forth in society, it sure doesn't get demonstrated much in the lives of as many people today. And the problem is exacerbated when this self-righteousness begins to play itself out in more than just in words and in verbal taunts. Eventually, if gone unchecked, this mindset goes from being just that—a mindset—to being acted out physically, through overt discrimination, to assault and even murder.

But these people doing all the judging often tend to forget that (1) they themselves aren't perfect, and (2) because they aren't perfect, they themselves will eventually face judgment. As Romans 14:4, 10, and 13 say, "Who are you to judge someone else's servant…You, then, why do you judge your brother? Or, why do you look down on your brother? For we will all stand before the judgment seat of God…Therefore, let us stop passing judgment on each other." In addition, 1 Corinthians 4:5 adamantly states, "Therefore, judge nothing before the appointed time; wait till the Lord comes. He will bring to light what is hidden in darkness and will expose the motives of men's hearts. At that time, each will receive his praise from G."

Now, a final way in which many people express immense dislike and outright hatred toward others is probably the most common of all—wanting to get back at someone who has hurt us, one way, or another. While many people wouldn't honestly find it a natural reaction to be envious or prejudiced toward others or not even find it easy to try to pass judgment on others, they often find it not only easy, but downright natural, to desire to take revenge, to even the score, to hurt someone back for the hurt that this other person gave to them.

Unfortunately, it seems to me, that the closer we get to the time of J's return, the more frequent and intense we see the attitudes (and related behaviors of) envy/greed, racism, and self-righteousness throughout society. But even though I don't have any factual statistics to back this up, I'm will to say that a prevalence of the mindset for a want for revenge has got them all beat easily. After all, many people take very seriously the adage "I don't get mad, I get even." Ha, ha, very funny (sarcastically).

But as the Bible in its text declares, in Leviticus 19:18 and Proverbs 20:22 and 24:29, "Do not seek revenge or bear a grudge against one of your people, but love your neighbor as yourself...Do not say, 'I'll pay you back for this wrong!' Wait for the Lord, and he will deliver you...Do not say, 'I'll do to him as he has done to me; I'll pay that man back for what he did.'"

Now, it's true that, if we happen to have someone in our life we'd call an enemy, even if we never actually acted out on our hatred of that person/those people, but simply thought about how much we hate them and occasionally said something that indicated just how we felt, something as simple as that could get us in a whole lot of trouble. At an afternoon tea for officers and their wives, the commanding general of the base delivered a seemingly endless speech.

A young lieutenant, listening with obviously disfavor, grumbled to the woman at his table, "What a pompous, unbearable old windbag that slob is."

The woman turned to him, her face red with rage, and said, "Lieutenant, do you know who I am?"

"No, ma'am."

"I'm the wife of the man you just called an unbearable old windbag."

"Indeed," began the lieutenant, looking steadfast and unruffled, "and do you know who I am?"

"No, I don't," stated the general's wife.

"Thank goodness!" exclaimed the lieutenant, as he quickly got up from the table and slipped into the crowd.

We need to realize, folks, that the passage found in 1 John 4:19–21 indicates that even though we say that we love God, if we hate our neighbor at the same time, the Bible at that point calls us a liar. A liar. That's pretty strong stuff.

You Can't Save the World Alone
1 Corinthians 12:4-31

A pastor approached one of the wealthiest members of his congregation about making a pledge to the church. The man informed the pastor that he had many obligations already. He asked if the pastor knew that the man's father was about to have his farm foreclosed, and that at the same time, his mother needed surgery. The pastor then admitted that he hadn't known those things. The wealthy man then went on to ask if the pastor had known that the wealthy man's bro hand recently been badly injured in an auto accident and that his bro-in-law was going to have to go to prison unless he was able to come up with the money to make up a shortage in his accounts by next week. The embarrassed minister admitted that he had not known any of these tragic circumstances in the life of this man. The pastor apologized for taking up the time of this man and started to leave. But the wealthy man wasn't finished with his tirade against the pastor: "Well, Pastor, if I'm not going to give a single dime to my family in times of need, what makes you think that I'm going to give any to the church?"

In all seriousness, if we were all to stop and think for a moment, we could all probably come up with at least half dozen situations where someone we know is suffering or someone we know of—through someone else—is in pretty much a crisis situation. One of the starkest reminders of the prevalence of the many different kinds/types of problems in our society today is given through a commercial presently running on certain channels promoting the work of the Red Cross. The girl in the commercial begins by explaining that because the main employer in her town kept dumping its toxic waste in the nearby river, the river has effectively been polluted, the fish and plant life in and around the river are dying and the kids in the area are contracting various diseases and actually dying. So, the girl goes on to say, she organized a huge protest to get the big, bad company to be shut down.

Well, in the process of the company shutting down, the kids in town are now twice as sick, since they can't get health insurance through the company that their parents used to work for, which, remember, had been made to go out of business—by the girl and those with her—because they had been the source of the original problem (the pollution) in the first place. The commercial then ends by the statement being made that none of us can solve all the problems of the world, but we can make a difference by each of us giving blood whenever we have that chance. You see, everybody must do their part so that no one else feels like they are responsible to make up for all the work that everyone else is leaving undone.

That's why I believe the apostle Paul wrote the following words, according to 1 Corinthians 12:4–31: "There are different kinds of spiritual gifts, but the same Spirit give them. There are different ways of serving, but the same Lord is served. There are different abilities to perform service, but the same G gives ability to everyone for their service. The Spirit's presence is shown in some way in each one, for the good of all. The Spirit gives one man a message of wisdom, while to another man the same Spirit gives a message of knowledge. One and the same Spirit gives faith to one man, while to another man he gives the power to heal. The Spirit gives one man the power to work miracles; to another, the gift of speaking G's message; and to yet another, the ability to tell the difference between gifts that come from the Spirit and those that do not. To one man, he gives the ability to speak in strange tongues, and to another, he gives the ability to explain what is said. But it is one and the same Spirit who does all this; he gives a different gift to each man, as he wishes."

Our bodies have many parts, but the many parts make up only one body when they are all put together. So it is with the body of Christ. Each of us is a part of the one body of Christ. Some of us are Jews, some are Gentiles, some are slaves, and some are free. But the HS has fitted us all together into one body. We have been baptized into Christ's body by the one Spirit, and all have been given that same HS. Yes, the body has man parts, not just one part. If the foot says, "I am not a part of the body because I am not a hand," that does not make it any less part of the body.

And what would you think if you heard an ear say, "I am not part of the body, because I am an ear, and not an eye?"

Would that make it any less part of the body? Suppose the whole body were an eye—then how would you hear? Or if your whole body were just one big ear, how could you smell anything?

But that isn't the way G made us. He has made many parts for our bodies and has put each part just where he wants it. What a strange thing a body would be if it had only one part! So he has made many parts, but still there is only one body. The eye can't say to the hand, "I don't need you!" and the head can't say to the feet, "I don't need you!" On the contrary, those parts of the body that seem to be weaker are indispensable, and the parts that we think are less honorable, we treat with special honor. The parts that are not presentable are treated with special modesty, while our presentable parts need no special treatment. But G has combined the members of the body and has given greater honor to the parts that lacked it so that there should be no division in the body but that its parts should have equal concern for each other. If one part suffers, every part suffers with it; if one part is honored, every part rejoices with it.

Now you are the body of Christ, and each one of you is a part of it. In the church, G has appointed first of all apostles, then prophets, then teachers, then workers of miracles and also those having gifts of healing, those able to help others, those with gifts of administration, and finally, those speaking in different kinds of tongues. Are all apostles? Are all prophets? Are all teachers? Do all work miracles? Do all have gifts of healing? Do all speak in tongues? Do all interpret? But eagerly desire the greater gifts.

Supporting roles of others helping their leaders are seen, for example, in Exodus 17:12: "When Moses' hands grew tired, they took a stone and put it under him and he sat on it. Aaron and Hur held his hands up—one on one side, one on the other—so that his hands remained steady till sunset." And there's the example found in 2 Samuel 21:15–17: "One again, there was a battle between the Philistines and Israel. David went down with his men to fight against the Philistines, and he became exhausted. Ishbi-Benob, one of the descendants of Rapha, whose bronze spearhead weighed seven and a half pounds and who was armed with anew sword, said he would kill David. But Abishai, son of Zeruiah, came to David's rescue; he struck the Philistine down and killed him." You see, here were two examples of great leaders from the Bible—Moses and David—who, at times, desperately needed the contribution of those around them. Why? Because they couldn't "save the world alone."

When everybody pitches in, that's that much less work and effort other people have to contribute to the cause. For a number of years, Andrew Carnegie, whose wife loved classical music, made up the annual deficit of the New York Philharmonic Society. Then one year, at a meeting of the directors, he made the suggestion that the responsibility to make up the lack of funding should not be his alone. He said, "From now on, I think the burden should be shared. You raise half the deficit from other donors, and I'll give you the remaining half." A few days later, the directors informed the philanthropist that his condition had been met. He was pleased by the news.

He said, "I told you the money could be raised easily enough. Where did you get it from?"

The directors replied, "From Mrs. Carnegie."

And you know, it may have nothing to do with how much money we're asked to give in order to keep a part of the world from "going down the tubes." Maybe it's that we're been requested to spend a lot of time and energy on a certain project...Time and energy that, to be honest, we just don't have. Not to sound selfish, but honestly, we all only have some much time to get the things done we need to get done, and only so much strength and energy to do all of it with. In addition, it might be that we're being pressured to participate in a type of altruistic activity that requires talents and abilities that we just don't have. Folks, God is not going to ask us to do something for him that we're not gifted, by him, to do—although people might ask us to do something like that. It's not wrong for us to say 'no' to taking part in a certain type of church or ministry activity if we truly don't feel that we have "the gift." That's why G endowed different people with different gifts—so that no one has to feel like they must save the world alone.

Unfortunately, though, there are those people who feel as though they are pretty much saving the world by themselves, even though the reality is that they're doing amazing little to make a difference. A young mother was holding her four-year-old son on her lap, telling him he was about to have a new baby brother. She explained that he could hold the baby's bottle, bring her a clean diaper when needed, and help push the carriage.

He then got off her lap, stood seriously in front of her and quizzed, "And what are you going to be doing, Mommy, when I do all the work?"

On the other hand, there are times when the person involved—for one reason or another—simply can't give/contribute, in any way, as much as they'd like to. That's all right—G just requires that we give what we can, and then, he will make up the difference. As Leviticus 5:7, 10 indicate when speaking of the Israelites bringing their assigned offering to the altar, "If someone can not afford a lamb, he is to bring 2 doves or pigeons to the Lord as a penalty for his sin…The priest shall then offer the other as a burnt offering in the prescribed way and make atonement for him for the sin he committed, and he will be forgiven."

When you stop to think about it—there are literally hundreds of worthy causes to either give your time or money to. Just the registered charities that focus on health and physical well-being, alone, number in the dozens/hundreds. I have chosen for myself three charities of different types to give to on a regular basis. The first is Compassion International, a Christian ministry that, for $32 a month, will feed, cloth, shelter, and give a Christian education to a needy child of your choosing, somewhere overseas. I then give to an outfit known as Watchman Fellowship, an organization that teaches Christians about the spiritual dangers of cults and false teachers, then I finally give to another organization that promotes love and harmony between people of different races and classes in society. That's why, when I get a phone call from someone asking me to make a $50 donation to help save the yellowbellied, sap-sucking tree owl from extinction, that I politely tell them that while I believe in the cause their fighting for, I simply can't give to their charity, at least not at this time. Why do I turn down giving to this charity? It's not because I don't care about the yellow-bellied, sap-sucking tree owl—I'm sure they're cute animals and they're important to the ecological balance in nature. But after having committed myself to helping feed the poor, educating people about false prophets, and promoting peace and harmony, I just don't have anything left over for the poor owl. I'll have to leave him up to someone else who feels called to take up its cause, because I know I can't save the world alone.

As a Christian, now, when deciding to forgo helping out a certain valid charity or ministry, let's remember to conduct ourselves appropriately and not scream/yell at the charity rep but treat them with respect. After all, they firmly believe in their program, even if we do not. So if the follower of Hare Krishna approaches you at the airport, asking for a donation, gently tell him, "I gave in a previous lifetime."

You know, instead of feeling like we have to carry the world on our shoulders, solving everybody's problems on our own, we need to remember to delegate some of the responsibility that's fallen on us to other people. Notice I said to delegate some of the responsibility, not all—we still need to help out. But when we all work together, we're much more effective in the work we do, and nobody has to run themselves into the ground to do it. Again, Scripture gives some perfect examples in this area, where many people worked together (some offering "temporary help") in order to get major tasks accomplished.

2 Chronicles 29:34, for instance, states, "The priests were too few to skin all the burnt offerings; so their kinsmen the Levites helped them until the tasks was finished and until other priests had been consecrated." The same Bible book states in chapter 32, verses 2–4, "When Hezekiah saw that Sennacherib had come and that he intended to make war on Jerusalem, he consulted with his officials and military staff about blocking off the water for the springs outside the city, and they helped him. A large force of men assembled, and they blocked all the springs and the stream that flowed through the land."

If you're presently looking for a place of service in your church or community, I would advise you to consult G, and ask him where you should serve. If you need to discover first where your talents/abilities lie, great. Do it. But don't try to save the world alone. Admit to yourself your interests and abilities are and what they aren't. What issues, problems, and difficulties of the world are you really passionate about trying to find a solution? Most likely, they're areas of life that you have an amount of talent/expertise in. Make that particular area of difficulty "your baby," then run with, but don't try to save the world yourself. Believe me, it will not work.

September 1, 2008 You Might Be a Christian If...
Romans 10:9; Galatians 5:22-23

More than likely, everybody in here has at least heard of, if not been familiar with the work of, Jeff Foxworthy. If you happen to be one of those who is not familiar with him, Mr. Foxworthy is a comedian who has built his fame and fortune on a comedic routine he developed around the short, simple phrase "You might be a redneck, if..." Let me give you some examples. You might be a redneck if (1) you ever cut your grass and found your car in the process; (2) you think a chain saw is a musical instrument; (3) your mother lists "ammunition" for an item on her Christmas wish list; and (4) you've ever been kicked out of the zoo for heckling the monkeys.

You see, Foxworthy's premise is that you can be considered a redneck if you have ever been connected with any of these particular behaviors. Well, I'd like to suggest to you this morning that likewise, Christians, too, can be identified easily enough if someone who isn't a Christian should witness them living their lives as Christians are supposed to live.

Now, for instance, the Bible plainly states in Romans 10:9, "If you confess with your mouth that J is Lord and believe in your heart that G raised him from the dead, you will be saved."

Well, all I can say to that is, a lot of people can profess to believe, but what really matters is how they choose to live their life, once they actually make that profession. So maybe a better "test of faith" to see if we ourselves are truly at least attempting to live the life of a Christian is to look at a Scripture passage like the one found in Galatians 5:22–23: "But the fruit of the Spirit is love, joy, peace, patience, kindness, goodness, faithfulness, gentleness and self-control."

You see, what this passage points out to us is that the Spirit leads us away from sin, but not by overwhelming us, forcing us to do G's will. Instead, he offers his gifts, power, and guidance, expecting us to follow him. He gives new life in Christ. Naturally, we should walk in his life of love, joy, peace, and the like. The Christian life, then, is a mystery, given to us of course by G, who provides us with the standards of love. G himself gives the Spirit who alone can enable Christians to live up to the standards of the faith.

Now, though it's the Holy Trinity that enables us to live the life were called to live in Christ, it is the individual Christian's responsibility to co-operate in this endeavor. We must live the kind of life to which we are called, trusting G rather than ourselves. The metaphor of love as a fruit in verse 22 captures the paradox in a single phrase. The Christian must bear the fruit, but only the spirit can produce it. Yes, you could very well be a Christian if you're pretty much constantly exhibiting love, joy, peace, patience, kindness, goodness, faithfulness, gentleness, and self-control in your life.

So to get back to the "redneck theory" developed by Jeff Foxworthy, for a second, Foxworthy has pointed out—and pretty accurately, I might add—that you might actually be a redneck if you've ever found yourself involved in a custody fight over a hunting dog. Also, if people tend to hear your car coming down the street before they can actually see it, you might be a redneck. And, if you've always been under the impression that The French Riviera is a type of foreign car, you just might be a redneck.

Well, to help to continue to illustrate the signs that would help identify a Christian, let me give you an opposite example of what a Christian is supposed to be like. You know, sometimes you can learn a lot about how to do/be something, by seeing for yourself an extremely poor example set by someone else. You can think to yourself then, "I know how to do/be such and such...all I have to do is do/be the exact opposite of the way I see so and so do it."

Once again, the apostle Paul gives us an example to see along these lines according to the Living Bible's version of 1 Corinthians 3:1–9. It's there the Bible says, "Dear Brothers, I have been talking to you as though you were still just babies in the Christian life, who are not following the Lord, but your own desires: I cannot talk to you as I would to healthy Christians, who are filled with the Spirit. I have had to feed you with milk and not solid food, because you couldn't digest anything stronger. And even now, you still have to be fed on milk. For you are still only baby Christians, controlled by your own desires and not G's. When you are jealous of one another and divide up into quarreling groups, doesn't that prove that you are still babies, wanting your own way? In fact, you are acting like people who don't belong to the Lord at all. There you are quarreling about whether I am greater than Apollos, and dividing the church. Doesn't this show how little you have grown in the Lord?

"Who am I and who is Apollos, that we should be the cause of a quarrel? Why, we're just G's servants, each of us with certain special abilities, and with our help, you believed. My work was to plant the seed in your hearts, and Apollos' work was to water it, but it was G, not we, who made the garden grow in your hearts. The person who does the planting or watering isn't very important, but G is important, because he is the one who makes things grow. Apollos and I are working as a team with the same aim, though each of us will be rewarded for his own hard work. We are only G's coworkers. You are G's garden, not ours; you are God's building, not ours."

You see, the early Christians in the church of Corinth had two main problems here, according to what Paul is saying. First of all, they couldn't seem to comprehend important advanced teaching Paul had ready to pass on to them because of their stalled spiritual growth. Lesson 1 here, then, as far as what *not* to do in order to be recognized by ourselves and others as a real Christian is to not allow ourselves to be biblically illiterate and spiritually ignorant, to study and absorb the Bible enough to be able to carry on an intelligent conversation that contains terms and doctrines of the Christian faith that even the most recent of converts to the faith should be able to understand. So even after having been in the church for some significant amount of time, if we honestly still need for fellow church members to relate to us the most basic of teachings, we just might *not* be a Christian.

And the second lesson in this passage is that Christians have no excuse for living in such a way that it naturally creates division, strife and tension in the church. Let me remind you what Paul said on this topic, in verses 3 and 4, from the Living Bible's version: "For you're still only baby Christians, controlled by you own desires, not G's. When you are jealous of one another and divide up into quarreling groups, doesn't that prove that you are still babies, wanting your own way? In fact, you are acting like people who don't belong to the Lord at all. There you are, quarreling about whether I am greater than Apollos, and dividing the church. Doesn't this show how little you have grown in the Lord?" So it would stand to reason that, taking into account what we just saw Paul talking about, that if you almost seem to get enjoyment out of causing strife, tension, and division in a local body of Christian believers, you might not be a Christian.

Yes, it's amazing how easily and quickly some people can be identified, according to certain signs and signals. For instance, once again, Jeff Foxworthy points out how we can easily locate a redneck when he points out, "If you've ever lost a tooth in the process of opening a beer bottle, you might be a redneck." If your wife's hairdo has ever been ruined by a ceiling fan, you might be a redneck. Or if you consider the fifth grade as your senior year, you might be a redneck.

See, the thing every Christian should want to do is to not only live their life in such a way that other people can easily identify them as Christians, but also live in a way that would inspire others to do the same. Face it, when we live hypocritical Christian lives, that's a turn-off to most people. When people in the world see us living very much unlike what we say we believe, that kind of thing gives them every reason in the world to not want to become a Christian. But when we determine for ourselves to live strong, committed, dedicated and devoted lives in J, that often encourages others to do the same.

This is why Paul wrote in 1 Thessalonians 2:6–8, "So you became our followers and the Lord's; for you received our message with joy from the HS in spite of the trails and sorrows it brought you. Then, you yourselves became an example for all the other Christians in Greece. And now, the word of the Lord has spread out from you to others everywhere, far beyond your boundaries, for wherever we go, we find people telling us about your remarkable faith in G."

It's the same reason why Paul writes in 1 Timothy 4:12, according to the Jerusalem Bible, "Don't let people disregard you because you are young, but set an example to all the believers in the way you speak and behave, and in your love, faith and purity."

So in the first of those two Scriptural examples, we can see that the Thessalonians had a wonderful testimony of Christ within themselves. This testimony, then, rang out far and wide, because they had learned well to live and witness through Paul's example. G calls witnesses to be examples to others, even in times of suffering.

The idea, then, is to live the Christian life seriously enough that no one who is unsaved around us would ever be able to "get it wrong" by observing the way we live. As Titus 2:7 instructs us, "In everything, set them an example by doing what is good. In your teaching, show integrity, seriousness and soundness of speech that can't be condemned, so that those who oppose you may be ashamed because they have nothing bad to say about us." You see, integrity is a quality found in church members whose motives are pure. Some attach themselves to the church out of a need for status and attention. The dedicated and devoted Christian should be motivated by love for people and love for truth. Christians must not give reason for criticism of their conduct or their work in the Lord.

Yes, sometimes all you have to do is to look at a person, and you can pretty get an idea of who they are and what they stand for. Most times, however, it takes a little bit more than just a glance at them. You may, in other words, have to really get to know a person, before putting a label on them. It's by spending a lot of quality time with a person that you would come to find things out about them that would definitely cue you in on just exactly what kind of person they are. For instance, if you discovered that a particular friend of yours always got a Christmas card every year from the company that makes Redman Chewing Tobacco, your friend might very well be a redneck. If you know somebody who is under the impression that beef jerky and moon pies are two of the four major food groups, yep, you guessed it—they're probably a redneck.

But maybe the best and most obvious way for people to recognize "a Christian is action" is to see loved demonstrated in our lives. After all, love was the main character trait that J stressed over and over for us to have, as he did in John 13:34–35, when he said, "A new command I give you: Love one another. As I have loved you, so you must love one another. By this all men will know that you are my disciples, if you loved one another."

You see, an important dimension of the general "neighbor-love" we Christians are supposed to have for everyone around us is the area of "disciple love." If we Christians can't love each other properly, how in the world can we expect to reach out to unbelievers in love, as G directs us to? J was saying here that the disciples' love for one another would identify them to others as his true disciples. The lack of love for one another raises confusing questions for others about the church and Christian discipleship. Attitudes such as hatred, fighting, jealousy, and snobbery have no place among disciples. Not only do such things harm the church itself, it does absolutely no favors, either, for the witness we bring to the world around us.

In addition, you can often tell whether someone is truly a Christian or not by the type of result they get when they witness to others about their faith. A truly educated, committed and loving Christian will eventually help lead others to the Lord who will exhibit those same kinds of characteristics. But someone who believes in erroneous theological doctrine or who is much less than committed in their faith or loving in their relationships with others is most likely a false believer of Christ. That why J said in Matthew 7:15–20, "Watch out for false prophets; they come to you looking like sheep on the outside, but they are really like wild wolves on the inside. You will know them by the way they act. Thorn bushes don't bear grapes, and briers do not bear figs. A healthy tree bears good fruit, while a poor tree bears bad fruit. A healthy tree cannot ear bad fruit, and a poor tree can't bear good fruit. Any tree that does not bear good fruit is cut down and thrown in the fire. So, then, you will know the false prophets by the way they act."

But once again, how can others tell if we might be a Christian? Well, we just might very well be a Christian, if we follow what J flatly stated in John 13:34– 35: "A new command I give you: Love one another. As I have loved you, so you must love one another. By this, all men will know that you are my disciples, if you love one another."

Yes, if you have two or more bros named Bubba or Junior, ever financed getting a tattoo, called your boss Buddy on a regular basis, or been fired from a construction job because of your appearance, people might recognize you as a redneck. Well, do you demonstrate enough characteristics that are described in scripture so that people are likely to correctly label you as a Christian?

About the Author

Rev. Roger Austin presently pastors the Bridgewater Baptist Church in Virginia and has pastored five other Virginia churches in the past. He has written one other book of his messages, *I'd Like to Die, but I've Got Stuff to Do*. He has also written and recorded two albums of contemporary Christian music, *Between the Dragon and the Lamb* and *Sin Isn't Pretty*.